T0214932

This book sets out the principles of parallel computing in a way which will be useful to student and potential user alike. It includes coverage of both conventional and neural computers. The content of the book is arranged hierarchically. It explains why, where and how parallel computing is used; the fundamental paradigms employed in the field; how systems are programmed or trained; technical aspects including connectivity and processing element complexity; and how system performance is estimated (and why doing so is difficult).

The penultimate chapter of the book comprises a set of case studies of archetypal parallel computers, each study written by an individual closely connected with the system in question. The final chapter correlates the various aspects of parallel computing into a taxonomy of systems.

Parallel computing
principles and practice

Parallel computing
principles and practice

T. J. FOUNTAIN
Department of Physics and Astronomy, University College London

CAMBRIDGE
UNIVERSITY PRESS

CAMBRIDGE UNIVERSITY PRESS
Cambridge, New York, Melbourne, Madrid, Cape Town, Singapore, São Paulo

Cambridge University Press
The Edinburgh Building, Cambridge CB2 2RU, UK

Published in the United States of America by Cambridge University Press, New York

www.cambridge.org
Information on this title: www.cambridge.org/9780521451314

First published 1994
This digitally printed first paperback version 2006

A catalogue record for this publication is available from the British Library

Library of Congress Cataloguing in Publication data

Fountain, T. J. (Terry J.)
Parallel computing : principles and practice / T. J. Fountain.
    p.   cm.
Includes bibliographical references and index.
ISBN 0-521-45131-0
1. Parallel processing (Electronic computers)   I. Title.
QA76.58.F67   1994
004'.35–dc20   93-36763   CIP

ISBN-13 978-0-521-45131-4 hardback
ISBN-10 0-521-45131-0 hardback

ISBN-13 978-0-521-03189-9 paperback
ISBN-10 0-521-03189-3 paperback

Contents

Preface

The study of parallel computing is just about as old as that of computing itself. Indeed, the early machine architects and programmers (neither category would have described themselves in these terms) recognised no such delineations in their work, although the natural human predilection for describing any process as a sequence of operations on a series of variables soon entrenched this philosophy as the basis of all normal systems.

Once this basis had become firmly established, it required a definite effort of will to perceive that alternative approaches might be worthwhile, especially as the proliferation of potential techniques made understanding more difficult. Thus, today, newcomers to the field might be told, according to their informer's inclination, that parallel computing means the use of transputers, or neural networks, or systolic arrays, or any one of a seemingly endless number of possibilities. At this point, students have the alternatives of accepting that a single facet comprises the whole, or attempting their own processes of analysis and evaluation. The potential users of a system are as likely to be set on the wrong path as the right one toward fulfilling their own set of practical aims.

This book is an attempt to set out the general principles of parallel computing in a way which will be useful to student and user alike. The approach I adopt to the subject is top-down – the simplest and most fundamental principles are enunciated first, with each important area being subsequently treated in greater depth. I would also characterise the approach as an engineering one, which flavours even the sections on programming parallel systems. This is a natural consequence of my own background and training.

The content of the book is arranged hierarchically. The first chapter explains why parallel computing is necessary, where it is commonly used, why the reader needs to know about it, the two or three underlying approaches to the subject and those factors which distinguish one system from another. The fundamental paradigms of parallel computing are set out in the following chapter. These are the key methods by which the various approaches are implemented – the basic intellectual ideas behind particular implementations. The third chapter considers a matter of vital importance, namely how these ideas are incorporated in programming languages.

The next two chapters cover fundamental technical aspects of parallel computers – the ways in which elements of parallel computers are connect-ed together, and the types of processing element which are appropriate for different categories of system.

The following chapter is of particular significance. One (perhaps the only) main reason for using parallel computers is to obtain cost-effectiveness or performance which is not otherwise available. To measure either parameter has proved even more difficult for parallel computers than for simpler systems. This chapter seeks to explain and mitigate this difficulty.

The penultimate chapter of the book comprises a set of case studies of archetypal parallel computers. It demonstrates how the various factors which have been considered previously are drawn together to form coherent systems, and the compromises and complexities which are thereby engen-dered. Each study has been written by an individual closely connected with the system in question, so that a variety of different factors are given promi-nence according to the views of each author.

The final chapter correlates the various aspects of parallel computing into a taxonomy of systems and attempts to develop some conclusions for the future.

Appropriate chapters are followed by exercises which are designed to direct students' attention towards the most important aspects of each area, and to explore their understanding of each facet. At each stage of the book, suggestions are made for further reading, by means of which interested readers may extend the depth of their knowledge. It is the author's hope that this book will be of use both to students of the subject of parallel com-puting and to potential users who want to avoid the many possible pitfalls in understanding this new and complex field.

1 Introduction

Before attempting to understand the complexities of the subject of parallel computing, the intending user or student ought, perhaps, to ask why such an exotic approach is necessary. After all, ordinary, serial, computers are in successful and widespread use in every area of society in industrially developed nations, and obtaining a sufficient understanding of their use and operation is no simple task. It might even be argued that, since the only reason for using two computers in place of one is because the single device is insufficiently powerful, a better approach is to increase the power (presumably by technological improvements) of the single machine.

As is usually the case, such a simplistic approach to the problem conceals a number of significant points. There are many application areas where the available power of 'ordinary' computers is insufficient to obtain the desired results. In the area of computer vision, for example, this insufficiency is related to the amount of time available for computation, results being required at a rate suitable for, perhaps, autonomous vehicle guidance. In the case of weather forecasting, existing models, running on single computers, are certainly able to produce results. Unfortunately, these are somewhat lacking in accuracy, and improvements here depend on significant extensions to the scope of the computer modelling involved. In some areas of scientific computation, including those concerned with the analysis of fundamental particle interactions, the time scale of the computation on current single computers would be such as to exceed the expected time to failure of the system.

In all these cases, the shortfall in performance is much greater than might at first be supposed – it can easily be several orders of magnitude. To take a single example from the field of image processing, it was recently suggested to me that operatives of a major oil company, when dealing with seismic data, would wish to have real-time processing of 10^9 voxels of data. (A voxel is an elemental data volume taken from a three-dimensional image.) This implies a processing rate of the order of 10^{12} operations per second. Compare this with the best current supercomputers, offering about 10^{10} operations per second (which themselves utilise a variety of parallel techniques as we shall see later) and the scale of the problem becomes apparent.

Although technological advance is impressively rapid, it tends to be only

1

about one order of magnitude every decade for general-purpose computers (but see Chapter 6 concerning the difficulties of measuring and comparing performance). Furthermore, the rate of technological improvement is showing signs of falling off as fundamental physical limits are approached and the problems of system engineering become harder, while the magnitude of some of the problems is becoming greater as their true requirements are better understood.

Another point concerns efficiency (and cost-effectiveness). Serial computers have a number of conceptual drawbacks in some of the application areas we are considering. These are mainly concerned with the fact that the data (or the problem) often has a built-in structure which is not reflected in the serial computer. Any advantage which might accrue by taking this structure into account is first discarded (by storing three-dimensional data as a list, for example) and then has to be regained in some way by the programmer. The inefficiency is therefore twofold – first the computer manipulates the data clumsily and then the user has to work harder to recover the structure to understand and solve the problem.

Next, there is the question of storage and access of data. A serial computer has, by definition, one (for the von Neumann architecture) or two (in the case of the Harvard system) channels to its memory. The problem outlined above in the field of image processing would best be solved by allowing simultaneous access to more than one million data items, perhaps in the manner illustrated in Figure 1.1. It is at least arguable that taking advantage of this possibility in some parallel way would avoid the serious problem of the processor-memory bottleneck which plagues many serial systems.

Finally, there is the undeniable existence of parallelism, on a massive scale, in the human brain. Although it apparently works in a very different way from ordinary computers, the brain is a problem-solver of unsurpassed excellence.

There is, then, at least a *prima facie* case for the utility of parallel computing. In some application areas, parallel computers may be easier to program, give performance unobtainable in any other way, and might be more cost-effective than serial alternatives. If this case is accepted, it is quite reasonable that an intending practitioner in the field should need to study and understand its complexities. Can the same be said of an intending user?

Perhaps the major problem which faces someone confronting the idea of parallel computing for the first time is that it is not a single idea. There are at least half a dozen significantly different approaches to the application of parallelism, each with very different implications for the user. The worst aspect of this is that, for a particular problem, some approaches can be seriously counter-productive. By this I mean that not only will some techniques be less effective than others, but some will be worse than staying with conventional computing in the first place. The reason is one which has been

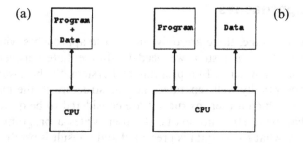

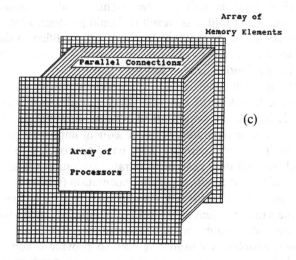

Figure 1.1 Overcoming the serial computer data bottleneck (a) von Neumann (b) Harvard (c) Parallel

mentioned already, namely that the use of parallelism almost always involves an attempt to improve the mapping between a computer and a particular class of problem. The kernel of the matter, then, is this:

> *In order to understand parallel computing, it is necessary to understand the relationships between problems and systems.*

One starting point might be to consider what application areas could benefit from the use of parallelism. However, in order to understand why these are suggested as being appropriate, it is first necessary to know something about the different ways in which parallelism can be applied.

1.1   Basic approaches

Fortunately, at this stage, there are only three basic approaches which we need to consider. As a first step, we need to differentiate between programmed and trained systems. In a programmed system, the hardware and software are conceptually well separated, i.e. the structure of the machine and the means by which a user instructs it are considered to be quite independent. The hardware structure exists, the user writes a program which tells the hardware what to do, data is presented and a result is produced. In the remainder of this book, I will often refer to this idea as *calculation*. In a trainable system, on the other hand, the method by which the system achieves a given result is built into the machine, and it is trained by being shown input data and told what result it should produce. After the training phase, the structure of the machine has been self-modified so that, on being shown further data, correct results are produced. This basic idea will often be referred to as *cognition* in what follows.

The latter approach achieves parallel embodiment in structures which are similar to those found in the brain, in which parallelism of data and function exist side by side. In programmed systems, however, the two types of parallelism tend to be separated, with consequent impact on the functioning of the system. There are therefore three basic approaches to parallel computing which we will now examine – parallel cognition (PC), data parallel calculation (DPC) and function parallel calculation (FPC). In order to clarify the differences between them, I will explain how each technique could be applied to the same problem in the field of computer vision and, as a starting point, how a serial solution might proceed.

The general problem I consider is how to provide a computer system which will differentiate between persons 'known' to it, whom it will permit to enter a secure area, and persons that it does not recognise, to whom it will forbid entry. We will assume that a data input system, comprising a CCTV and digitiser, is common to all solutions, as is a door opening device activated by a single signal. To begin, let us consider those aspects which are shared by all the programmed approaches.

1.1.1   Programmed systems

The common components of a programmable computer system, whatever its degree of parallelism, are illustrated in Figure 1.2. They comprise one or more data stores; one or more computational engines; at least one program store, which may or may not be contiguous with the data store(s); and one or more program sequencers. In addition to these items of hardware, there will be a software structure of variable complexity ranging from a single, executable program to a suite including operating system, compilers and

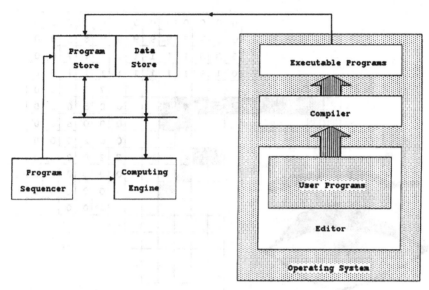

Figure 1.2   The common components of programmable systems

executable programs. Leaving aside the variability, the structure is simply program, store, sequencer and computer. How are these components employed to solve the problem in hand?

1.1.1.1 Serial

The data which is received from the combination of camera and digitiser will be in the form of a continuous stream of (usually) eight-bit numbers, changing at a rate determined by the clock rate of the digitiser. This should, ideally, be very high (of the order of 50 MHz) in order to reproduce faithfully the high-frequency components of the information in the image. The first requirement is to store this data in a form which will both represent the image properly and be comprehensible to the computer. This is done by considering the image as a set of pixels – sub-areas of the image sufficiently small that the information they contain can be represented by a single number, called the grey-level of the pixel. The data stream coming from the digitiser is sampled at a series of points such that the stored data represents a square array of pixels similar to those shown in Figure 1.3. The pixel values may be stored in either a special section of memory, or in part of the general computer memory. In either case they effectively form a list of data items.

The computer will contain and, when appropriate, sequence a program of instructions to manipulate this list of data to obtain the required result. A general flow chart of the process might be that shown in Figure 1.4 – each block of the chart represents an operation (or group of operations) on

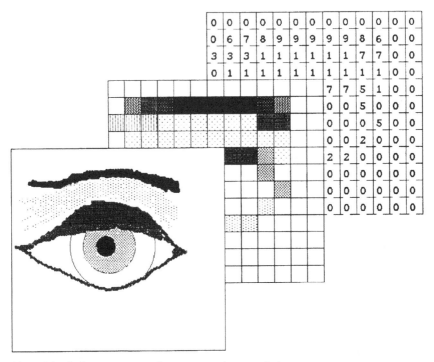

Figure 1.3 An image represented as an array of square pixels

either the original image data or on some intermediate result. At each stage, each instruction must be executed on a series of items, or sets of items, of data until the function has been applied to the whole image. Consider the first operation shown, that of filtering the original data. There are many ways of doing this, but one method is to replace the value of each pixel with the average value of the pixels in the local spatial neighbourhood. In order to do this, the computer must calculate the set of addresses corresponding to the neighbourhood for the first pixel, add the data from these addresses, divide by the number of pixels in the neighbourhood, and store the result as the first item of a new list. The fact that the set of source addresses will not be contiguous in the address space is an added complication. The computer must then repeat these operations until the averaging process has been applied to every part of the original data. In a typical application, such as we envisage here, there are likely to be more than 64 000 original pixels, and therefore almost that number of averaging operations. Note that all this effort merely executes the first filtering operation in the flow chart!

However, things are not always so bad. Let us suppose that the program has been able to segment the image – that is, the interesting part (a human face) has been separated from the rest of the picture. Already at this stage

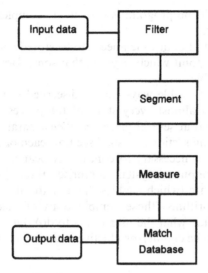

Figure 1.4   A serial program flow chart

the amount of data to be processed, although still formidable, has been
reduced, perhaps by a factor of 10. Now the program needs to find the
edges of the areas of interest in the face. Suitable subsets (again, local neighbourhoods) of the reduced data list must be selected and the gradients of
the data must be computed. Only those gradients above some threshold
value are stored as results but, along with the gradient value and direction,
information on the position of the data in the original image must be
stored. Nevertheless, the amount of data stored as a result of this process is
very significantly reduced, perhaps by a factor of 100.

Now the next stages of the flow chart can be executed. Certain key distances between points of the edge map data are computed as parameters of
the original input – these might be length and width of the head, distance
between the eyes, position of the mouth, etc. At this stage the original input
picture has been reduced to a few (perhaps 10) key parameters, and the final
stage can take place – matching this set of parameters against those stored
in a database of known, and therefore admissible, persons. If no match is
found, admittance is not granted.

A number of points are apparent from a consideration of the process
described above. First, a very large number of computations are required to
process the data from one image. Although it is unlikely that a series of
would-be intruders would present themselves at intervals of less than a few
seconds, it must be borne in mind that not all images obtained from the
camera during this period will be suitable for analysis, so the required repetition rate for processing may be much faster than once every second. This
is going to make severe demands on the computational speed of a serial

computer, especially if the program is sufficiently complex to avoid unacceptable rates of error.

Second, the amount of data which needs to be stored and accessed is also very large – a further point which suggests that some form of parallel processing might be suitable.

Third, at least two possible ways can be discerned in which parallelism might be applied – at almost every stage of the process *data* parallelism could be exploited, and at several places *functional* parallelism could be of benefit. In the following sections we shall see how each of these approaches might be used, but it is necessary to continually bear in mind that a programmed parallel computing system comprises three facets – hardware (self-evidently), software (which enables the user to take advantage of the parallelism) and algorithms (those combinations of machine operations which efficiently execute what the user wants to do). Disregarding any one of the three is likely to be counter-productive in terms of achieving results.

1.1.1.2   *Parallel data*

In this and the next two sections I shall assume that cost is no object in the pursuit of performance and understanding. Of course, this is almost never the case in real life, but the assumption will enable us to concentrate on developing some general principles. We might note, in passing, that the first of these could be:

> *Building a parallel computer nearly always costs more than building a serial one – but it may still be more cost-effective !*

I have already stated that all our systems share a common input comprising CCTV and digitiser, so our initial data format is that of a string of (effectively) pixel values. Before going any further with our design, we must consider what we are attempting to achieve. In this case, we are seeking out those areas of our system design where data parallelism may be effectively applied, and this gives us a clue as to the first move. This should be to carry out an analysis of the parallel data types in our process, and the relationships between them. Our tool for doing this is the data format flow chart, shown in Figure 1.5.

The chart is built up as follows. Each node of the chart (a square box) contains a description of the natural data format at particular points of the program, whereas each activity on the chart (a box with rounded corners) represents a segment of program.

The starting point is the raw data received from the digitiser. This is passed to the activity *store*, after which the most parallel unit of data which can be handled is the image. This optimum (image) format remains the same through the operations of filtering and segmentation, and forms the input to the *measurement of parameters* activity. However, the most parallel

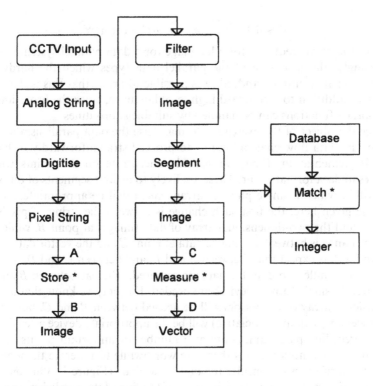

Figure 1.5   A data format flow chart

data unit we can obtain as an output from this operation is a vector of parameters. This is the input to the final stage of the process, the matching of our new input to a database. Note that a second input to this activity (the database itself) has a similar data format. The ultimate data output of the whole process is, of course, the door activation signal – a single item of data.

Having created the data format flow chart, it remains to translate it into the requirements of a system. Let us consider software first. Given that we are able to physically handle the data formats we have included in the flow chart as single entities, the prime requirement on our software is to reflect this ability. Thus if the hardware we devise can handle an operation of local filtering on all the pixels in an image in one go, then the software should allow us to write instructions of the form:

$$\text{Image\_Y} = \textit{filter}\ \text{Image\_X}$$

Similarly, if we have provided an item of hardware which can directly compute the degree of acceptability of a match between two vectors, then we should be permitted to write instructions of the form:

$$\text{Result1} = \text{Vector\_X } match \text{ Vector\_Y}$$

Thus, the prime requisite for a language for a data parallel system is, not surprisingly, the provision of the parallel data types which the hardware handles as single entities. Indeed, it is possible to argue that this is the only necessary addition to a standard high-level language, since the provision of appropriate functions can be handled by suitable subroutines.

Since the object of the exercise is to maximise the data parallelism in this design, the data flow chart allows us to proceed straightforwardly to hardware implementation. First, we should concentrate on the points where changes in data format occur. These are likely to delimit segments of our system within which a single physical arrangement will be appropriate. In the example given here, the first such change is between the string of pixels at point A and the two-dimensional array of data (image) at point B, while the second change is between the image data at point C and the vector data at D. We would thus expect that, between A and B, and between C and D, devices which can handle two data formats are required, whereas between B and C and after D, single format devices are needed. Further, we know that a two-dimensional array of processors will be needed between B and C, but a vector processor (perhaps associative) will be the appropriate device after D.

The preceding paragraph contains a number of important points, and a good many assumptions. It is therefore worthwhile to reiterate the ideas in order to clarify them. Consider the data flow chart (Figure 1.5) in conjunction with Figure 1.6, which is a diagram of the final data parallel system. At each stage there is an equivalence between the two. Every block of program which operates on data of consistent format corresponds to a single parallel processor of appropriate configuration. In addition, where changes in data format are required by the flow chart, specific devices are provided in the hardware to do the job.

Most of the assumptions which I have made above are connected with our supposed ability to assign the proper arrangement of hardware to each segment of program. If I assume no source of knowledge outside this book, then the reader will not be in a position to do this until a number of further chapters have been read. However, it should be apparent that, in attempting to maximise data parallelism, we can hardly do better than assign one processor per element of data in any given parallel set, and make all the processors operate simultaneously.

A number of points become apparent from this exercise. First, the amount of parallelism which can be achieved is very significant in this type of application – at one stage we call for over 64 000 processors to be operating together! Second, it is difficult (perhaps impossible) to arrange for total parallelism – there is still a definite sequence of operations to be performed. The third point is that parallelisation of memory is just as important as that

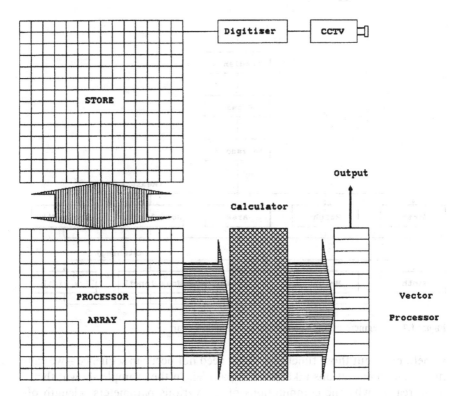

Figure 1.6 A data parallel calculation system

of processors – here we need parallel access to thousands of data items simultaneously if processing performance is not to be wasted. Finally, any real application is likely to involve different data types, and hence differently configured items of parallel hardware, if maximum optimisation is to be achieved.

1.1.1.3 Parallel function

Naturally enough, if we seek to implement functional parallelism in a computer, we need a tool which will enable us to analyse the areas of functional parallelism. As in the case of data parallelism, we begin with a re-examination of the problem in the light of our intended method. At the highest level (remembering that we are executing the identical program on a series of images), there are two ways in which we might look for functional parallelism. First, consider the segment of program flow chart shown in Figure 1.7.

In this flow chart, some sequences are necessary, while some are optional. For the moment, let us suppose that there is nothing we can do about the necessarily sequential functions – they have to occur in sequence because the input to one is the output of a previous operation. However, we can do

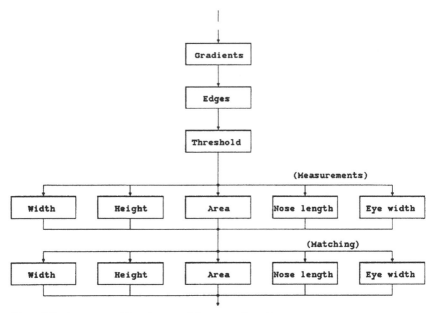

Figure 1.7   A segment of function parallel program flow chart

something about those functions which need not occur in sequence – we can make the computations take place in parallel. In the example shown, there is no reason why the computations of the various parameters – length of nose, distance between eyes, width of face, etc. – should not proceed in parallel. Each calculation is using the same set of data as its original input. Of course, problems may arise if multiple computers are attempting to access the same physical memory, but these can easily be overcome by arranging that the result of the previous sequential segment of program is simultaneously written to the appropriate number of memory units.

In a similar fashion, the matching of different elements of the database might be most efficiently achieved by different methods for each segment. In such a case, parallel execution of the various partial matching algorithms could be implemented.

There is a second way in which functional parallelism might be implemented. By applying this second technique, we can, surprisingly, address that part of the problem where sequential processing seems to be a requirement. Consider again the program flow chart (Figure 1.7), but this time as the time sequence of operations shown in Figure 1.8. In this diagram, repeated operation of the program is shown, reflecting its application to a sequence of images. Now imagine that a dedicated processor is assigned to each of the functions in the sequence. Figure 1.8 shows that each of these is used only for a small proportion of the available time on any given image.

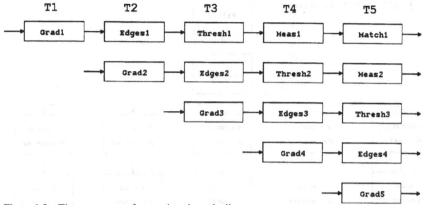

Figure 1.8 Time sequence of operations in a pipeline

However, this is not a necessary condition for correct functioning of the system. We could arrange matters so that each unit begins operating on the next image as soon as it has completed its calculations on the previous image. Results are then produced – images are processed and decisions are made – at the rate at which one computing element executes its own segment of program. When processing has been going on for some time, all the processors are working in parallel and the speedup is proportional to the number of processors.

There are therefore (at least) two ways of implementing functional parallelism and applying it to the problem in hand, and the resulting system is shown in Figure 1.9. Note that the amount of parallelism we can apply (about 10 simultaneous operations) is unlikely to be as great as with data parallelism, but that the entire problem can be parallelised in this way.

What we have not yet considered is the type of programming language which might be necessary to control such a computer. In this context, the two techniques which have been used need to be considered separately. The first, where parallel operations were identified within a single 'pass' of the program, is ideally served by some kind of parallelising compiler, that is a compiler which can itself identify those elements of a program which can be executed concurrently. As we shall see in a later chapter, such compilers are available, although they often work in a limited context. An alternative to this is to permit the programmer to 'tag' segments of code as being sequential or parallel as appropriate.

The second technique used above to implement functional parallelism has, surprisingly, no implications for user-level software at all. Both the program which is written and the sequence of events which happens to a given image are purely sequential. Again, the equivalent of a parallelising compiler must exist in order to distribute the various program segments to

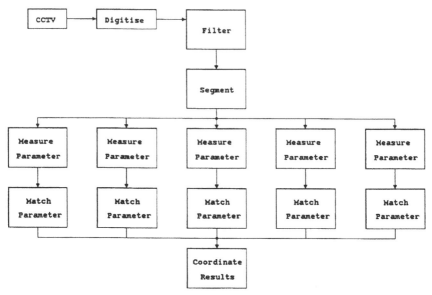

Figure 1.9   A function parallel computation system

the proper places on the system, and to coordinate their interactions, but the user need know nothing of this process.

It is of interest to note that, for both data parallel and function parallel systems, the identification of parallelism is much more easily carried out at the level of a flow chart (Figures 1.5 and 1.7) than within a program. This seems to indicate that, if software systems are to execute this function automatically, they may need to be presented with program specifications at this higher level.

1.1.2   Trainable systems

A completely different approach to implementing parallel computers to solve problems of the sort considered here has been inspired by considerations of how human brains attack such questions. (Because of this background, the approach is often called *neural* or *pseudo-neural*.)

It is obvious that the brain does not exist from the moment of birth as a completely operating structure, awaiting only the input of a suitable program to begin problem solving. Instead it undergoes a period of development – training – which eventually enables it not only to solve problems which it has encountered before, but to generalise its problem-solving techniques to handle new categories of question. It is this generalisation which is so attractive to proponents of this idea. In their book *Cognisers – Neural Networks and Machines that Think*, which forms an excellent introduction to the ideas and philosophy underlying this approach, Johnson and Brown coined the word cognisers to categorise systems which work in this way.

When applied to the field of computers, the basic idea is an exact analogue of the training and use of a human brain. A structure is devised which can absorb two types of input simultaneously. The first type of input is data – in our example data corresponding to the set of pixels making up an image. The second input is only valid during the training phase. This input informs the computing structure which *class* the data input falls into – in our example either accepted or rejected. On the basis of these two inputs, the computer adjusts its internal states (which roughly equate to memories) to produce an output which corresponds to the class input. This process is repeated an appropriate number of times until the operators believe the system is sufficiently well trained, and it is then switched into the operating mode. Each sub-class of the data (each person) produces a positive response at a particular output node and in order to arrive at an overall accept or reject decision these outputs must be combined. If the machine is correctly designed, and we shall see specific examples of such devices in later chapters, upon receiving further data inputs it will properly classify them into the required categories. The system will perform this operation with sufficient flexibility that modified versions of images (perhaps with the addition of beard or glasses) in the acceptable classes will still be accepted, whereas all other images will be rejected.

At first sight it would seem that the process with which we began the previous two sections – an analysis of the problem in order to discover areas of parallelism – is inappropriate here. That this is not, in fact, so reflects the level at which we previously specified the problem – a program. For a similar technique to be valid in this context we must move back to a higher level of abstraction. The level we need is a statement of the sort:

> *Classify images from a TV camera into two classes, one class resulting in a door being opened, the classification to be carried out with 99% correctness. The members of the 'open door' class are completely known, but their images are not fully specified.*

With the problem phrased in this manner, there are a number of hints, both that the problem might be amenable to solution by a cogniser, and that a parallel implementation may be needed. First, the input data is highly parallel, whereas the desired result could scarcely be simpler – close or open a door. This implies that a many-to-one mapping is required. Second, the problem is one of adaptive classification – no numerical results of any sort are needed. Finally, there is the implication that the classification is between a small number of known classes and a much larger, unknown class. All these are characteristics of the sort of problem which cognisers might be expected to solve.

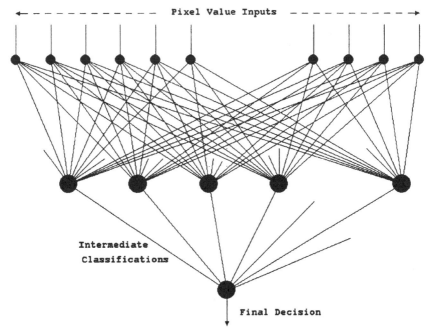

Figure 1.10   A parallel cognitive system

At the risk of pre-empting some of the material to come in later chapters, let us envisage a computer-like system which might carry out such a task. The first requirement is to store the input images (as they arrive) in a frame store. Our parallel computing network will take as its inputs the values (or, more likely, a subset of the values) of the elements of the store, i.e. the pixel values. The computing structure itself will be similar to that shown in Figure 1.10 – a highly-connected set of nodes with many inputs but rather fewer intermediate outputs and only one final output. Each node is a threshold unit whose output is one if the sum of its inputs exceeds a predetermined threshold, but is otherwise zero. Connections between nodes are by means of variable resistors. Operation of the system is as follows.

In training mode, the first image is input to the frame store and the values of the connecting resistors are modified so that a chosen output is either one or zero, depending on the status of the input image (admissible or not). This procedure is repeated with a large number of input images, the adjustment of resistors being carried out in such a way as to allow a consistent set of results, i.e. each admissible image gives a one at a specified output, all inadmissible inputs give zeroes at all outputs. That this is, in fact, possible we shall see in later chapters, but one obvious requirement is that the system must be sufficiently complex, that is, it must be sufficiently parallel.

In operating mode, the system will classify any input as either accepted or rejected. If the training has been sufficiently thorough, and if the algorithm used to adjust weights in the system allows consistency, and if the capacity of the system is sufficient, then the classification will (usually) be correct.

We can see from this that the system requires no programming as such – the ingenuity which usually goes into writing software must be redirected towards he development of adaptive training algorithms and interconnection methods. Of course, if the system developer is separate from the system user, then the user will have an easier time – except that the process of training such a machine can be somewhat tedious. It is also apparent that the differentiation between parallelism of data and function, present in the programmed systems, has disappeared. If, very roughly, we think of data as being distributed amongst the connecting resistors and function as being distributed amongst the nodes, parallelism of both types is present, although the specific details of what is happening are obscure – we have no exact representation of the internal states of the machine.

1.2   Fundamental system aspects

Before proceeding to a consideration of those application areas which might be suitable for the use of parallel computing, let us reiterate those basic aspects of parallel systems which distinguish one type from another, and from which we can infer information about their likely use. Table 1.1 summarises those factors. I have used shorthand labels to differentiate the approaches described above.

The first two factors in the table are those which I have used to define the various categories of system, but the others require some comment. The amount of parallelism in the three categories is likely to reflect closely the amount identifiable in the target applications of each. Thus, since both DPC and PC systems involve parallel data, and areas of application exist where this is (almost) infinite, the amount of parallelism is likely to be high. Similarly high levels have not so far been discovered in applying functional parallelism.

The amount of connectivity within a given system, that is the number of other processors in the system to which a given processor is connected, reflects that required by the relevant applications. Parallel data is often highly correlated in the spatial domain, so only short-range connectivity is needed between processing elements. Processor assemblies operating in the function parallel mode may all need to exchange data frequently, so that the provision of more connections of higher bandwidths is needed. The neural idea, embodied in cognisers, depends substantially for its efficacy on a dense interconnection network.

As far as accuracy is concerned, both DPC and FPC systems are likely to

Table 1.1. *Distinguishing features of computing systems*

System	Serial	DPC	FPC	PC
Control technique	Program	Program	Program	Train
Type of parallelism	None	Data	Function	Both
Amount of parallelism	None	High	Low	High
Connectivity	–	Low	High	High
Accuracy	High	High	High	Medium
Flexibility	Medium	Low	Low	High

be involved with high-precision calculation, whilst PC systems can be regarded as having a more approximate response. Similarly the programmed devices will have poor tolerance to conditions outside their planned field, whereas a PC system should be more flexible in its response.

Thus, of the parallel systems, the cogniser (PC) is potentially the most effective in applying parallelism, since it scores highly on all the relevant parameters in the table, whereas the other two approaches embody both good and bad points. This is not to say, of course, that a neural system is always the best to use. It must continually be borne in mind that it is the fit between problem and solution which is important – otherwise valuable resources will be wasted.

From Table 1.1 we might make some initial deductions about the type of problems which might map well onto the different categories of parallel approach. If we have to perform (relatively) simple processing on large, structured data sets, a DPC system is likely to be suitable. If data sets are smaller, but the amount of computation to be applied to each datum is large, then a FPC system may be appropriate. If the problem is for some reason ill-posed, that is, if the specification of input data or function is at all imprecise, then a cogniser system may be the best bet. Let us therefore look at some of the problem areas where parallelism has been applied, and see if the suggested correspondence is maintained.

1.3   Application areas

Naturally enough, the first major group of application areas comprises those problems where parallelism is apparent, although not exploited, in current serial solutions. These almost all fall into the area of data parallelism.

1.3.1 Image processing

The heading of this section may be misleading for some readers. I mean it to include image transformation, image analysis, pattern recognition, computer vision and machine vision, all terms which are used (sometimes interchangeably) to specify different aspects of the same general field.

The first reason why image processing is an appropriate area for the application of parallel computing has two aspects. The first concerns the sheer quantities of data which may be involved. Table 1.2 summarises the data content (in bytes) of some typical images. The second aspect lies in the speed at which processing of these images is required to proceed, and there are two quite separate ways in which this requirement arises.

First, many image processing applications occur in environments where the repetition rate for processing images is fixed by some external constraint. This may be the rate at which parts are constructed by an automated production line, the image repetition rate of a standard CCTV camera, or simply the rate at which a human inspector could perform the same task. In a rather different context, the controlling rate may be that at which an Earth-mapping satellite or a particle collision experiment is producing images. Table 1.2 gives typical values for some of these rates. The implication of these two factors taken together is clear – processing rates far in excess of anything available from conventional computers are required.

The second aspect of the need for speed lies in the requirement to program (or train) systems to perform the required tasks. The experience of many researchers in this field (including that of the author) is that, when developing the algorithms to perform a particular task, the response speed of the development system is crucial to successful development. This need for speedy response itself has a number of aspects, of which sheer processing power is only one. Equally important, from a hardware point of view, is the need for fast data input and output channels to data capture and display devices and to permanent storage. Neither of these is particularly easy to arrange, since most such devices are designed for operation with serial computers in which the data path already has a number of bottlenecks.

Table 1.2 *Data content of images*

Image	Pixel Resolution	Byte Resolution	Amount of Data (bytes)	Processing Time (seconds)	Processing Time/byte (seconds)
TV camera	2.5×10^5	1	2.5×10^5	0.02	8×10^{-8}
Landsat	1.6×10^7	10	1.6×10^7	60	4×10^{-7}
Map of UK	1.5×10^{12}	5	8×10^{12}	2×10^6	3×10^{-7}

−1	−2	−1
0	0	0
1	2	1

Figure 1.11   An image transform based on local operations

However, for parallel systems, one end of the data path is already of potentially high bandwidth, so the problems are somewhat reduced. In a later chapter we shall see how specific systems have dealt with this problem. A second additional requirement is the need for appropriate systems software. It is tedious in the extreme if, having decided to make a minor change in, for example, a convolution kernel, a time-consuming sequence of editing, compiling, linking and running must be executed before the result can be seen. Obviously, some kind of interpreted, interactive environment is required.

There is a second major reason why image processing is such an apposite area of application for parallel computing. It lies in the structured nature of the data sets (and operations) involved. Earlier in this chapter I emphasised that the key to the successful application of parallel computing lies in matching the structure of the computer to that of the problem. Images have a particularly obvious property which renders this process rather easier than in some other contexts – the data has high spatial correlation, that is, in transforming the value of an input data pixel to another value in a result image, the information required is frequently likely to be that data close to the original input pixel.Consider the situation depicted in Figure 1.11. In order to calculate values for the gradients (edges) in the input image, it is only necessary to convolve the image, at each point, with the 3×3 window of values shown. The convolution process works as follows. If the set of pixel values in the window is w_i, where $i = 1,...,9$, and the set of values in the convolving window is g_i, where $i = 1,...,9$, then the new value for the central pixel is R, given by:

$$R = \sum_{i=1}^{9} g_i w_i$$

This is an example of a local neighbourhood operator, very commonly used at this level of image processing. It is apparent from this example that the most typical technique in this field is the application of data parallelism, although there are certainly areas where a cognitive approach has been found to be worthwhile. The former is typically used where mensuration of image data is required, the latter where classification is needed. The technique of functional parallelism is sometimes implemented at this level in the form of the pipeline (see the next chapter).

As a counter to this optimistic view of the relation between image processing and parallel computing, it is worth pointing out that, if higher-level vision operations such as model matching or graph searching are required, serious problems associated with changing data format can be encountered.

1.3.2 Mathematical modelling

In many areas of endeavour in the fields of engineering and science, problems are solved by the technique of mathematical modelling. The technique involves describing the entity in question (which may be a complex structure, a chemical or biological process or a mathematical abstraction) in terms of equations which embody both constants and variables. One familiar example from the field of engineering is the technique of finite element analysis. The technique is illustrated in Figure 1.12.

The idea is as follows. The structure of an automobile shell (a suspension sub frame is shown in the diagram) can be approximated by a series of

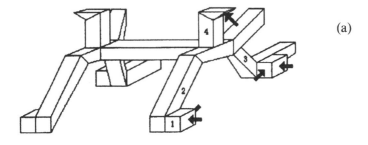

(a)

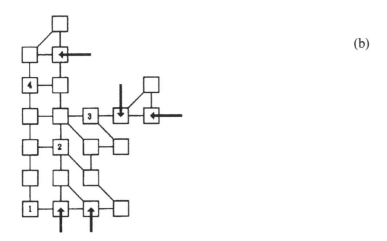

(b)

Figure 1.12   Finite element analysis of an automobile structure (a) The structure (b) Mapping to processors

plane elements (in this case rectangles and triangles), whose mechanical properties can be accurately described by equations embodying such constants as the tensile strength of steel, and variables which might include the thickness of the material and the stresses which are applied at defined points of the element. Naturally, such stresses are usually applied to a given element by the adjoining elements (which in turn are affected by their neighbours), so that the series of equations which define the whole structure are linked in reasonably simple ways. At the start of the process the structure is unstressed, and the model is then exercised by applying external forces such as inputs from the suspension, aerodynamic pressure, etc. Matters are arranged so that results are produced which detail the deformation of the body shell and, ultimately, its breakdown modes.

It should be apparent that, since real automobile bodies are made up of complex curves, the accuracy of results from such a process will depend on the fineness of the modelling elements. This in turn implies that, for such a complex structure, many thousands of elements are likely to be used. Here, then, is an obvious area for the application of parallelism. An appropriate technique would be one known as *relaxation*. Consider the situation shown in Figure 1.12 – a section of the finite element model near to a suspension mounting point.

The figure shows both the original element structure and a parallel computing structure where the calculations relating to each element are carried out on a dedicated processor. The processors are linked by channels which correspond to the shared edges of the elements. Calculations proceed by a process of iteration through a series of time steps.

At step one, when an external stress is first applied, only the processor corresponding to the element connected to the suspension point calculates a new value of its outputs – the stresses it passes to neighbouring elements. At step two, the processors corresponding to these elements calculate new results – as does the first element, since the transmission of stresses will be a two-way process. At each step, more and more elements are involved until, once all the processors are operating, the whole network settles down to a state representing a new static configuration of the body shell. Figure 1.13 illustrates the first few steps in the process. In this example, the figures do not represent any real parameter of stress calculations, although the algorithm used to generate them was typically iterative, and involved feedback as well as feed-forward. Although such a process can clearly be (and has frequently been) modelled on a powerful serial computer, it maps ideally onto a parallel network, such as that suggested, with consequent improvements in performance and/or precision of results.

Unusually, an argument could be made for the suitability of each of the three basic ideas of parallel computing for this application area. The problem could be regarded as data parallel, in that models could be designed in which the computation required at each element is identical, with only the parameters being different. It could be regarded as function parallel, if the computation at each element were tailored to the exact requirements of the element. Finally, it could be suggested that the process corresponds to a cogniser technique known as global minimisation, which we shall come to in the next chapter. The choice of an appropriate technique would obviously then depend on more detailed analyses of efficiency.

The example described above is obviously not unique. Other areas of application would include modelling of world-wide weather systems, investigations of particle interactions within crystalline or amorphous materials,

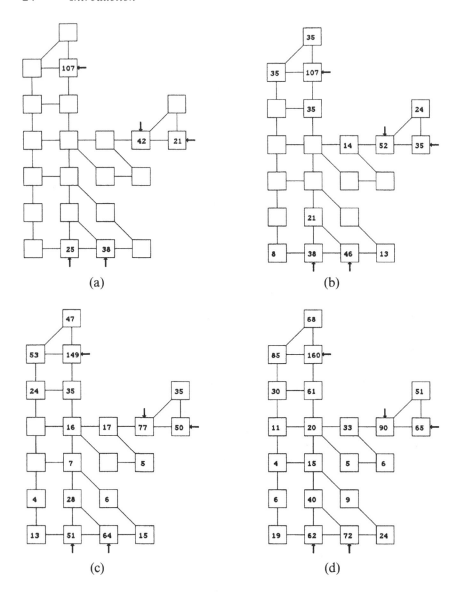

Figure 1.13   The process of relaxation (a) Stage 1 (b) Stage 2 (c) Stage 3 (d) Stage 4

and calculations connected with the stability of complex molecules. These areas, and many others, have aspects which can readily be mapped onto parallel structures of one sort or another.

1.3.3   Artificial intelligence

Artificial intelligence (AI) has been defined as:

> *Part of computer science, concerned with computer systems which exhibit human intelligence: understanding language, learning new information, reasoning, and solving problems.*

This definition is taken from *Artificial Intelligence – A Personal, Commonsense Journey* by Arnold and Bowie, which is a good, understandable introduction to the subject.

There are, in fact, several particular aspects of the field which suggest that the application of some form of parallel computing might be appropriate. The first is what I might call the anthropomorphic argument. Since the aim of the field is to emulate the operation of human intelligence, it seems intuitively obvious that a parallel cogniser, which mimics the structure of the brain, will be the proper tool for the job. Although in my view this argument has considerable force, it would probably be anathema to the majority of practitioners of AI.

To the mainstream practitioner of the field, AI is based firmly on a few core ideas. The first of these is that of a *database* of knowledge. Such databases, at least at this level of consideration, fall into two classes – databases of objects and databases of rules. It is easiest to explain these concepts with the aid of an example. Suppose that the problem to be solved is to design and construct a plumbing system for an apartment. The objects in this instance are the obvious items, such as pipes, washbasins, drains, etc., which make up the plumbing, as well as less obvious items such as the pressure of incoming water, the physical measurements of the rooms, and facts such as 'we want the bath over there'. It should be apparent from this that the class of objects has two important characteristics – each object may be very complex (in the jargon, it has many *attributes*) and there may be a very large number of objects, even in a tightly defined field such as that considered here. Taken together, these two facts provide the first indication that the amount of data being manipulated is very large, and that therefore parallelism may be necessary. It is worth noting, in passing, that conventional AI wisdom suggests that the effectiveness of an AI system depends heavily on the size of its database, so that there is continual pressure to increase the amount of data involved.

The rules of an AI system comprise the definitions of what to do next in order to solve the problem in hand – such things as:

> If you want to connect the washbasin tap to the wall spigot, first measure the distance between them.

Of course, rules are likely to be hierarchical. In this case 'measure the distance' might have a set of rules for application in different circumstances –

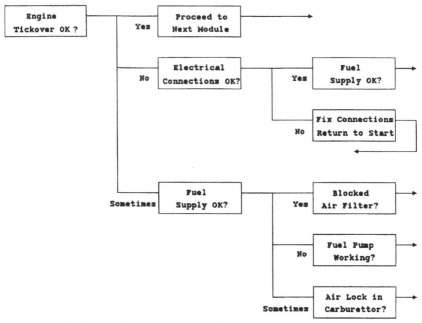

Figure 1.14   The hierarchical structure of a rule base

if the connection isn't a straight line, for example – and these rules may link with others, and eventually with the object database, in a complex structure. Figure 1.14 gives a flavour of the sort of structure which is usually involved, typically a tree or graph. In this case, the problem area is that of automobile maintenance.

One important point to be borne in mind is that such structures often allow searches for the best (or only) way to solve a problem amongst what may be a multitude of possibilities. This gives us another clue as to the applicability of parallelism. There is no reason why numbers of avenues of possibility cannot be explored in parallel (provided some mechanism is in place to resolve conflicts or assess alternatives).

There are therefore at least three reasons to suppose that applying parallelism might be a suitable way to attack such problems – but do appropriate parallel techniques exist to make the application effective? Let us first consider the cognitive approach suggested at the beginning of this section.

Artificial intelligence systems first learn about the world (or, at least, about that small part of it which constitutes the problem domain) and then attempt to solve problems which they haven't 'seen' before. At first glance, this appears to match exactly with the sort of thing I described cognitive systems as doing earlier, but there are important differences. First, the solution to an AI problem is likely to be much more complex than a simple categorisation of input data (which is what I described cognisers as doing).

There are some limited cases where this approach might be suitable – if, for example, the first question has the form 'What illness is this patient suffering from?' the answer might well be one of many predefined categories. However, even in such cases, the second problem still exists. This concerns the fact that inputting data into an AI system is almost always an interactive process – the data needed at later stages depends on the answers to earlier questions. At present, cogniser systems are very far from this stage of development, so we should (reluctantly) conclude that, in spite of the intuitive match, parallel cognisers are not yet appropriate for application to AI.

All is not lost, however. Some sort of function parallel calculator might very well be a suitable platform for an AI system. This is because, as we shall see in the next chapter, there exist techniques specifically intended to manipulate the type of graph structure which comprises the rule base of an AI system. It is in this area that we find parallelism an applicable technique to the computing requirements of artificial intelligence.

1.3.4 General database manipulation

As was pointed out above, artificial intelligence depends for much of its efficacy upon the use and manipulation of databases. In fact, this is just one particular example of a much wider field of application, that of database manipulation in the administrative and financial context.

The amount of money and time spent on computing in general administration is far greater than the equivalent expenditure in the areas of science and engineering applications which I have considered above. Although, in general, a lower proportion of this expenditure is devoted to problems demanding the power of parallel computing, applications in this area constitute a significant proportion of the total and therefore should not be ignored.

An example will illustrate why parallel computing might be useful in certain straightforward database manipulation operations. First, consider the magnitude of the record keeping requirements of the central taxation authorities in a country of moderate size and wealth such as the United Kingdom. This country has, at any one time, perhaps thirty million taxpayers. The data entry on each of these might well constitute (to judge solely from the complexity of tax forms!) upwards of one hundred fields, each comprising up to one hundred bytes of information. A straightforward serial computer would require perhaps one millisecond to execute one field matching operation (typical of database operations) per taxpayer. A full scan through the database (operating on only a single field) would therefore take thirty thousand seconds – about thirty hours! More complex multiple functions would take correspondingly longer.

The most simplistic application of parallelism, whereby each byte of data to be matched at a given moment was assigned to its own processor, could speed this up by perhaps two orders of magnitude – reducing the time required to less than twenty minutes. Alternatively, segments of the database could be assigned to each of a set of parallel processing elements, offering an improvement in performance proportional to the number of elements employed.

That such improvements in performance could be easily achieved in database manipulations is inherent in the structured nature of the data, and the repetitive nature of the operations which are being performed. Thus either data parallel or function parallel techniques might prove appropriate and easily implemented. It is unlikely that, in the present state of the art, any kind of cognitive system would prove suitable for the types of operation required.

1.4   Summary

Let us, then, summarise what has been (dis)covered in this first chapter. The first point concerns the need for parallel computing. It was argued that, whatever advances occur in the technology of serial computers, there are certain fields of application where their present or foreseeable available power is quite insufficient for the task, and the required power can only be supplied by parallel systems of some sort.

Second, in order to make valid judgements about parallel computing, it is necessary to understand how particular problems will map onto specific implementations of parallelism. Without an appropriate matching, the application of parallel techniques can be inefficient and even, under some circumstances, counter-productive.

Third, there are three radically different basic approaches to parallel computing – those I have called data parallel calculation (DPC), function parallel calculation (FPC) and parallel cognition (PC) – the application of which lead to significantly different parallel implementations. I have suggested that it is possible to discover how each idea can be applied to a particular problem by analysing the problem at the appropriate level. To assess the relevance of parallel cognition, it is necessary to specify the problem at the highest conceptual level. To discover whether the ideas of data parallel calculation or function parallel calculation are appropriate, specifications at the level of, respectively, the data format flow chart and the program flow chart are needed.

Fourth, a number of particular application areas can be identified in which many problems suitable for the application of parallel computing are to be found. These areas include image processing, mathematical modelling, scientific computation, artificial intelligence and database manipulation.

Given an analysis of an appropriate problem using the methods described, the next step will usually be to assess the most effective approach. In general terms, we have seen that the three basic ideas are distinguished by different scores on parameters such as amount of parallelism, degree of inter-processor connectivity, accuracy and flexibility. This represents, however, a very preliminary stage of assessment, and to proceed further it will be necessary to look at how these basic ideas are implemented. The first stage of this process is to understand the paradigms which underlie the implementations. These paradigms are described in the next chapter.

2 The Paradigms of Parallel Computing

The *Shorter Oxford English Dictionary* defines the word *paradigm* as meaning pattern or example, but it is used here in its generally accepted sense in this field, where it is taken to imply a fundamental technique or key idea. This chapter, therefore, is concerned with describing the fundamental ideas behind the implementation of parallel computation.

Two matters need to be dealt with before we begin. First, the reader should avoid confusion between the basic approaches set out in Chapter 1 and the paradigms described here. In the final chapter of this book, I develop a taxonomy of parallel computing systems, i.e. a structured analysis of systems in which each succeeding stage is based on increasingly detailed properties. In this taxonomy, the first two levels of differentiation are on the basis of the three approaches of the first chapter, whereas the third level is based on the paradigms described here. This is shown in Figure 2.1.

Next, there is the whole subject of optical computing. In one sense, an optical component, such as a lens, is a data parallel computer of dedicated functionality (and formidable power). There is certainly an overlap in the functions of such components and those of, say, an image processing parallel computer of the conventional sort. A lens can perform a fourier transform (a kind of frequency analysis) on an image, literally at the speed of light, whereas a conventional computer requires many cycles of operation to achieve the same result. An argument could therefore be made for the inclusion of this type of optical computing as one of the paradigms covered in this chapter. Beyond noting the possibility, I have chosen not to do so on the basis that the approach is sufficiently specialised, and sufficiently different from the others in this book, to warrant separate treatment.

In other quarters, the phrase *optical computing* is taken to mean the use of devices, whose status is modified by optical rather than electrical means, to emulate the kind of circuits found in electronic computers. Again, beyond noting this as an alternative technical approach, I believe a proper treatment is better attempted elsewhere. A satisfying introduction to both aspects is given by Feitelson in his book *Optical Computing: A Survey for Computer Scientists*.

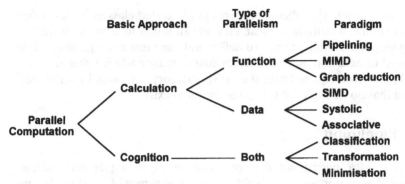

Figure 2.1   The first levels of a taxonomy

2.1   Flynn's taxonomy

Whilst there are, as we shall see later, certain relationships to be perceived between the paradigms described here, it is probably best, in the first instance, to treat them as completely independent. I begin with those ideas which may be somewhat familiar from the field of conventional computing, and proceed to those which might be regarded as more exotic or complex. Before doing so, however, in order to clarify the headings given to some of the following sections of this chapter, it is necessary to consider one of the earliest, and perhaps most useful, attempts at classifying computer systems.

In 1966, M. J. Flynn published a seminal paper in the *Proceedings of IEEE* [1] concerning a taxonomy of computer architectures. The central idea was that this could be carried out in terms of data streams and instruction streams, and the singularity or multiplicity of each. Possible categories of architecture therefore comprised *SISD* (single instruction stream, single data stream); *SIMD* (single instruction stream, multiple data stream); *MISD* (multiple instruction stream, single data stream) and *MIMD* (multiple instruction stream, multiple data stream). These convenient shorthand labels passed into the language of parallel computing but, as with many other well-used words, the meanings became subtly altered from those intended by their originator. The two labels which have most currency today are SIMD and MIMD, which are taken to mean:

SIMD A parallel array of processing elements, all of which execute the same instruction at the same moment. The processors are usually mesh-connected, and the basic approach is data parallelism.
MIMD An assembly of processing elements each of which can carry out any task, either independently of, or in concert with, other processors. The connectivity between the elements is not usually specified. The basic approach is often, but not always, function parallelism.

It is unfortunate that these acronyms fall into that class of words which embody sufficient latitude to mean (almost) all things to all men. In the following sections, I shall attempt to define and use them more precisely. It is of interest to note that, at one time, the first paradigm which I shall describe – pipelining – was equated with the MISD category, although Flynn himself claimed that no examples of this category could exist.

2.2 Pipelining

The basic idea underlying the technique of pipelining is very simple. Suppose that a process can be split up into a sequence of identifiable sub-processes. A calculation which can be handled in this fashion is the following:

$$F(x,y) = \sqrt{93(x+y)}$$

In this case the sub-processes are the functions *add, multiply* and *square root*. Further, suppose that a substantial set of such calculations is needed in immediate succession. The idea of pipelining is applied as follows.

Assign to each of the sub-processes a particular computation unit. (For the sake of simplicity at this stage we assume that each processor can carry out its assigned task in unit time.) Arrange that the output of each processor is connected to the input of the succeeding unit. Further, arrange that data are input sequentially to the first processor at the appropriate rate. Figure 2.2 illustrates the arrangement required.

We now assume that a synchronising clock is started, and that at each tick of the clock every unit executes its defined calculation, and fresh inputs are presented to the first unit.

At the first tick, processor 1 adds the first two numbers (let us call them x_1 and y_1) and presents the result to the input of unit 2. At the second tick, processor 2 multiplies the first result (z_1) by the constant value (93) and presents the result to the inputs of processor 3. At the same time processor 1 is adding together x_2 and y_2 and presenting them to the input of processor 2. At the third tick, three things happen simultaneously. Processor 3 calculates the square root of $93z_1$; processor 2 multiplies z_2 by 93; processor 1 adds together x_3 and y_3. We have now, after three ticks of the clock, produced our first result. However, as long as data continue to be presented to the inputs of processor 1, a new result is produced at every tick. The speedup in performance is therefore the maximum which we could expect from a three-processor parallel system – a factor of three. Furthermore, the system which we have implemented is particularly simple in terms of connectivity – in particular, the results all come out in one place.

This example, simple though it is, illustrates a number of important

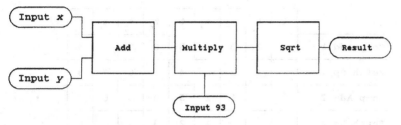

Figure 2.2   The elements of a computational pipeline

points about pipelining. First, in common with all other parallel computing paradigms, it relies for its efficacy on being applied to an appropriate problem. In this case, the requirements are that a suitably large set of identical computations need to be executed; that each computation can be split up into a sequence of sub-functions; and finally that the output of each sub-function is the input to the next. Second, although a pipeline produces one result per clock period once it is full, there is always a *latency* associated with the system, this being one clock period per unit of the pipeline (in the case of our example, three clock periods). The latency is the time between starting the system and getting the first result. Third, because pipelining is itself a sequentially organised operation, programming techniques require little or no modification from the users' point of view, and optimisation is easy to automate. Fourth, the improvement in performance which can be expected is almost exactly equivalent to the resources allocated – the speedup factor is the same as the number of stages in the pipeline. Small departures from the exact relationship are caused by the latency of the system and by difficulties in ensuring that all stages of the pipeline do equal amounts of work.

Finally, however, a little thought reveals one of the significant drawbacks of the pipelining technique under some circumstances. Suppose that, instead of the example given above, a different calculation were to be required, for example:

$$F(x,t) = 2\pi \int \frac{\alpha + \beta}{\sin(x)} \, dt$$

In this case, a different pipeline of different elements would need to be set up. In other words, each specific calculation which the computer is required to execute needs a specific configuration of pipeline. Whilst it is feasible to implement a reasonably general arrangement which would allow a large number of configurations, complete generality is impossible to achieve and, in any case, the need to reconfigure the system between each computational segment is likely to be both tedious and time-consuming. These strictures do not apply if each unit of the pipeline is programmable, but maintaining

	t_1	t_2	t_3	t_4	t_5	t_6	t_7	t_8	t_9
Comp Add 1	1	2	3	4	5	6	7	8	9
Fetch Op 1		1	2	3	4	5	6	7	8
Comp Add 2			1	2	3	4	5	6	7
Fetch Op 2				1	2	3	4	5	6
Comp Result					1	2	3	4	5
Comp Add 3						1	2	3	4
Store Result							1	2	3

Figure 2.3   Timing relationships within a machine-level pipeline

the requirement for each element to operate in unit time then becomes more difficult. The further problem of optimising the pipeline length to be the same as that of the program remains, however.

The example of pipelining given above was chosen for its simplicity, rather than its realism. In fact, the technique is unlikely to be applied to problems of this sort. There are two areas where use of the method is more profitable and therefore more widespread – at the machine instruction level and at the algorithm level.

The argument for use of the technique at the lowest machine level is as follows. The great majority of machine instructions in a computer can be broken down into a common sequence of operations:

(1) Compute address for first operand
(2) Fetch first operand
(3) Compute address for next operand
(4) Fetch next operand
(5) Repeat (3) and (4) as required
(6) Execute the required computation
(7) Compute address for result
(8) Store result

Given that most instructions will need this sequence of operations, it is obviously well worthwhile to set up a pipeline to deal with the situation and thereby sequence instructions at the relevant clock rate, rather than every five to ten clock periods. Figure 2.3 shows how the timing of the various elements is related. At t_1 only the first unit of the pipeline is active, but by t_7 each unit is operating on a segment of a different instruction, and the first result has been stored. Thereafter, results are produced at each clock period. Of course, there are some classes of instruction which cannot be han-

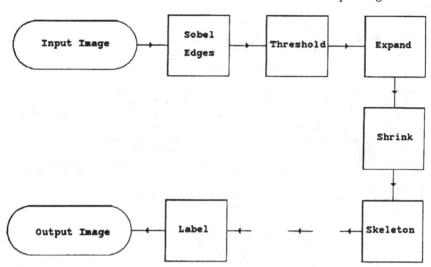

Figure 2.4 An image processing pipeline

dled in this way, particularly conditional branches, but it is relatively simple to set up arrangements to deal with these. Because an approximately five-fold improvement in performance is simple to achieve at low cost by this method, it is a widely used technique.

A second area where pipelining has been profitably employed is in the construction of special-purpose computers, in particular those intended for use in image processing applications. In this context, the paradigm has been used to implement both data and functional parallelism, sometimes (confusingly!) in the same system.

Let us consider the functionally parallel aspect first, since that is the method embodied in the two examples given so far. The argument used is that, since we are considering a special-purpose computer, the design (and the program) can be optimised for a particular application. Further, most image processing application programs comprise relatively few instructions, and it therefore makes sense to assign one element of a pipeline to each instruction, even if some instructions are repeated at various points in the program.

Image processing employs algorithms which may not be familiar to the general reader. This book is not the place to attempt a full exposition of these and any reader who requires such a treatment is recommended to study *Digital Image Processing* by Gonzalez and Wintz. It is not, however, necessary to have a complete understanding of the algorithms employed in order to appreciate the form of the pipeline shown in Figure 2.4. Important points to note are that such a system is likely to comprise a large number of elements (perhaps as many as 100); that each element will execute a complete operation of some sort; and that the value of the system is only realised when a large sequence of images is to be processed, perhaps from

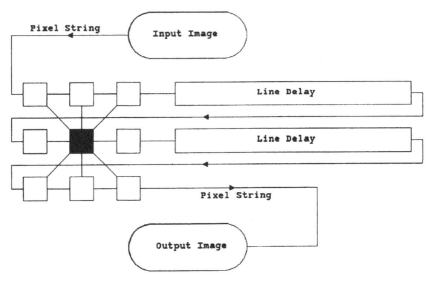

Figure 2.5   A data parallel pipeline arrangement

continuous CCTV input.

The data parallel aspect of pipelining can be appreciated by focusing down on one of the functional elements of Figure 2.4. Let us choose the first of those shown – finding object edges. The operation is one of a class known as local neighbourhood operators, that is, the result at each pixel depends on the values of the input pixels which comprise a 3 × 3 *neighbourhood* around the pixel under consideration. The point here is that this neighbourhood of data can be presented to a computational element automatically, without the necessity for complex addressing schemes, by pipelining the pixel data through an arrangement such as that shown in Figure 2.5. The active processing element in the system is the black square – all the other components are storage elements whose purpose is to continually present the correct configuration of data to the processor. At every tick of the clock, data is shifted through the structure so that, once sufficient data is in the pipeline, a new result is created at every tick, and the results are produced in the correct order as a new image. This technique has been used to advantage in a number of systems including the Cytocomputer [2].

Finally, it is of some interest to consider the question raised earlier – is a pipeline an MISD system? I believe that Flynn intended this designation to mean that, in a single data stream, at a given moment a single item of data was being acted upon by multiple instructions. In this sense, a pipeline is clearly not MISD. Nevertheless, multiple instructions are operating simultaneously and usefully on what is, after all, a single input data stream. The confusion here is probably only one of semantics, or possibly of interpretation, and is probably reflected in the fact that, whereas the word *pipeline* has wide acceptance, the designation *MISD* is rarely used. In this instance, my advice to the reader is to conform to popular usage and thereby avoid any controversy over the MISD designation.

2.3   MIMD

This is the second parallel computing paradigm which is in widespread use, in one form, in many so-called serial computers. In this context the argument which underlies its use is as follows. Any substantial computer program is likely to embody a number of quite different classes of operation – on one level these might include arithmetic computation, program sequencing, disc control and raster display formatting. Given a suitable lack of cost constraints, and an appropriate requirement for performance, it would obviously be advantageous to assign a dedicated unit to each identifiable function – every operation would thereby be executed with maximum efficiency. Further, there are often likely to be circumstances (in a multi-user configuration, for example) when simultaneous operation of some of these units would be both possible and desirable. A suitable arrangement which might satisfy these requirements is shown in Figure 2.6.

The basic method of operation is this. Although each element of the assembly is permitted to carry out operations autonomously, one of the elements, usually the program sequencer, is assigned to coordinate all the activities. Thus, when a segment of program is encountered which requires

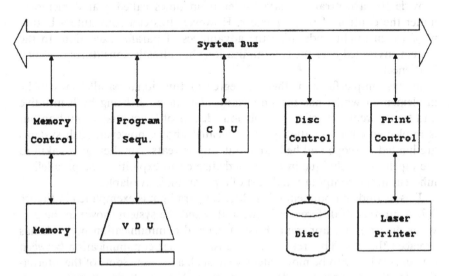

Figure 2.6   A possible MIMD system

a data file, held on disc, to be printed on the laser printer, the following sequence takes place:

(1) The sequencer sends the necessary instructions and parameters to the disc controller and to the printer controller
(2) The disc controller reads data from the disc to a buffer
(3) The disc and printer controllers cooperate to transfer data from the disc buffer to the printer buffer
(4) The printer controller causes the data to be printed

This simple process illustrates a number of important points. First, as soon as operation (1) above is completed, the sequencer is free to continue executing further segments of the program. Of course, if these sections require use of the disc or printer, or even use of the bus on which they are communicating, then the anticipated parallelism cannot occur. If this is not the case, however, functional parallelism has been achieved.

Second, all three of the devices in use may need to communicate with each other at various points in the process. This means that mechanisms have to be in place whereby each device is continually 'listening out' for messages from other devices and evaluating the priority of commands or requests to take action.

Third, because the disc in particular is a real-time device – it rotates at a fixed rate quite independent of the time at which a request for data arrives – some form of data buffering has to be provided with which other devices can communicate. It is worth noting that one type of arrangement would provide for a centralised data buffer (sometimes called shared memory) under the control of the sequencer. However, this can constitute a bottleneck which might undermine the advantages of parallel execution. In the system envisaged here the communications bus already constitutes one such bottleneck.

In this simple fashion, then, a degree of functional parallelism can be implemented which has the important advantages of being both intuitive and transparent – it reflects an obvious degree of functional separation but is implemented automatically. As indicated above, however, such systems are limited in scope and hedged about with caveats. An alternative, akin to the pipelining technique in that it is dedicated to exploiting the parallelism inherent in the computational part of a program, is available.

This second embodiment of the MIMD paradigm is exemplified in Figure 2.7. A number of differences between this and the system shown in the previous diagram are apparent. First, a general communication network has replaced the bus. This reflects the realisation that communication between elements is likely to be more intensive in such a system. Some of the alternatives for this network include those set out in Figure 2.8, which are:

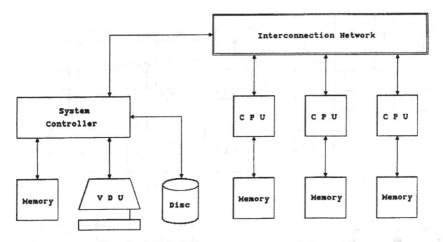

Figure 2.7 An alternative MIMD system

(a) Arranging the processing elements (PEs) in a regular structure, such as a two dimensional grid, and providing direct communications between the physically nearest elements only

(b) Providing multiple buses between the set of elements, so that the probability of finding an unused channel when needed is high

(c) Connecting the processors by means of an N-dimensional hypercube. This arrangement is fully described in Chapter 4, but it is sufficient to note here that, for a set of N elements, the maximum number of steps between any two is 2^N

(d) Supplying a full crossbar switch between the elements. This arrangement guarantees that a direct channel between two elements exists, but does not guarantee that this channel will always be available if other devices are communicating

The main point to note here is that the more complex of these networks are often viable alternatives for MIMD systems only because of the relatively limited numbers of processors which are usually incorporated.

The second general point to note is that all the elements (except the system controller) which are attached to the communication network are general-purpose processors. This means that, as long as a suitable means is provided to distribute processing and keep track of the overall situation, program segments can be distributed homogeneously. (This is only approximately true for some of the connection networks shown in Figure 2.8.)

The technique for operating such a network is usually as follows. The controlling processor (frequently dedicated to this task) has software structures which keep track of the following items:

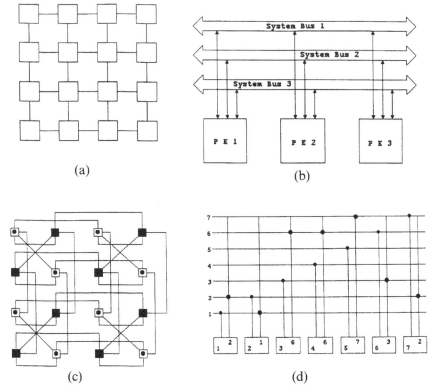

Figure 2.8 Some alternative interconnection networks (a) Mesh (b) Multiple buses (c) Hypercube (d) Crossbar switch

(a) The computational segments which need to be executed
(b) The results of computation which may subsequently be required
(c) Those processing elements which are currently active
(d) Those elements which are inactive, either because they are currently computing or because they have been deemed to be faulty

Each computational element can signal its status to these structures and request data from, and send results to, them. The obvious difficulties with such a system are threefold. First, if the overall program cannot be split up into enough parallel segments, resources will be wasted. Second, if too much inter-processor communication is required, the network may become overloaded. Third, if the amount of time spent keeping track of the whole process is too great, the value of achieving parallelism may be lost. It is of some interest to note that this problem is the main reason why single bus-connected systems are often inappropriate in this context. Such systems can become saturated with as few as sixteen processors, so that adding more processors actually decreases the absolute performance [3].

Another point concerns the amount of operator interaction with the process of segment allocation and processor communication. As we shall see later, this can range between zero and (almost) infinity. Some programming languages demand that the programmer should define the placement of each parallel segment and the route for every communication. Others will act as parallelising compilers and execute the whole process automatically, although usually with less efficiency. The choice is thus the usual one between convenience and cost-effectiveness.

We may therefore summarise the main aspects of the MIMD paradigm as follows. First, its use implies a particular combination of software and hardware – a software system which supports the idea of functional parallelism, either at the gross or detailed level, and a hardware system which is an assembly of processing elements, each of which can operate autonomously and which may be either specialised or general-purpose in operation, together with a suitable communication network. Second, the processing elements are certain to be complex in structure (each is, after all, an autonomous computer) but are likely to be relatively few in number. Finally, such systems are likely to offer some speedup in execution times on almost any program, although optimum efficiency will only be obtained for appropriately structured problems. They are probably the most versatile of all parallel systems for the general-purpose user.

A discussion of MIMD systems would be incomplete without mention of the transputer. This splendid name was coined by (among others) Iann Barron, who subsequently founded the Inmos company to produce the devices. The transputer (in its many guises) is a microprocessor specifically designed to be the basic computing component of MIMD systems such as those described above. It was the first such device to recognise the paramount importance of communications in obtaining the anticipated performance from assemblies such as these and therefore became popular in their implementation. A fuller description of this device will be found in Chapter 7D.

2.4 Graph reduction

The third of the paradigms in the general class of FPC ideas is not, necessarily, a parallel technique at all. It can be implemented perfectly satisfactorily in strict sequential fashion, but it is a method which apparently lends itself so well to parallel implementation that a number of systems based upon the idea have been constructed. I therefore include it here. I will begin by describing the method of graph reduction *per se*, and then explain the modifications which are required for parallel implementation.

The basic idea is this. Any computational program can be expressed as a *graph*. As an example, consider the following function:

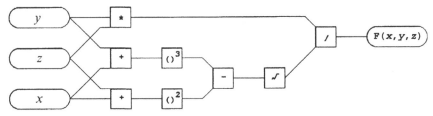

Figure 2.9   A computation graph

$$F(x,y,z) = \frac{\sqrt{(x+y)^3 - (x+z)^2}}{xy}$$

where $x = 7$; $y = 4$; $z = 9$;

This expression can be represented by the graphical structure shown in Figure 2.9, which is known as the *computation graph*. Graph reduction proceeds by repeatedly evaluating sub-graphs which are reducible, that is, single functions which have parameters which are all either constants or evaluated expressions. The process of reduction normally proceeds, therefore, from the left of the graph to the right, and continues until no further reductions can take place. At this point the *normal form* of the expression has been reached. For the present example, the first pass consists of replacing the parameters x, y and z with their specified values. At the second stage the expressions (+) and (×) can be evaluated; at the third stage ()^2 and ()^3 can be calculated; at the fourth stage (−), at the fifth the square root and at the sixth the final division can be evaluated. (Note that, for the levels at which more than one reduction occurs, I have neglected to define which shall be evaluated first.) Various stages in the reduction of the graph are shown in Figure 2.10.

Everything which I have described so far can proceed satisfactorily in a serial manner. It is, however, apparent that at least three stages of the process are susceptible to parallel evaluation. For example, there is no reason why the computation of $(x+y)$, $(x+z)$ and (yz) should not proceed at the same time but, before considering what type of systems might be suitable for such parallel implementations of this idea, it is necessary to introduce a related concept, that of *dataflow*. (It is probably worth noting here that some practitioners of parallel computing, in particular those working with graph reduction or dataflow systems, would consider the two ideas to be quite separate paradigms within the FPC area. I hope that it will shortly become apparent to the reader why I choose to consider them here as closely related flavours of the same idea.)

Consider again the computation graph shown in Figure 2.9. There are two ways in which the parallel execution of this graph might be controlled. The first is by the normal program flow method, illustrated by the following segment of pseudo-code:

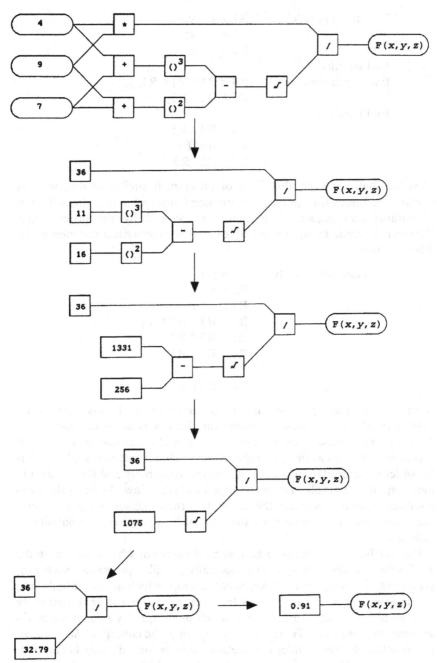

Figure 2.10   The process of graph reduction

Execute in parallel: R1 = x + y;
                         R2 = x + z;
                         R3 = y * z;
End parallel:
Execute in parallel: R4 = R1 * R1 * R1;
                         R5 = R2 * R2;
End parallel:
                         R6 = R4 − R5
                         R7 = sqrt R6
                         R8 = R7 / R3

As we shall see later, this form of program is similar to that used in Occam (the Inmos transputer programming language) in that the definition of parallel and sequential segments is specified by the programmer. However, it would be equally possible (and valid) to write a program in the following form:

Evaluate when ready: R1 = x + y
                         R2 = x + z
                         R3 = y * z
                         R4 = R1 * R1 * R1
                         R5 = R2 * R2
                         R6 = R4 − R5
                         R7 = sqrt R6
                         R8 = R7 / R3

With the important proviso that the order in which the instructions are written by the programmer is irrelevant. This is because the instruction 'Evaluate when ready' means 'evaluate any and all of the next group of expressions as soon as the data input which each requires is available'. Thus the order of computation is governed by the availability and flow of data in the computation graph – hence the appellation dataflow. As far as the computation graph is concerned, this means that the execution of any particular node must await the receipt of tokens which indicate the availability of valid data.

One further factor needs to be taken into account when considering the application of this paradigm to realistically complex programs. Such programs may include, for example, iterative loops which are potentially infinite in extent. In such cases, a new (parallel) process could be started every time around the loop – a technique which might quickly swamp the available parallel resources. To avoid this happening, the concept of *lazy evaluation* is often invoked. Under this method, calculations are only begun once it is known that the result is required. Systems which use the technique are usually called demand driven, although the method is really a refinement of data driven reduction.

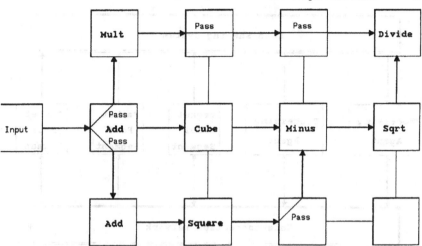

Figure 2.11 Mapping a computation graph onto an MIMD mesh

There are, then, two main ways of achieving the desired graph reduction – data driven and instruction driven – with the natural inference that there are likely to be, correspondingly, two types of system used for implementation. In fact, there are really three main possibilities. The first of these is a general-purpose MIMD assembly, which could be arranged to implement either approach. An example of how the graph given in Figure 2.9 might be mapped onto a general-purpose MIMD mesh (such as the Meiko system [4]) is shown in Figure 2.11.

Of the two dedicated approaches which might be used, the key difference lies in the control of the system. In both cases, the computation graph must be mapped onto the physical arrangement of processors. In the first case, one of the elements is designated as the controller, and must determine when other elements are made active, according to the control flow of the program. In the second case, control of the system is achieved by the flow of data tokens between participating elements.

The example given above is a very simple segment of program, and it is therefore correspondingly simple to map the program graph onto an arbitrary arrangement of processors. In more complex programs, it would obviously be desirable to avoid a complex hand-mapping procedure, and this can be achieved if special-purpose systems are used. Figure 2.12 shows the overall architecture of the ALICE [5] graph reduction system. Segments of graph, awaiting either reduction or valid parameters, are held in one or another of the packet pool segments . The processing elements obtain sections of graph for reduction from these, and pass results back, via the interconnection network, which in the case of the ALICE system is a multi-stage switching network (see Chapter 4). The whole process is arbitrated by the load sharing system.

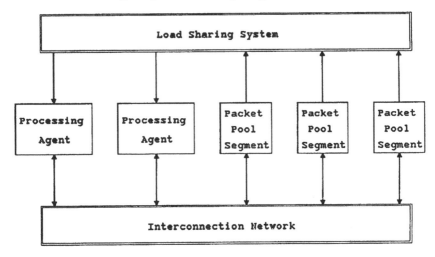

Figure 2.12   The ALICE graph reduction system

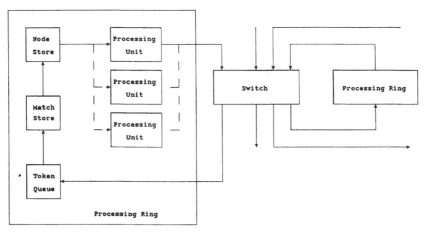

Figure 2.13   The Manchester Dataflow machine

Figure 2.13 illustrates the architecture of the Manchester Dataflow machine [6]. Each processing ring is a self-contained unit which may contain one or more processing units. Multiple processing units may be used in a single ring because of the mismatch in performance between segment processing time and segment matching. Additional performance can be obtained by adding further processing rings, in which case the multiple rings communicate via the switch.

Naturally, there are many subtleties involved in the implementations of both graph reduction and its close cousin, dataflow. A number of papers covering specific development programs can be found in *Multiprocessor Computer Architectures*, edited by Fountain and Shute. To summarise briefly the central ideas behind these paradigms: graph reduction consists first of casting the problem as a computation graph and then executing elements of that graph, in parallel where possible and sequentially where necessary. The dataflow idea involves the same technique, but allows the availability of valid data to control the order of execution of the program.

2.5 SIMD

We now move on to the first of the paradigms under the general data parallel calculation category – SIMD. As described earlier, the acronym implies a single instruction stream operating on multiple data streams, and a few moments' consideration should convince the reader that there must be a conflict between the general interpretation of the term and its exact definition.

Consider the four situations shown in Figure 2.14. Part (a) shows what must be an SISD system – a single stream of instructions is operating on a single stream of binary data. A serial stream of binary data must represent a 'single' data stream, since any further reduction of the information in each bit reduces it to no data at all. Parts (b) and (c) show what most of us would regard as normal von Neumann computers (one eight-bit and the other 64-bit) which are therefore, by implication, also SISD systems – in both cases a single instruction stream is unarguably operating on a single stream of data. But it is also true that more data (eight bits) is being operated upon by each instruction in (b) than in (a), and yet more still (64 bits) in (c). Why aren't these classed as SIMD architectures? Apparently because our single data stream is defined in terms of a stream of single coherent entities, not necessarily of single bits. Now consider part (d) of the diagram.

Here we are on less familiar ground. This is a depiction of the classical SIMD array processor – there is a massive amount of parallel data (thousands of pixels) being operated on at once. However, all those pixels constitute a respectable data entity in their own right, namely an image, so we're back to single instructions acting on a single stream of data items. Does this mean there is no difference between any of the parts of Figure 2.14?

I have not set up this apparent paradox merely to confuse the reader, but to point out that the terms one is likely to encounter in the field of parallel computing are not always as logically defined as their users might claim. The practical difference between SISD and SIMD is as follows. If data is in the form of a single stream of *numbers* (which may, of course, represent any symbolic entities), then the computer is a serial one. However, if each data item being acted upon cannot be described by a single number without further qualification, then the system is parallel and, in the case we are considering, SIMD. Thus an image, to follow the example given above, cannot be described by a single number, however large, without extra knowledge of

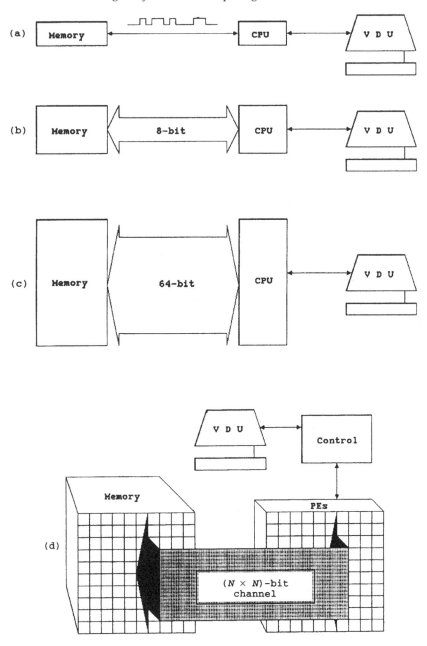

Figure 2.14   Where does SIMD begin? (a) Serial data (b) 8-bit data (c) 64-bit data (d) Parallel data

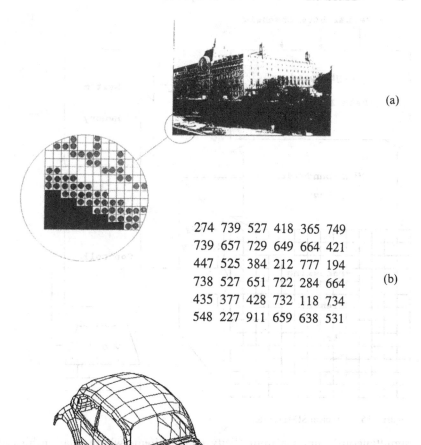

(a)

274 739 527 418 365 749
739 657 729 649 664 421
447 525 384 212 777 194
738 527 651 722 284 664   (b)
435 377 428 732 118 734
548 227 911 659 638 531

(c)

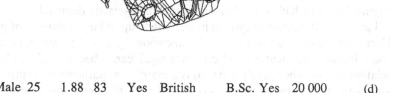

Male 25   1.88 83   Yes British   B.Sc. Yes 20 000   (d)

Figure 2.15 Typical parallel data sets (a) An image (b) A matrix (c) An engineering model (d) A database entry

the relationship between, say, digits in the number and some two-dimensional spatial arrangement.

The essence of the SIMD paradigm, then, is this. If a single instruction stream (that is, what is conventionally understood by a serial program) acts

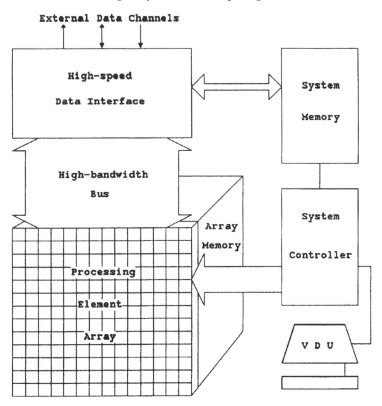

Figure 2.16 A typical SIMD system

simultaneously upon a multiplicity of data items whose relationships are important but undefined within the data set, then the SIMD paradigm is in operation. It is usually the case that the relationship is either spatial, or can be expressed by a spatial analogue. To understand this point, consider Figure 2.15, in which a number of parallel data sets are depicted.

Part (a) of the figure shows an image, made up of large numbers of pixels. Here, the relationship is a real two-dimensional one – the data value corresponding to a particular pixel only has significance because of its physical relationship to other pixels. Part (b) is a matrix – a mathematical entity. The values in the matrix might be associated with physically distributed variables but, equally, they might be connected with a distribution of states in energy space. In either case, however, the mathematical operations which need to be carried out are facilitated by the two-dimensional spatial representation. Part (c) is a representation of an automobile body shell which has been subjected to finite element analysis. Here, it is important that topological relationships are maintained in any mapping – the spatially-warped representation necessary to map to a uniform array is acceptable. Finally, part

(d) of the figure shows an item from a database entry. In this case, the positioning of elements along the vector is relatively unimportant, but it is vital that the same relationship be maintained for all items in the database.

Parallel processing of any of these types of data set (and many others) is perfectly feasible using the SIMD paradigm. The key factors in system design are matching the configuration of the parallel set of processing elements to the target data, and providing the appropriate connectivity between those elements. This connectivity is almost always between nearest neighbours in whatever set of dimensions is relevant. The question of near-neighbour connectivity is considered fully in Chapter 4, so it is sufficient here to note that the dominant example is the so-called four-connected square mesh, shown in Figure 2.16.

The same figure also shows a typical SIMD system design. Apart from the array itself, of which more in a moment, critical areas of design include the interface between the system controller and the array, which includes provision for distribution and synchronisation of control signals over the array, and any special purpose data input/output devices and the arrangements for interfacing them to the array.

These factors are both vital to the efficient performance of the system for the following reason. Probably the main advantage of the SIMD paradigm, and of systems which utilise it, is the sheer amount of parallelism which can be achieved. This, in turn, is possible both because the degree of parallelism in the target data sets is often enormous (parallel data sets of millions of items are not uncommon) and because the systems themselves are (theoretically) extensible to whatever degree is required. It is little more difficult to make and program an SIMD system of one million processing elements than one of a hundred (though considerably more costly). No new concepts are required, no additional overheads accrue, and the increase in performance is proportional to the additional numbers of elements, no matter how large the system becomes. This does, of course, cause problems concerned with distribution of global control signals, and power and earth lines, but these are not insurmountable. A far more serious difficulty can arise in supplying such systems with data at a suitable rate, and this is why special-purpose interfaces are often required.

The only other major point which needs to be considered at this stage is that of the design of the processing elements. The problem here is one of keeping overall system complexity within reasonable bounds. One factor which helps is that none of the elements require program sequencers or program memory – each or these is needed only once, in the system controller. However, until the very recent past, system designers have adopted a policy of maximising numbers of processors rather than their complexity, even though this has usually meant using single-bit elements, which in itself can lead to additional software complexity. Nevertheless, the processing elements are always complex enough to execute a full range of arithmetic and logical operations, in particular being provided with efficient mechanisms for gathering data from their neighbours.

Thus we may summarise the SIMD paradigm as implying a (substantially) normal programming language, running on an ordinary von Neumann computer, within which certain instructions act in parallel on very large structured data sets. The computations for these operations take place on a correspondingly large and correspondingly structured array of simple processing elements, each usually connected to its nearest neighbours in all dimensions of the implemented array. The major advantage of SIMD systems lies in the prodigious amount of parallelism which can be achieved and utilised [7].

2.6   Systolic

The second of the paradigms which utilises data parallelism is the idea of a systolic system. The word is derived from the biological term *systole* – the regular contraction of heart and arteries which pumps blood through the body. In computer terms, the idea is that data is pumped through a (parallel) computing structure in a similarly regular fashion. In the most simple implementations of the idea, the action of each stage of the array is identical, the array is usually two-dimensional and the only control signal broadcast to the processors is from a clock. One of the simplest systems which might be said to embody these principles is illustrated in Figure 2.17.

The purpose of the system is to add together, in a parallel manner, a set of numbers. (It may be remarked here that similar arrangements are often used as complements to SIMD arrays for the purpose of computing a sum of a subset of data items in the array.) The systolic principles which the arrangement embodies are:

(a) Data flows in only one direction across the array
(b) Each element of the array performs the same function, in this case addition
(c) The only control signal broadcast to all elements is from a clock

At the first clock pulse of the system, each pair of input numbers is added. At the second clock pulse, these sums of pairs are themselves added in pairs, and so the computation proceeds until a complete sum is produced at the output. The system is rendered internally systolic by the interpolation of a storage register at each stage of addition. (It is equally possible to devise a system where the complete addition takes place in one clock cycle, with no intermediate storage being required.) It should also be noted that the resulting system has many of the characteristics of a pipeline, so that, as in any such arrangement, a series of sets of numbers may be added, with a

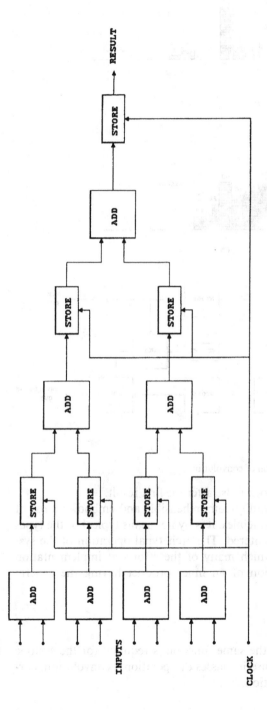

Figure 2.17 A systolic adder tree

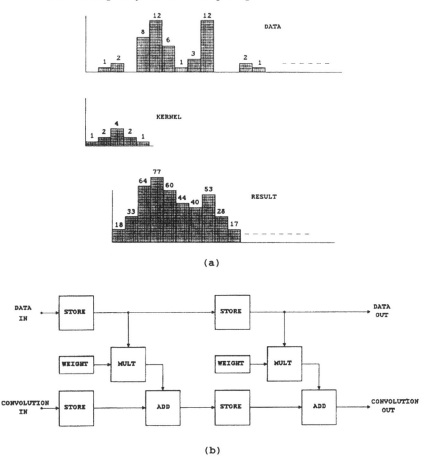

Figure 2.18   A systolic implementation of convolution

new sum appearing at every clock pulse after the first result.

Although this example is readily comprehensible and embodies most of the originally stated systolic principles, it is by no means typical of the types of systolic array usually encountered. The archetypal operation of the systolic processor element, on which many of the efforts at implementation concentrate, is the computation of an inner product having the general form:

$$Y_{i+1} = Y_i + (X_{i+1} \times W_i)$$

This is principally because the same function is required for the systolic computation of at least three useful classes of operation – convolution, correlation and matrix multiplication.

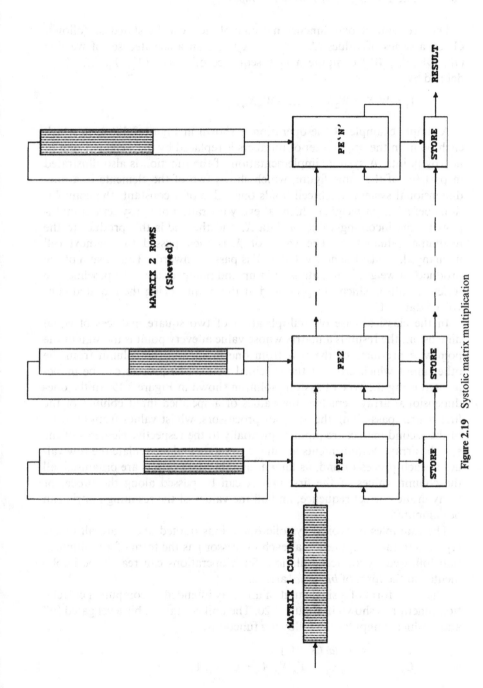

Figure 2.19 Systolic matrix multiplication

The problem of one-dimensional convolution can be stated as follows. Given a series of values $(X_1, X_2, ..., X_n)$ and an associated set of weights $(W_1, W_2, ..., W_m)$ compute a new sequence of values $(Y_1, Y_2, ..., Y_{n-m+1})$ defined by:

$$Y_i = W_1 X_i + W_2 X_{i+1} + ... + W_m X_{i+m-1}.$$

A simple example of the operation is shown in Figure 2.18(a), in which each point in the original set of numbers is replaced by the weighted sum of nearby points. A systolic implementation of the function is also illustrated in part (b) of the same figure, which shows two of the elements in a one-dimensional system. Each cell holds one value of a constant (the convolution coefficient or weight) which, at every operation of the system, it multiplies by the incoming value of data X, and then adds this product to the incoming value of Y. The value of X is then passed to the next cell unchanged, whilst the new value of Y is passed onwards. Thus a sum of the products of weights and data is built up and pumped down the pipeline, the series of values which are produced at the output being the required convolved data set.

In the classical case of multiplication of two square matrices of equal dimension, the result is a matrix whose value at every point is the sum of the pointwise products of the row from one input and the column from the other input which cross at the specified point. The process can be implemented using the type of systolic solution shown in Figure 2.19. In the one-dimensional array depicted, the values of a specified input column of the first matrix pass along the array of processors, whilst values from all rows of the second matrix are input sequentially to the respective elements of the systolic array. Arrangements are made to retain and recirculate the row values at each processor and, as long as suitable data offsets are organised, all the column values of the first matrix can be passed along the processor array in the correct sequence, and all the values of the resulting matrix can be computed.

The examples of typical systolic operations quoted above are all of the type where the computation at each processor has the form of a multiplication followed by an accumulation. Such operations can readily be implemented in the form of *bit-serial* arrays.

The basic form of a single unit of an array intended to compute a correlation function is shown in Figure 2.20. The unit contains a bit-level gated full adder which computes the following functions:

$$Y \qquad = Y_{in} \, @ \, (X_{in}.A_{in})$$
$$C_{out} \quad = Y_{in}.C_{in} + Y_{in}.X_{in}.A_{in} + C_{in}.X_{in}.A_{in}$$

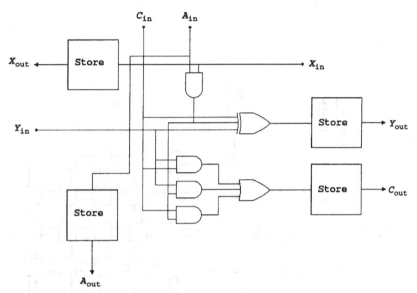

Figure 2.20   A bit-serial systolic array element

where   @ = exclusive OR
                 + = OR
                 . = AND

The arrangement of these cells into an array forming a correlator is shown in Figure 2.21, together with the arrangement of time-skewed data which is required. Results also appear in the time-skewed form shown and are, in effect, the set of binary coefficients

$$Y_{in} \qquad n = 0,1,...,m$$

which taken together form the binary number Y_i given by:

$$Y_i = Y_{i0}2^0 + Y_{i1}2^1 + ...$$

The size of the array is determined by the precision of data and coefficients used, whilst any real convolver chip would have additional peripheral cells. In general such devices require particular skewing of the data to be presented to the array and in some cases the circuits required to implement this, and the equivalent de-skewing of results, are integrated onto the same very large scale integration (VLSI) device. Because the devices are optimised for a particular operation (and are, as a corollary, unable to perform any other) their performance is extremely good. VLSI devices manufactured by GEC operate at 20 MHz and the correlator chip can therefore execute, for example, a sixteen-stage correlation on 9-bit data over a 512 × 512 pixel image in about 13 ms. This is sufficient to maintain single-function frame-rate image processing using a single chip. It is apparent, therefore, that a

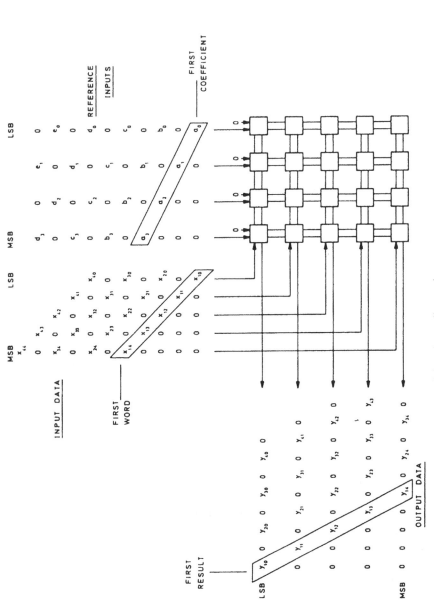

Figure 2.21 A systolic correlator array

collection of systolic chips of this type, assembled into a pipeline, would provide a reasonable solution in applications where:

(a) An overall processing algorithm is known
(b) Systolic algorithms are available for each stage of the process
(c) A relatively small number of components make up the overall algorithm

There are, however, drawbacks to the approach in other situations. Programs which need to deal with complex problems often utilise hundreds of different algorithms to produce a result. Even supposing that this variety could be substantially reduced by recasting the solution in a systolic mould, it is probable that many tens of different systolic chips would be needed. Although due allowance must be made for the likely fact that the building-block elements of many would be similar, this still represents a daunting programme of VLSI design and construction. A further problem is that many programs involve the use of the same algorithms at several different stages, so that the total number of operations executed may be much greater than the number of different algorithms used. In such situations, assemblies of systolic chips suffer the same problem as other linear pipelines, in that a chip must be provided for each time the algorithm is used.

Another difficulty exists in a research environment where solutions to problems are being developed. The type of SIMD array described in the previous section permits such development in a natural manner. Because physical rearrangement is inevitably more time-consuming and difficult than programming, the use of specific-function systolic chips is entirely inappropriate to this sort of research.

In summary, we may conclude that the systolic principle, applied in particular to operations such as convolution and matrix multiplication, has led to the implementation of VLSI chips whose conceptual simplicity produces important improvements in computational power over alternative devices. In addition, systolic algorithms, designed for implementation on other types of system, provide worthwhile new approaches to some classes of computation [8].

2.7 Association

The third of the data parallel paradigms of parallel computing has arisen from the need to discover relationships between data items in some problems. Again, the technique is not necessarily parallel, but can map very comfortably onto the appropriate parallel system. The basic idea can be illustrated by considering the functioning of a program to check the spelling in a document. For each word in the document, it is required to check for a

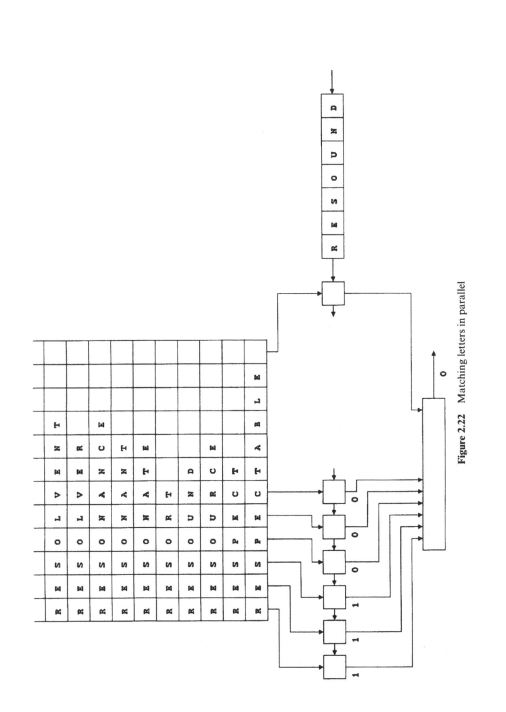

Figure 2.22 Matching letters in parallel

match in spelling between that word and a database of known spellings – a dictionary. Since we are dealing with text files, each word will be represented by a string of ASCII characters, the limits of the string being defined by 'space' characters. A serial computer must check each pair of elements – one from the document word and one from the dictionary word – sequentially, accumulating a 'pass' or 'fail' record as it proceeds. This process must then be repeated for the current word against every dictionary entry, and then for all other words in the document. The potentialities for parallel operation are therefore formidable. (I should note here that this example is not untypical of the general class of database matching problems, although the potential for parallelism is probably greater than most.)

In this particular example, there are three levels where parallelism might be introduced. The first method, illustrated in Figure 2.22, would allow all the letters in each word to be matched simultaneously. Each of the parallel comparison units gives rise to a local 'match' bit, and these are logically combined to produce an overall answer. The number of parallel elements would be relatively small (equal to the number of letters in the longest word in the database) and the speed advantage would be correspondingly limited.

A more parallel technique would be that shown in Figure 2.23. A large number of parallel comparator units is provided, perhaps equal to the number of words in a page (typically about 500). The dictionary contents are then streamed past each comparator until the checking process is complete for that page, when the next section of text is brought forward.

A further, almost certainly unrealistic, level of parallelism would be to provide a comparator for each dictionary entry (at least tens of thousands of items) and stream the text past all processors simultaneously.

Anyone with more than a passing acquaintance with real database accessing systems will realise that the approaches outlined above are simplistic. In almost every case (and certainly in the example used here), some form of hierarchical searching algorithm can pay enormous dividends. To continue with our example, once a match has been obtained for the first letter of a word, only the section of the dictionary under that letter needs to be searched. The same is then true for the second letter, then for the third and so on. Such a directed search is quite easy to set up in a serial computer, but can it be carried out by any parallel method? One technique might work as follows.

(1) For each word, compare the first letter to each letter of the alphabet
(2) Use the match to direct the next stage of the search to the proper section of the dictionary
(3) For all subsequent letters, repeat the process of (1) and (2) until all letters of the word have been processed

This technique is serial in the number of letters in the word, but can be

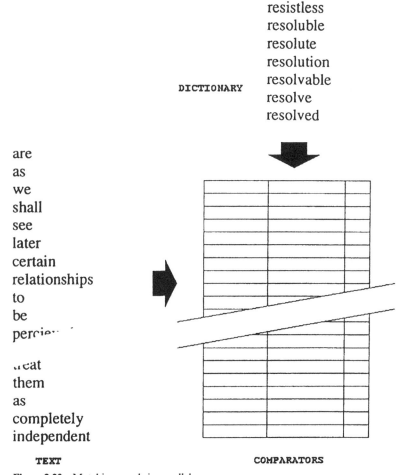

Figure 2.23   Matching words in parallel

parallelised in all other respects – each letter can be matched to the alphabet in parallel, and a parallel set of words in the text could be processed in parallel. Of course, such a technique is only reasonable because of the particular structure of the example used here. For other database searching problems, other approaches might be required.

There is a further level of subtlety to associative processing which we should consider here. Many problems do not require an answer of the form 'match or fail'. Frequently a user wishes to know which is the nearest match to a complex item of data, or perhaps requires a measure of how nearly his data matches some ideal. The major difficulty in such cases is the determination of a suitable measure to define the quality of match. In the case of the spell checker, this might require a formula of the following sort:

$$Value = \frac{1}{N}(T - F)$$

where
N = number of letters in word
T = number of matching letters
F = number of unmatched letters

Even this approach might be thought to be too simplistic, in which case some variable weighting connected with position of letters in the word might be desirable.

In other cases, for instance where an item of data is being matched to some numerical parameter, then the matching metric could well be a simple numerical difference. However, quite arbitrary qualitative judgements sometimes need to be made. Is a bicycle more like a motorcycle (because it has the same number of wheels) or more like a skateboard (because both are human-powered)? Such questions can make the definition of associative systems (whether parallel or not) much more complex than the computational requirements might indicate.

In summary, then, we might say that the associative paradigm can lend itself rather well to data parallel implementations, particularly because of the amount of parallelism which can be achieved. However, problems connected with the subtlety of the concept of association may mean that implementation is not completely straightforward. In extreme cases, it may be that a functionally parallel approach may be just as (or more) appropriate.

In most of the sections of this chapter so far, we have been concerned, understandably, with the basic process of calculation. This is a process quite familiar to any reader of this book – although the methods of implementation may have been unfamiliar to varying degrees. Only in the last section, concerned with associative processing, is the idea introduced that qualitative, rather than quantitative, results may be important. This forms a convenient precursor to a consideration of the cognitive paradigms, since these are most frequently concerned with obtaining qualitative results. It is worth considering for a moment how this comes about.

In order to do so, we need to think about the purposes of computation in general. There are really two quite separate classes of question which a user can ask of a computing system. Examples of the first type are:

How many people in greater New York have blood group (AB Rh neg.)?
What is the mean error on the length of this machined part?
What does the diameter of this bridge support need to be to allow a safety factor of 100%?

All these questions require numerical answers. Examples of the second class of question might include:

Is this tissue sample diseased?
What is the translation of this English text into French?
What is the most likely outcome in voting intentions if we increase federal income tax by 1%?

Each of these questions requires a symbolic answer although, given our cultural predilection for numerical computing, an answer for each could be obtained by calculation. However, in considering the three cognitive paradigms – classification, transformation and minimisation – we shall see that answers to these types of questions can be obtained in a non-numerical fashion.

2.8   Classification

The idea of classification is, at first glance, extremely simple. For example, few of us would have any difficulty deciding whether an apple is a fruit or a vegetable. Similarly, we know that a banana is a fruit, whereas a cabbage is a vegetable. But suppose you were presented with a kumquat? Or maybe a yam? Certainly there are a group of readers who know what these are, but how would we decide if we didn't?

I make this point to illustrate that, in the absence of some knowledge of the subject in question, even a human might have difficulty in deciding on a classification. However, you might decide that the kumquat looked more like a fruit (because of its colour) and tasted more like a fruit (usually sweeter than a vegetable) and therefore probably was a fruit. In other words, you would use the training you had received (by eating other foods) to make a decision based on probabilities. It is just such a technique which is used by a cognitive classifier. Without worrying yet about the nature of the cognitive machine to be used, the process is as follows.

First, data about a series of objects (the training set) are fed to the computer. These data include both the parameters used to describe the object (these are often, but not necessarily, in picture form) and the specified classification. When the training phase is complete, the computer will decide on categories for new data which include only the parametric description.

The key to the use of this paradigm is the question of implementation. In order to explain how this can be done, it is probably useful to begin with some of the ideas of multivariate analysis. Consider the situation shown in Figure 2.24. In each of the three parts of this diagram, a graph has been plotted whose axes are two parameters of a set of objects – let us suppose they are the length and width of rectangles. For some (unspecified) reason, we wish to classify these rectangles into a small number of classes, based on

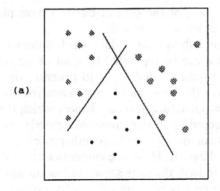

(a)

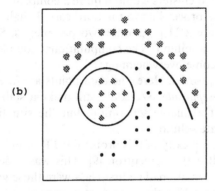

(b)

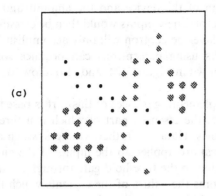

(c)

Figure 2.24 The classification of data sets (a) Linearly separable (b) Separable
(c) Non-separable

the values of the parameters. For the sake of clarity I have plotted three classes, in each case using different symbols.

In part (a) of the diagram I show a set of data which is linearly separable, that is, the three categories can be separated by a set of straight lines, as shown. Such a situation would be quite easy to program on a standard computer – the equations of the lines can be written analytically. However, even in this case, we might introduce another element which the computer would classify wrongly according to our predefined criteria. Furthermore, this type of situation is uncommonly simple. A rather more realistic case is shown in part (b) of the diagram. Here, the categories are still separable, but not by straight lines. Indeed, the lines shown follow no simple analytic formula at all. It would obviously be more difficult to program a standard computer to perform the required classification, and any additional data falling outside the designated clusters would require a complete re-programming exercise. Now, before proceeding to the third case, I shall introduce a further complication. Figure 2.24 plots only two parameters. Suppose we had ten, or a thousand, or a million? The computational complexity of the situation could quickly become overwhelming.

Finally, let us consider case (c). Here, the data points are intermingled – the data are, in fact, *non-separable*. We could still make a stab at a set of lines which gives the best available separation, but the situation is only amenable to an approximate solution.

Considerations of the complexity of this problem led Rosenblatt, in 1957, to propose a solution called the perceptron [9]. This was a device which accepted two classes of information. The first class were those which corresponded to parametric data, whilst the second set were used, during a training phase, to modify the internal states of the device to produce the required classification. If the design of the device and the amount and method of training were both satisfactory, new inputs would then be classified satisfactorily. Although a single-layer perceptron will only accomplish linear separation, multi-layer circuits using perceptrons can produce some sort of answer for all the cases shown in Figure 2.24, and also allow for significantly large numbers of inputs.

One feasible way of implementing devices of this sort is based on the circuit shown in Figure 2.25, the essential part of which is a threshold gate. The circuit works as follows. Data (or, rather, voltages which are proportional to input data values) are applied to the inputs of the circuit, at the left. Each input is connected to the threshold gate through a variable resistor. The threshold gate sums the values of the currents which flow into it, and applies a threshold to this value, so that the output of the gate is either one or zero, corresponding to the summed input being above or below the chosen threshold. During the training phase, the values of the variable resistors are changed so that the desired output is obtained for each set of input

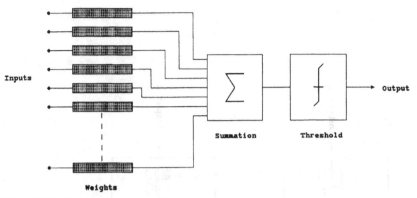

Figure 2.25   An implementation of the perceptron

data. In this case, the variable resistors are used to vary the effect of each input, i.e. the 'weight' which each is given. (Obviously, a suitable strategy is required so that changes are made in a consistent fashion. Appropriate techniques for doing this will be discussed in Chapter 3.) This circuit is a single classifier – it will accept one class of objects and reject all others. If multiple classes are present, at least one such circuit is needed for each class, resulting in the arrangement shown in Figure 2.26.

In the early history of these devices, there was some doubt over their generality and, in a classic debate, it was demonstrated that such devices could not perform a particular type of logical manipulation (an exclusive-OR operation). This led, unfairly, to their being ignored until the recent upsurge of interest in pseudo-neural circuits. In fact, in the original form, now called the single-layer perceptron, the applicability of the circuits is unnecessarily limited. If they are combined into the type of structure shown in Figure 2.27 (known, unsurprisingly, as the multi-layer perceptron), two things become apparent. First, the circuit becomes more flexible, more powerful and therefore more generally applicable. This is principally because the intermediate (hidden) layers of nodes represent intermediate features which are not those representing the ultimate classification.

As an example of how this can work, consider the case (which is often encountered) where the input data represent a subset of pixels from an image, and the required classification is into squares, rectangles, circles and ovals. In real cases of this sort, it is often discovered that a more efficient system results if there are intermediate nodes which correspond to ideas such as curvedness, straightness, symmetry and asymmetry. The outputs of these can then be combined to deliver the final result.

The second factor which becomes more apparent as the complexity of the multi-layer perceptron circuits builds up is the similarity to neural structures – there is the same distributed and unspecified functionality and the

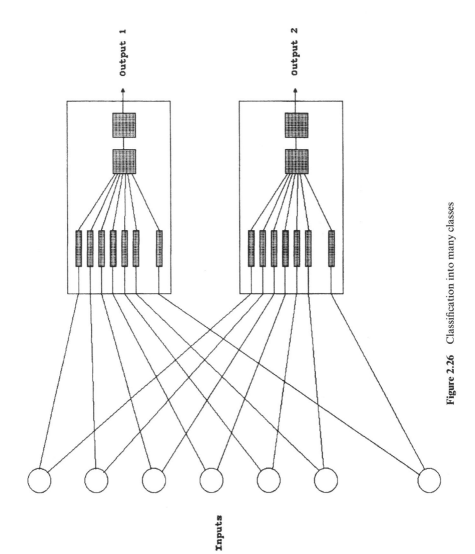

Figure 2.26   Classification into many classes

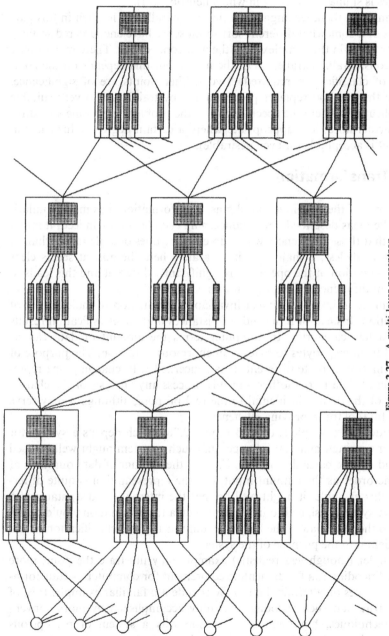

Figure 2.27 A multi-layer perceptron

same complexity and distribution of connections. Even the functioning of the nodes is similar to the way in which neurons work.

In summary, then, we might note that the parallelism implicit in this paradigm is of a somewhat different sort to those we have encountered so far – it mainly exists in the complexity of the interconnections. There may or may not be considerable parallelism of the nodes, but this depends on the complexity of classification required. Two further points are of significance. Because this method replaces programming by training, it is very suitable for applications where the specification of the problem is in some way difficult. Furthermore, it is appropriate where a certain degree of fuzziness in the result is acceptable (or even desirable).

2.9   Transformation

The second of the cognitive paradigms, transformation, has many similarities to the ideas described above concerning classification – indeed, it might be said that those differences which do exist are ones of scale rather than of kind. Nevertheless, I shall treat it separately here, because it seems clear that the intention of the operation is significantly different and this leads to important differences of implementation.

Classification involves, almost invariably, a reduction in the quantity of information. Instead of thousands of instances of data, classification results in just a few categories. In computer terms the amount of data can be reduced from megabytes to bytes – an enormous reduction. The purpose of transformation is quite different. It is concerned with changing one representation of data into another – in this process any analysis of the characteristics of the data is incidental to the real purpose, although it may serve as a useful tool for improving efficiency.

Consider the example shown in Figure 2.28, which depicts a system for converting written material into speech. (Such a system might well be used as an aid for the partially sighted.) Clearly, the amount of data output is of the same order as the amount input, but the representation is quite different. In this example, it might well be that the internal (hidden) states of a cognitive system designed to implement such a transformation would correspond to the *phonemes* of the language, but this internal classification would be incidental to the purpose of the system.

A simpler (though less realistic) example may illustrate the point more clearly. Encoding is a fundamental requirement for computers – transforming key strokes on a terminal into ASCII code is a familiar example. It is, of course, true that such encoding is readily accomplished by more conventional techniques, but there is no reason why a system of perceptrons should not be used for the purpose. In such a case, the system would output one data item (the ASCII code) for every data input.

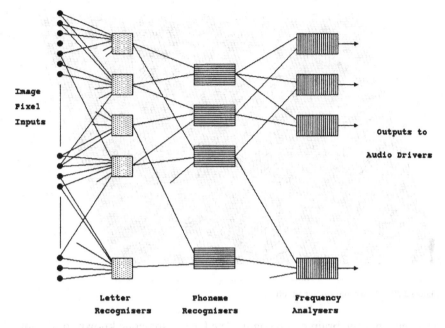

Figure 2.28   A text reading system

It is apparent from these examples that the transformation paradigm usually employs implementations which are similar to those of classification, with one important difference. Whereas classification implies a many-to-few operation, it is quite likely that transformation will require a many-to-many system, with each data input producing a unique output. For the sake of efficiency, it may be that the output data are themselves produced in an encoded form, so that the physical number of output lines from a system may be few, but this does not invalidate the principle of the operation.

2.10   Minimisation

The third cognitive technique, that of minimisation, is used in a rather different way from the other two, and demands a different starting point in order to arrive at a proper understanding of its operation. Figure 2.29 is a three-dimensional plot of a surface in parameter space. It can be readily observed that the value of the z-parameter has a number of points which are local minima , that is, starting from one of these points, any small change in either of the x- or y-parameters results in an increase in the value of z. It is also observable that there is a global minimum value of the z-parameter – any change in x or y, of whatever magnitude, results in an increase in z.

This representation enables us to visualise two types of problem. The first of these is the problem of recognition. In the sphere of human action, it is

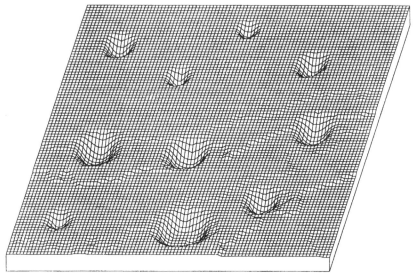

Figure 2.29   A two-parameter function

apparent that the brain can recognise the face of someone known to it from the most fragmentary glimpse. It appears that the brain can associate the fragmented picture with stored information, and recall the stored information in its entirety. The second is the type of problem where the z-parameter represents a cost function, and we wish to arrive at a solution which will minimise this cost. Let us examine an example of each of these cases.

2.10.1   Local minimisation

The classic embodiment of this technique is the Hopfield network [10], devised by John Hopfield in 1982. The network comprises a set of all-to-all connected binary threshold logic units with weighted connections between the units. The state of each unit of the system can be either one or zero (this is sometimes modified to minus one or plus one). The idea is that a number of patterns are stored in the network, by modifying the weights according to a specific rule (the Hebb rule [11]). The rule defines the weights in terms of the states of the elements of the system. This rule-based approach to defining the interconnection weights is in contrast to the training employed for the same purpose in the two cognitive paradigms described above. The patterns correspond to particular sets of values of the variables of the problem under consideration – in typical examples these are the values of pixels in a picture. Figure 2.30 gives some idea of the complexity of such a network, in which a significant difference from the multi-layer perceptron lies in the presence of feedback. Each connection shown in the diagram represents a two-way path.

Pattern Inputs

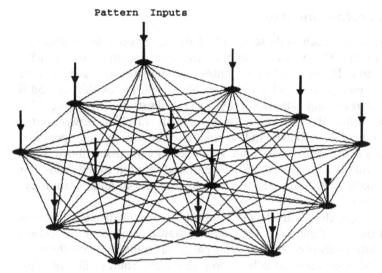

Figure 2.30   A Hopfield network

The object of the exercise is to present to the network a partial pattern (or one corrupted by noise) and allow the network to determine which of its stored patterns is the closest to it. The network achieves this by taking the input pattern as its starting state and evolving by means of serial, element-by-element, updating. A system 'energy' can be defined which is a mathematical function of the system weights and the states of the system elements. Because of the rule which has been used to define the weights in the system, this results in the system evolving towards the nearest energy minimum, which should correspond to the stored pattern which is most like the input. Thus the second important difference from the multi-layer perceptron approach is that the production of the answer is an iterative process (which may take a considerable time).

There are, in fact, a number of serious difficulties in achieving useful implementations of this technique. The number and quality of the stored images is severely limited – if there are too many, or they are too similar, then the energy minima are either too diffuse or too close together, both cases leading to a high incidence of false recognitions. The one remedy for this – a substantial increase in the number of elements – has its own drawbacks. There is a physical problem, in that all-to-all connectivity becomes increasingly difficult to implement as the number of elements increases. A second problem is the added time required to implement the serial updating algorithm over a larger number of elements. For these reasons, amongst others, although there is still considerable theoretical interest in such techniques, a more immediately applicable method is that of global minimisation.

2.10.2   Global minimisation

Hopfield networks, such as those described above, are suitable for discovering local minima. If the global minimum (or some approximation to it) is required, then a different technique, known as simulated annealing, can be applied. A classic problem which is amenable to solution by this method is the so-called travelling salesman problem [12], illustrated in Figure 2.31. The idea is to find the best route for a salesman travelling between retail outlets in a number of cities and so minimise the cost of the operation, which in this case corresponds to the system energy discussed above. If the number of cities is large, an exhaustive analytical solution to the problem is computationally unrealistic, but the technique of global minimisation can offer a solution.

In this example the parameters of the problem are the distances between cities, and the cost function is the overall distance covered on the chosen route. It is intuitively obvious that some particular route will have the minimum cost, but it is almost equally obvious that many routes will give a reasonable approximation to this minimum. Two possible routes around the same set of cities in North America are suggested in the diagram.

There are a number of significant differences from the local minimisation procedure described above. First, the rule for defining the system weights is different. In the present case, the weights are defined as a function of the distance between cities – each specific problem of this type will have its own, unique, definition. Second, the element updating procedure, whilst still being a serial operation, is no longer deterministic. At every stage of the algorithm, a probabilistic calculation determines whether or not a given alteration (corresponding, here, to a change in routing) is accepted or rejected. Any alteration which reduces the overall cost of the route will be accepted, but there is a finite chance that a change which increases the overall cost of the route will also be accepted. This probability is related to a factor which is often called *temperature* (in continuation of the energy analogy). The higher the temperature, the greater the probability that a higher-cost route change will be accepted. Eventual convergence of the system towards the global minimum often involves gradually reducing this temperature from an initially high value. Low values are not often used from the outset because they can lead to the system becoming trapped in states far from the global minimum.

By allowing the system to evolve under these conditions from some arbitrary starting configuration, solutions very close to the minimum cost can often be found, and in some cases the minimum itself can be achieved.

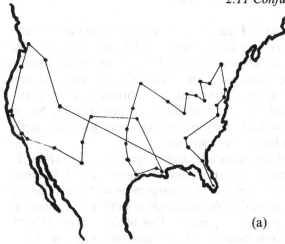

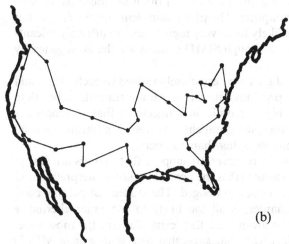

Figure 2.31   The travelling salesman problem (a) A plausible route (b) A less costly route

2.11   Confusion compounded

This chapter is probably, for the beginner, the crucial part of the entire book. Chapter 1 is, hopefully, a fairly easy introduction to the basic ideas of parallelism – parallel data, parallel functions and systems like brains which somehow combine both. In the present chapter the reader has been exposed to ideas of considerably greater subtlety, depth and complexity. Before embarking on any added complications, is there any way to hang on to some key ideas?

An excellent starting point is Figure 2.1. An understanding of the relationships implicit in this diagram gives a firm foundation to what follows. There are three function parallel paradigms, and these share some common ideas – systems embodying these paradigms have to be programmed, and the programming may be more complicated than normal serial programming. Such systems are likely to have complex processing elements but, in parallel terms, rather few of them. They are perhaps more general in application than those resulting from other approaches.

Within this group there are, naturally, some significant differences. In particular, the pipelining paradigm, whilst conforming to most of the group characteristics, allows virtually the normal serial approach to programming to be used. It is also unusual in that the technique is valid, under some circumstances, under the data parallel approach. One of these three, MIMD, is the most generally applicable paradigm of any described in this chapter.

The characteristics of the three data parallel paradigms are, in many respects, the opposite of those of the function parallel approaches. Whilst they must be programmed, the programming is often as simple as, or simpler than, that of a serial computer. The processing elements are simple, but the degree of parallelism is likely to be very high. They are often significantly specialised in application, although SIMD systems are the most generally applicable of the group.

The three cognitive paradigms are very closely related to each other, and are quite dissimilar to the previous categories. All are trained, rather than programmed, all are more highly parallel in connectivity than in processors (although the degree of processor parallelism is not insignificant) and all operate in the milieu of symbols rather than numbers.

It would be quite unrealistic, however, to suppose that matters are always so simple. The first thing to note is that the present author's interpretation of the situation is not universally acknowledged. The student of parallel computing, having read this chapter, is all too likely to encounter alternative viewpoints and so should be aware that they exist. Perhaps the most widespread usage which conflicts with that suggested here is to equate MIMD with functional parallelism and SIMD with data parallelism. In one sense this has some justification, but I believe my own approach leads to a more comprehensible structure. Similarly, as I indicated earlier in this chapter, some practitioners prefer to consider dataflow as a paradigm in its own right and, again, it is difficult to deny this alternative on strictly logical grounds. Finally, it is certain that not all experts on cognitive systems would agree with my particular choice of paradigms – many might consider classification and transformation to be two sides of the same coin. Readers should gather from this that taxonomy, at least as applied to parallel computing, is not yet an exact science, and be prepared to exercise their critical judgement at an early stage by choosing whatever methods enhance their understanding of the subject.

A second problem concerns the overlaps between the various paradigms presented here. It is apparent, for instance, that some of the ideas of associative processing have much in common with those underlying classification. Similarly, a one-dimensional systolic array might be seen as indistinguishable from a pipeline of the appropriate configuration. Perhaps worse, pipelines exhibiting data parallelism exist side-by-side with those executing parallel functions. At this stage I can only recommend that the reader should retain a certain flexibility of attitude. It is important that you should understand the processes going on in any particular system, and should be able to converse about them intelligently, not that you must apply one specific label to a given process in place of another. To illustrate this point, let us analyse the type of parallel system which is probably the most widespread, and perhaps the most significant, at the present time – the vector supercomputer.

2.11.1 The vector supercomputer

When powerful computers are considered or discussed, the most likely type to spring to mind is the vector supercomputer, epitomised by the Cray series of machines (although examples are also supplied by Fujitsu, IBM, CDC and a few others). In the context of this book, we should consider whether such machines embody parallelism and, if so, in what form. It is a, perhaps natural, assumption that vector supercomputing is a paradigm in its own right. As I shall show briefly here, such systems embody at least two, and often three, of the paradigms set out earlier in this chapter.

The first of these paradigms is SIMD or, to be slightly more precise, vectorisation (hence part of the name). One source of the power of these systems derives from the execution of each instruction on large vectors of data, of the order of 64-256 bits long. Just as with any other SIMD system, appropriate data configuration is required if effective performance is to be achieved.

At the same time as data is configured into these long words, the words themselves are configured into sequences of data items which can be manipulated in the same way. This permits the next paradigm – pipelining – to be implemented efficiently at the microinstruction level described in Section 2 of this chapter.

Although the power derived from the use of these two paradigms (combined, of course, with that derived from the most up-to-date technology) permitted the first generation systems to process data at prodigious rates, many of the problems to which they were applied demanded still greater performance. This was achieved in systems such as the Cray Y-MP, by utilising yet another paradigm, that of MIMD. Thus, effectively, a small number of first generation systems were combined in a tightly coupled cooperating group amongst which the overall problem was shared.

The penalty which has to be paid for this complexity is, of course, that the full available power of such systems can be realised for only a small class of problems and, in almost every problem, the mapping of application and data onto the system has itself to be carried out by a combination of sophisticated compiler and powerful computer (often referred to as the *front-end* system). It is apparent, from the comparatively widespread use of such systems, that there are many cases where this effort is considered well worth while.

We have now arrived at a point where the ideas underlying parallel computing have been set out in some sort of order. The obvious next step is to consider how these ideas are (or might be) implemented, and the first move must be to understand how the parallel elements are to be controlled. I have emphasised all along that the key to the successful use of parallel computers is to obtain an appropriate mapping between problem and system. This is achieved, in the first instance, by understanding how the parallel elements can be made to do what is required, and this, in turn, is determined by the techniques of programming (or their equivalents) used on the various systems. The next chapter, therefore, is concerned with the programming of parallel computers.

2.12 Exercises

1. Explain the differences between:
   (a) Calculation and cognition
   (b) Functional and data parallelism

2. List the nine parallel computing paradigms and suggest an application for which each would be suitable. Explain your choices.

3. Sketch the block diagram of a pipeline suitable for speeding up the execution of arithmetic operations in a single-processor computer. Estimate the improvement in performance which your pipeline would achieve on the following operation:

   For $i = 1 - 10$
   Do
   $F_i = a_i + b_i + c_{i+1}$

What other applications of pipelining can you suggest?

4. You are required to execute the following calculations:

> For $i = 1 - 10$
> Do
>
> $$F_i = \sqrt{\frac{(x_i + y_i)^3 - (x_i + z_i)^2}{yz}}$$

Suggest two parallel paradigms which might be applied to speed up the execution, and compare their respective merits and disadvantages.

5. Given the following calculation, estimate the speedup obtained by applying the dataflow technique.

> For $i = 1 - 10$
> Do
>
> $$F_i = \sum_{k=1}^{k=5} (a_i + b_i^3)^k$$

Explain any assumptions which you make. Sketch a suitable implementation and explain how it works.

6. Compare and contrast the three data parallel paradigms. Which of them would you expect to be most effective at matrix manipulation? Justify your answer with some brief calculations.

7. Give examples of three types of data sets for whose manipulation the SIMD paradigm might be suitable. Can you suggest any circumstances in which the application of the MIMD principle might be preferable?

8. Explain the travelling salesman problem. Indicate how a cogniser might solve the problem, stating which paradigm would be involved, and why.

9. Sketch a Hopfield network and explain its purpose, and show how it might be implemented and used.

10. Describe how a vector supercomputer combines a number of different aspects of parallel computing, and estimate the improvement in performance which it derives from each of these aspects.

3 Programming Parallel Computers

In order to make sense of the way in which users control parallel computers, we shall have to adopt a rather wider definition of the idea of programming than that which is usually taken. This is principally because of the existence of systems which are trained rather than programmed. Later in this chapter I shall attempt to show the equivalence between the two approaches but it is probably best to begin by considering how the conventional idea of programming is applied to parallel systems.

3.1 Parallel programming

There are three factors which we should take into account in order to arrive at a proper understanding of the differences between one type of parallel language and another and to appreciate where the use of each type is appropriate. These are whether the parallelism is hidden or explicit, which paradigm is employed and the level of the language. Although there is, inevitably, a certain amount of overlap between these factors, I shall treat them as though they were independent.

3.1.1 The embodiment of parallelism

There is really only one fundamental choice to be made here – should the parallelism embodied in a language be implicit or explicit? That is, should the parallelism be hidden from the programmers, or should it be specified by them? The first alternative is usually achieved by allowing the use of data types, in a program, which themselves comprise multiple data entities. Although this style of program is usually connected with vector or array processors and, by association, with the SIMD control paradigm, it is in fact much more widespread. Consider a conventional program which begins:

Declare integers:	one; two; people;
Declare longs:	many; lots; millions;

If integers are 16-bit numbers and longs are 32-bit, then whatever operations follow will embody more 'parallelism' if they are required to act on the longs than if they act on the integers. Although the functions which act upon them have the same name, longs comprise twice as many bits as integers. The amount of parallelism is hidden or implicit.

The following example serves to explain the differences which arise when, in one case, a parallel data structure does not map onto an underlying physical machine, whereas in the other case it does. A language designed to run on a single-processor device might take the following form to add two, two-dimensional arrays of data.

Declare: $A_{ij}; B_{ij}; C_{ij};$
                $i = 0, j = 0$
While $i < n$
                $i = i + 1$
While $j < m$
                $j = j + 1$
                $C_{ij} = A_{ij} + B_{ij}$

A program intended for implementation on a processor array, in which data arrays were a natural data type, would simply say:

Declare arrays: A; B; C;
C = A+B

The implicit (i.e. undeclared) parallelism reflects the parallelism provided in the target hardware and the programmer has no need to be concerned with the limits of the arrays, or with cycling through the elements in a logical or synchronised fashion.

However, there are some circumstances where it may be preferable to allow the programmer explicit control of a set of parallel operations, even though it might be possible to hide the operation. Such situations usually occur when the technique of functional parallelism is being used. Let us consider, as an example, the computational problem posed in Section 4 of Chapter 2:

$$F(x,y,z) = \frac{\sqrt{(x+y)^3 - (x+z)^2}}{yz}$$

and its implementation on an MIMD mesh. In Chapter 2, it was suggested that the following segment of pseudo-code would be appropriate to define the necessary parallel and sequential operations:

Execute in parallel: R1 = x + y;
                        R2 = x + z;
                        R3 = y * z;
End parallel:

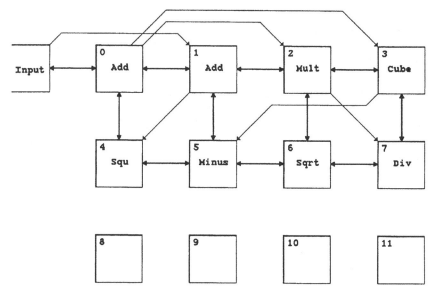

Figure 3.1   The result of arbitrary mapping

Execute in parallel: R4 = R1 * R1 * R1;
                        R5 = R2 * R2;
End parallel:
                        R6 = R4 – R5;
                        R7 = sqrt R6;
                        R8 = R7 / R3;

However, it is clear that this code is not sufficient to ensure the mapping illustrated in Figure 2.11. Any parallel computer has to be supplied with some sort of compiler which will allocate resources in the absence of specific instructions, but in many cases this will not result in the configuration desired by the programmer. Suppose that a compiler merely allocated resources in some numerical order, then the situation shown in Figure 3.1 might result. This would require already active processors to execute additional data passing operations (indicated by the lighter arrows), while some of the available resources (processors 8–11) remain completely idle. Whilst any real compiler is unlikely to be as unsophisticated in its approach as this, real problems are equally likely to be more complex, so that the mapping may well be similarly inefficient. The end result is bound to be slower execution of the program.

One way to avoid this problem would be for the programmer to explicitly state which processes should be mapped to which processors. Although this would be relatively easy for the type of example given above, more realistic programs, involving greater complexity, would be much harder to map. A more widespread technique, which has proved rather easier to manage, is to allow the programmer to define the communication channels between processes. If we assume the simplest possible syntax for our (imaginary) language, and allow our (equally imaginary) compiler sufficient sophistication to link input to output channels through inactive processing elements, then the following form of code might lead to the required implementation (shown in Figure 3.2).

Execute in series:	x -> I1;	
	y -> I1;	*/x,y and z are passed to
	z -> I1;	channel I1/*
Execute in parallel:	I1 — T2;	*/channel I1 is linked to channel T2/*
	I1 — T3;	*/channel I1 is linked to channel T3/*
End parallel:		
Execute in parallel:	(x+y) -> T1;	*/(x+y) passed to T1/*
	(x+z) -> T5;	*/(x+z) passed to T5/*
	(y*z) -> T4;	*/(y*z) passed to T4/*
End parallel:		
Execute in parallel:	T1 -> [cube] -> T7;	*/variables input on T1 are cubed and output on T7/*
	T5 -> [square] -> T6;	*/variables input on T5 are squared and output on T6/*
End parallel:		
	T7 -> T6 -> [–] -> T8;	*/T8 = T7 – T6/*
	T8 -> [sqrt] -> T9;	*/variables input on T8 are square-rooted and output on T9/*
	T9 -> T4 -> [/] -> O1;	*/O1 = T9 divided by T4/*

Of course, while this pseudo-code might lead to the desired mapping, the result would depend on the sophistication of the compiler and the resolution, in a real language, of potential ambiguities. The important point is to illustrate the idea that the program has made explicit both the parallel processing which is required and, equally important, the parallel communication. This is in stark contrast to the minimal added complexity which is required to implement implicit parallelism. It is apparent, then, that the complexity of a parallel language will depend heavily on the programming

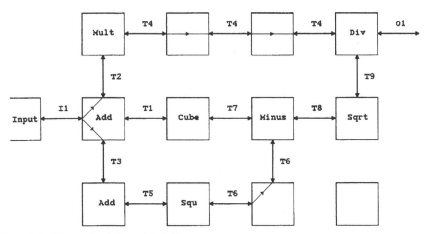

Figure 3.2   The result of channel definition

model on which it is based. We shall consider the alternatives in this area next.

3.1.2   The programming paradigm

It is unfortunate that a number of different metrics (not necessarily orthogonal) are in common use to describe the various paradigms of parallel computing languages. Thus, on the one hand, languages can be based on either message passing, dataflow or shared memory models, and on the other might be imperative or declarative in style. Further problems can arise over whether, for example, declarative languages are necessarily also logic languages, and whether either or both fall into the category of functional languages. The reader who requires a treatment of these matters in greater depth than I shall attempt here will find *Programming Models for Parallel Systems* by Williams a very accessible text. Indeed, the following treatment follows her categories as far as possible.

One approach to this section would be to consider the paradigms of Chapter 2, one-by-one, and describe the required language structure for each. In fact, some of those paradigms are, at heart, programming techniques. I shall follow this method to a limited extent but, where possible, I believe it is more illuminating for the reader to approach the question of programming from a slightly different viewpoint. It is as well to remember that what we shall be considering here are programming models, rather than machines, which gives us the freedom to adopt whatever level of program we choose – the next section of this chapter considers the alternative levels in more detail.

3.1.2.1 *Arrays and pipelines*

I choose to begin with a treatment of the appropriate paradigms for SIMD systems, systolic systems and pipelines, principally because programs for such systems are most likely to embody implicit parallelism, and are therefore the simplest to describe. This is because the parallelism in such systems is almost always hard-wired into the machines. From the user's point of view the programming models are very simple. All three are shown in Figure 3.3.

SIMD arrays can conceptually be of any dimensionality (this is considered more fully in Chapter 4), but the programming model is the same for all – additional data types are defined and embedded into a normal serial language, and dedicated subroutines are provided to supply all the necessary array functions. Although many of these will undoubtedly involve passing data between numbers of processors, the mechanics of this process are automatically arbitrated by the machine, and are invisible to the user. Usually, any mismatch between the size of the data set and that of the array is dealt with transparently.

Although pipelines are (usually) functionally parallel systems, the mechanics of both the mapping of processes to processors, and the communications between processes, can be hidden from the user, because both are automatically ordered by the system, with consequent simplification of the programming model. We should note, however, that a *reconfigurable* pipeline would not fall into this category. Alternative models exist for such systems, as we shall see later.

Systolic devices are even easier to deal with, in that a single such device is akin to any other type of special accelerator (like a floating-point unit), and can therefore straightforwardly be incorporated in a serial programming model. There do exist so-called systolic systems which comprise multiple programmable units, but these can usually be dealt with in the same way as pipelines.

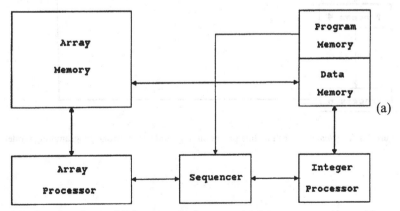

Figure 3.3 Programming models for some simple systems (a) Array programming model

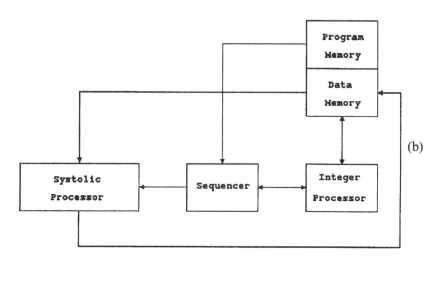

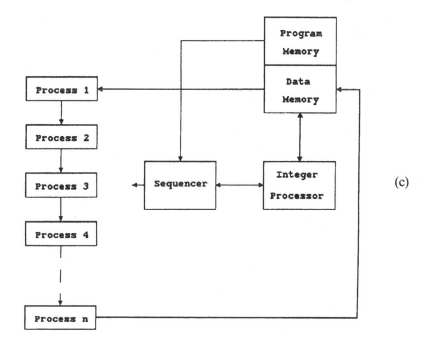

Figure 3.3 *(continued)*   (b) Pipeline programming model (c) Systolic programming model

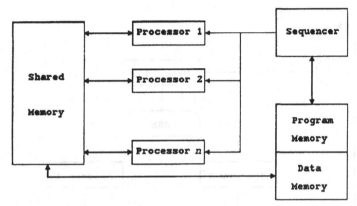

Figure 3.4 The shared memory model

3.1.2.2 Shared memory systems

The basic programming model for a shared memory system, shown in Figure 3.4, is superficially as simple as those discussed above, but conceals a number of difficulties. Before we deal with these, consider the advantages of the model. Given a number of processes which may be executed in parallel, there is no necessity to specify which processors tackle which task. It will, of course, be necessary to specify which operations in a program may be executed in parallel, and which must occur sequentially. With the further requirement that these processes must communicate data at some time, the shared memory provides the means to do so without needing to define specific communication channels. However, it is here that the problems lie concealed. It is necessary to introduce protocols which prevent the misuse of shared variables. If one of our processes modifies a variable at some (undetermined) time, whilst another process uses the variable at an equally indeterminate moment, the result of the second process will also be undefined unless some method of synchronisation is provided.

Two types of language construct have been widely used to specify the parallel and sequential parts of programs, categorised by Williams as *Fork and Join* and *Cobegin*. They operate as follows.

A fork statement either initiates one or more new processes and allows the current process to continue, or initiates two or more new processes and terminates the current process. Its dual, the join statement, either terminates one or more processes and continues with the original forking process, or terminates two or more processes and continues with a new process. The whole mechanism can be visualised as shown in Figure 3.5.

The cobegin construct allows the programmer to specify in a straightforward way those parts of the program which may be executed in parallel:

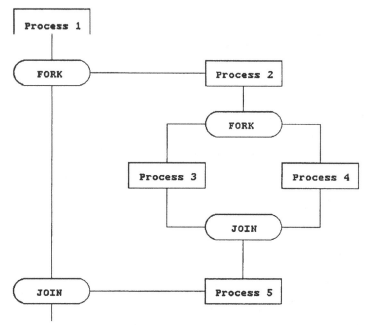

Figure 3.5 Defining parallel processes in the shared memory model

> cobegin
>
>> process 1
>> process 2
>> process 3
>> .
>> .
>> .
>> process n
>
> end

Neither of these constructs, of itself, provides the necessary protection of shared variables. Techniques which have been used to provide this protection include the use of *semaphores* and *monitors*. Semaphores are based on the *P* and *V* operators defined by Dijkstra [13] which are sometimes called the *wait* and *signal* operators.

A semaphore (*s*) is an integer variable which can take only non-negative values. *Wait(s)* causes the process calling the wait to be suspended, unless $s > 0$, in which case *s* is decremented by one. *Signal(s)* starts a process which has been suspended on the state of *s*, or increments *s* by one. The intention is that the use of these two operators should render critical sections of the code indivisible (i.e. the execution of that section of code cannot be interrupted). Two critical sections of different processes that must not be executed simultaneously are said to be *mutually exclusive*. The following example shows how the two constructs can be used to ensure that two processes are mutually exclusive, that all legal actions will eventually happen, and that deadlock (i.e. the program halting permanently part way through) cannot occur.

```
integer (s) = 1
cobegin
        process x
        begin
                repeat
                        wait(s)
                        critical part 1
                        signal(s)
                        remainder of x
                forever
        end
        process y
        begin
                repeat
                        wait(s)
                        critical part 2
                        signal(s)
                        remainder of y
                forever
        end
coend
```

An alternative to this process is the provision of a *monitor*. A monitor is a body of code which includes permanent variables and procedures, which is executed when a program is initiated. Its function is to provide a high-level method of synchronisation, and it achieves this by being invoked before any communication between two processes is allowed. The scheduling of the monitor's procedures is built in to the system, and access to specific procedures is only allowed to specific processes.

3.1.2.3 Message passing systems

Message passing systems are those where memory is private rather than shared, and in which, therefore, specific provision must be made for communications. This provision is made in the form of *channels* which allow messages to be sent by one process and received by another. A programming model for such a system is shown in Figure 3.6. In addition to methods for assigning parallelism, languages which are based on this model need to deal with two matters – the naming of the channels, and the method of controlling the messages that use the channels.

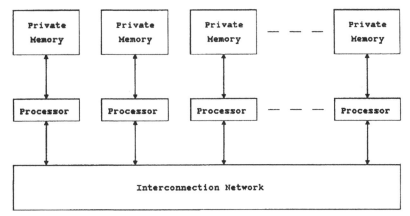

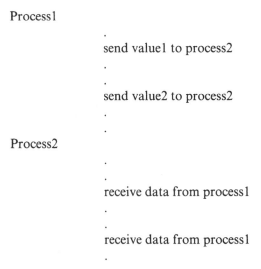

Figure 3.6   A message passing model

The first technique does not involve naming the channels at all, but names the communicating *processes*. This method works well provided that only one communication between two processes is required. Since in general the programmer cannot know how quickly each process will execute, a problem of synchronisation can arise if several communications are needed at different points. Consider the following segment of code:

Process1

.

send value1 to process2

.

.

send value2 to process2

.

.

Process2

.

.

receive data from process1

.

receive data from process1

.

Depending on the speed of execution of the two parallel processes, value1 may be lost, the correct data may be transferred, or data may be garbled. An alternative technique is to use a *global mailbox*. This is a program construct which may be the destination of any *Send* and the source of any *Receive* which names that mailbox. Such a process acts as a sort of shared memory area which is used for this specific purpose. Finally, channels themselves may be named in the way indicated in Section 3.1.1. Processes can then indulge in multiple communication as long as multiple channel names are used.

Message passing always requires appropriate constructs in both sending and receiving processes, but the actual process can be implemented either synchronously or asynchronously. Asynchronous message passing assumes a rather ill-specified communications network, rather like an electronic mail system. The initiating process sends a message to this network and, at some unspecified time later, the receiving process accesses the network to obtain the message. Such systems do not guarantee that messages are received in the order in which they are sent and, for this reason, are rarely implemented.

In a synchronous message passing system, a process which initiates a message waits after sending the message until the target process has accepted the message. If the target process reaches its receive statement first, then it must wait until the message is sent. Only after the transfer has been executed can both processes continue. Some models of the graph reduction paradigm, introduced in Chapter 2, are based on synchronous message passing.

3.1.2.4 *Declarative languages*

All of the software I have considered so far falls into the category of *imperative* languages – that is, the language specifies not only the problem which is to be solved, but also how it is to be solved. An alternative class is that of *declarative* languages, in which the problem is specified, but the order of execution of sub-problems is not. This paradigm has an obvious relationship to the idea of parallel processing, since the possibility is left open to implement processes in as parallel a way as resources will permit, although the method of implementation may not be immediately apparent.

Some declarative languages are also logic programming languages. Because readers may be less familiar with this idea than with the usual functional languages, and because logic programming is considered as being particularly appropriate for artificial intelligence programs (one of the major application areas suggested in Chapter 1), I choose to illustrate both sets of ideas simultaneously.

It will only be possible here to touch on the fundamental ideas of logic programming. A fuller treatment is available in *Programming in PARLOG* by Conlon which, as the title suggests, also deals very completely with the parallel logic language Parlog, described briefly in a later section of this chapter. The most important of these fundamental ideas is that program statements are evaluated not in terms of numerical values but in terms of their validity. Thus, the most basic type of statement is a proposition, which may be either true or false, having the form:

A: The computer is working.

The value of such a proposition (i.e. whether it is true or false) will probably depend on the validity of other propositions:

B: The power is on
C: The power supply is working
D: The hard disc is spinning
E: The login prompt has appeared
F: The printer is printing
G: A program is still running
H: The keyboard is active

The connections between these propositions can be defined with the use of a simple set of primitive connectives:

Connective	Function	Symbol
Conjunction	AND	&
Disjunction	OR	+
Implication	IF	<-

In the following way:

A <- E :   If the login prompt has appeared
            then the computer is working.

This is really the simplest sort of logical program statement. Two more complex sorts of expression are particularly relevant to the notion of parallel computing:

A <- B & C & D
A <- E + F + G

The first statement implies that if the power is on AND the power supply is working AND the hard disc is spinning, then the computer is working. (The fact that this is a rather limited definition of a working computer illustrates an important point. A logical program is not concerned with discovering truth in any higher sense, but in evaluating the validity of its expressions within the terms it has been given.) This is an example of AND parallelism: all the propositions on the right hand side must be true if the left hand side is to be true.

The second statement is an example of OR parallelism. If any of the statements on the right hand side is true, the left hand side is true also. Thus, the computer is working if the login has appeared, OR the printer is printing, OR if a program is still running. Naturally, the OR is not exclusive – any combination of the stated conditions implies a working computer too. These two types of statement have an important implication for parallel implementations. Assuming that all statements on the right are to be evaluated in parallel, B, C and D must all be fully evaluated to determine the validity of A. By contrast, as soon as any of E, F or G has been evaluated as true, the other evaluations can terminate, since A is now determined.

A program which comprised the list of propositions A – H given above, together with (say) the IF statement embodying OR parallelism, could be supplied with data corresponding to the validity of propositions B – H, and could return a value for proposition A. This is not, of course, the limit of what can be achieved with a declarative logic language. As suggested above, such languages are much more likely to be used in the context of artificial intelligence. Consider an implementation of an expert system. The rules of such a system correspond to the type of IF statements outlined above, whereas the database of system knowledge corresponds to the propositions. The operation of the expert system consists of evaluating statements (either one-by-one or in parallel) and determining the next statement to be accessed on the basis of the validity of the current statement.

We can begin to see, from the above, first, that declarative logic languages allow problems to be formulated in terms similar to those used in human reasoning and, second, that such formulation frequently allows the permissible parallelism in a set of functions to be made explicit. Since such languages do not necessarily imply that parallelism must be employed at any point, it is often said that they embody *concurrency*, that is, the potential for parallelism.

One further point is perhaps worth considering here. Although humans find the process of reasoning easy to execute, they often do this in a way which is difficult to implement on computers, known as bottom-up inference. Consider the situation where a crime has been committed, and certain facts are known about the perpetrator – that he is a man, over six feet tall, with a wooden leg, etc. – and about the crime – it was committed on a Monday, at midnight, in Paris. A database of known criminals exists, which includes their characteristics and information on their whereabouts. If a computer were to be required to match suspects with crime by bottom-up inference, it would need to apply the rules derived from the description of the crime to every person in the database – an exhaustive and exhausting process.

A better technique for computers, which leads to less work whilst still guaranteeing a complete solution, is to use the strategy of top-down inference. This requires the solution to begin with the highest-level 'rule' available, and derive from that a set of sub-rules which, if satisfied, will prove the initial rule. This process is repeated until the set of propositions (in this case suspects) is reached which satisfies the requirements of the program. It is perhaps easier to visualise this process as searching the network shown in Figure 3.7. Top-down evaluation begins at the apex of the structure and proceeds down only those paths which are necessary. Our supposed murder

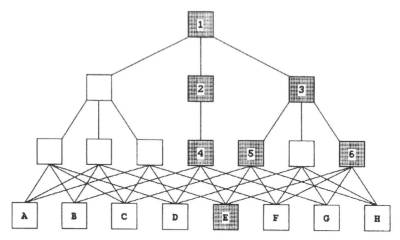

Figure 3.7 Evaluation strategies illustrated

(node 1) must have been committed by someone who was in Paris (node 2) and satisfies the description (node 3). In turn, the description is only satisfied by a male (node 5) with a wooden leg (node 6), whilst the suspect must have been in Paris at the correct time (node 4). Fortunately, only one suspect satisfies this (unlikely) set of conditions but, more to the point, only those links between the set of suspects A to H and nodes 4, 5 and 6 need to be evaluated. Bottom-up evaluation implies beginning at the base of the structure and evaluating all possibilities.

It may be appropriate, at this point, to note that this example demonstrates the difficulty which may sometimes arise in the process of choosing a suitable paradigm for a particular problem. A glance at Figure 3.7 might suggest an ideal match to the idea of graph reduction. In fact, this would only be true if bottom-up evaluation were to be implemented. If top-down evaluation is used, then the more general MIMD paradigm is more suitable. However, given that some particular paradigm can be selected for a given area of application, the question still remains as to what is the most appropriate level of software for the anticipated user. This question is considered in the next section.

3.1.3 The level of abstraction

Readers who are familiar with conventional computers may already understand the conceptual differences between high- and low-level languages. However, conventional wisdom often obscures the fact that there is a hierarchy of ways available in which a user may interact with a computer system. This fact is of particular significance for users of parallel systems, since one of the contradictions inherent in parallelism is between the need to allow a user to exploit it and the wish to protect the user from the consequences of its increased complexity.

Beginning at the lowest level, the possibilities which are available may be categorised as microcode, assembly-level, high-level, menus and graphical interfaces. For the sake of consistency, and because the details are familiar to me, I shall illustrate all these levels with reference to the body of software developed for the CLIP series of parallel computers built by the Image Processing Group at University College London. *Cellular Logic Image Processing*, edited by Duff and Fountain, provides much useful background on this series of machines.

3.1.3.1   Microcode

Writing programs in microcode is probably only for those few dedicated system developers who work on the dangerous frontier between hardware and software – I include a section on the process here for the sake of completeness, and as an illustration of the difficulties for the benefit of anyone who might contemplate using a machine which is programmed at this level. Microcode is a necessary evil, and an understanding of the principles involved may help the student of parallel computing to a better comprehension of the complexity of the subject. One point to bear in mind is that parallel computing is expensive, and its efficiency is therefore important. In those systems which use it, good microcode is a prerequisite of efficiency.

Figure 3.8 illustrates one of the processing elements which are at the heart of the CLIP7A system, a linear SIMD array of 256 such elements [14]. The total number of control lines to each element is about 80, which implies a total of 2^{80} possible control states for the system. Instances of these possible states must be built into sequences which define meaningful operations of the system. This is achieved by defining a series of microcode mnemonics, each of which specifies the active or passive state of every control line. Naturally, most simple operations (loading the local memory, for example) require very few lines to be active. To make the job of the microprogrammer easier, the default option is for all the lines to be in the passive state except those which are specified as active.

Definition of microcode proceeds as follows. First, all control lines are specified by their function and a corresponding number. A section of the definition file looks like this:

94	...
95	processor select obus 2
96	processor select obus 1
97	processor select obus 0
98	processor load D register
99	processor carry in 0

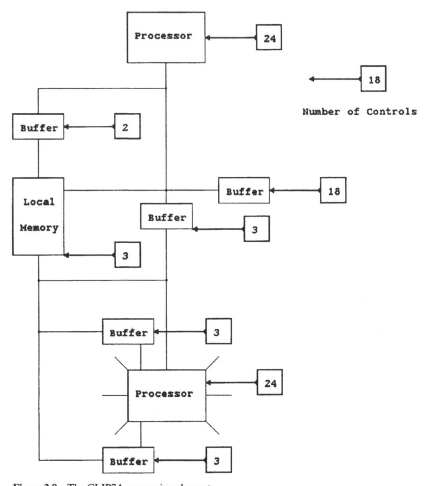

Figure 3.8   The CLIP7A processing element

100   processor carry in 1
101   processor select D source
102   processor clear N register
103   load RAM
104   ...

Second, simple operations are defined by specifying a mnemonic and the numbers of the active lines which that mnemonic must set (lines may be either active high (1) or active low (0)). A section of the mnemonic definition file, concerning functions of the processor arithmetic logic unit (ALU) and shift register, looks like this:

zero	:139 140 141 142 143	:	{output zero}
and	:140 141 142 143	:139	{logical AND}
pass_s	:141 142 143	:139 140	{output S register}
pass_b	:140 142 143	:139 141 132 133	{output B register}
add	:141 142	:143	{sum inputs}
sub	:142	:141 143	{difference inputs}
rotate_s	:139 140 141	:142 143	{set S mode to rotate}
lshift_s	:139 141	:140 142 143	{set S mode to logical shift}

Third, combinations of mnemonics, written on the same line, make up complete single lines of microcode, that is, each line specifies the control state of the system for one clock period. In general, this will not be sufficient to execute any meaningful processor element function so, finally, several lines of microcode are concatenated to produce single microcode functions:

```
#define    from1 53
#define    from2 84
#define    to1    19
main()
           address[from1]; read_ram; load_s
           address[from2]; read_ram; load_s; load_b
           add; read_b
           address[to1]; read_alu; load_ram
```

This function would extract two values from local memory, add them together and store the result. The reader should note that the physical form of this code is important – mnemonics on the same line define the control state in one period, the sequence of lines defines the sequence of control states. The parallelism in CLIP7A microcode is therefore, in this sense, explicit, whereas in another sense it is implicit, since the same operation is applied to all 256 processing elements at the same time.

Functions such as that shown above constitute the basic operations of a system (in this case CLIP7A). Any performance lost at this stage cannot be recouped by higher levels of software – in fact the opposite is usually the case. The great benefit of a microcoded system is that, if some particular operation is found to be critical to performance at a late stage of development, extra effort can be applied to optimise the microcode for that operation.

3.1.3.2   Assembly-level

Not all systems, serial or parallel, are microcoded. In some, the basic operations are hard-wired into either the processor or the controller. The CLIP4 machine has such a structure. In the case of such systems, these hard-wired functions form the components of the lowest level of software which can be implemented on the system, which is called assembly-level software. (In microcoded systems an assembly-level language often exists whose basic elements are the microcoded functions. This is so in the case of the CLIP7A system.) These languages form a sort of half-way house between the system-specific *how* of microcode and the non system-specific *what* of high-level languages. Thus, an assembly-level language will include an instruction to add together the contents of two registers (if registers exist in the system), but won't include a floating-point addition if no floating-point unit is provided in the system. Contrast this with a high-level language, which will allow floating-point operations as long as suitable subroutines have been written at assembly level to execute them.

The assembly-level languages used in the CLIP systems take the form of *virtual machines*. This implies that the instructions used do not exactly mirror every idiosyncrasy of their target machines, but attempt to provide a somewhat cleaner interface for the programmer. This approach reflects modern practice, but can lead to a degree of inefficiency if carried to excess. The main advance over programming at the microcode level, as far as parallel machines is concerned, is to allow all the facilities of a system to be accessed in a single language. Consider the following segment of code:

```
main()                                    */start of main program/*
{       CONTIG=1;
        FILE *fd, *fd1;
        charfile_name[50];                */definition of data structures/*
        data8 *new_image;

        .
        blur(fd, image);                  */subroutine call/*

        .
        c7vm_close();                     */end of main program/*

}

        .
void
        blur(FILE *fd, Vector *image)     */start of subroutine/*
        {
        .
        data8 *im_ptr;
        data8 array[256];                 */local data definitions/*
        Vector_16 anywhere;

        .
        for(int i=1; i<256; i++){         */repeat 256 times/*
        c7_setconstant16(temp[0],0);
        vm_av8tov16(im_ele[i-1],temp[1]); */calls to microcode routines/*
        vm_av8tov16(im_ele[i],temp[2]);
```

```
        vm_av8tov16(im_ele[i-1],temp[3]);
        vm_aadd16(temp[1],temp[2],temp[0]);      */single-vector add/*
        vm_aadd16(temp[0],temp[3],temp_v);
        vm_arshift16(temp_v,1,l_temp);           */single-vector shift/*

        vm_aadd16(rl_temp,temp_v,total);
        vm_adiv16(total,nine_v,quot,anywhere);
        vm_av16tov8(quot,image[i]);
        for(int x=0; x<256; x++){
        array[x] = (data8)(total[x]/9);
                }
        c7_enter_data(image[i+1],array);         */data I/O operation/*
        }
}
```

This is part of the code for calculating the average over a local neighbourhood of 3 × 3 pixels, at every point of a 256 × 256 pixel image. It displays the following typical features:

(a) A main program/subroutine structure
(b) The use of looping constructs
(c) The definition of a variety of data types
(d) The provision of low-level functions, executed on the parallel machine
(e) A standard base language (in this case, C)

This level of programming is the most efficient that a programmer is likely to encounter under normal circumstances. It closely reflects the functionality of the underlying machine, without submerging the programmer in hardware details. The example used here embodies implicit parallelism, but other such languages, as we shall see later, are explicit in their parallel constructs. It is again worth emphasising that the former reflects the data parallelism inherent in the CLIP systems, whereas the latter usually implies functional parallelism.

3.1.3.3   *High-level languages*

The CLIP research program uses the C language as the basis for its higher level software. Because the main application interest is in *Image Processing* the languages are called IPC4 (for CLIP4) and IPC7 (for CLIP7A). An extended version of Fortran, very similar in concept to these languages, is described later in this chapter, so I will confine myself to a few general remarks at this stage. The main point to note is that there are only two areas of modification needed to extend a high-level language into the area of parallel computing.

The first is the provision of appropriate parallel data or functional structures, the second is the addition of a suitable subroutine library (usually written in an appropriate assembly-level language) of specialised functions. This view depends for its validity on the use of implicit parallelism, and conceals one further important factor. Although the user's view of such a language may be satisfactorily undemanding, an enormous amount of work has to be done to the base language compiler in order to permit the indicated modifications, particularly in the case of functional parallelism. This only concerns potential users insofar as they may be inclined to doubt the robustness of such a structure if it has been produced with insufficient resources.

By far the greatest amount of computer programming is carried out by users at this level, but this situation may be changing. In many application areas, menu-based systems and graphical interfaces bid fair to become the most useful tools of the near future.

3.1.3.4 *Menus and graphical interfaces*

The basic idea of a menu-based language is very simple. Functions, be they high- or low-level, are packaged in a uniform way in respect of calling conventions, parameter passing, data I/O, etc. Data types, such as arrays, lists, database entries or images, are either implicit in the language or are themselves selected from a menu. The user of such systems is almost always unaware of the degree or type of any parallelism involved – it is entirely implicit.

The program of this type used on the CLIP systems is called YAM (Yet Another Menu!) which, in addition to a list of specialised image operators, permits ordinary arithmetic and program sequencing operations to be explicitly included. System-specific data I/O instructions are provided as well as general functions for data storage and retrieval and hard copy output. A typical YAM program listing begins with a header consisting of comments:

```
/*
** FILE:        logfile.yam
** DATE:        Mon Jun 7 13:36:08 1993
*/
```

And continues with combinations of simple mnemonics and program control functions:

```
Input   = grab(8)
        display(Input)
Av      = average(Input)
do 4
Av      = average(Av)
enddo
        display(Av)
```

```
Med     = median(Input)
          display(Med)
Corr    = div(Med,Av)
Con1    = 128
Norm    = mult(Corr,Con1)
          display(Norm)
Bin     = autothresh(Norm)
          display(Bin)
Thin    = skel(Bin)
Mid     = and(Thin,Input)
          display(Mid)
Res     = volume(Mid)
          display(Res)
```

The function mnemonics all commence with lower-case letters, the image names with upper-case. The program listing shown takes in an 8-bit image, performs several spatial neighbourhood averages to obtain a representation of background variation; uses this to produce a normalised, corrected image which is thresholded; finds the skeleton of the binary image; ANDs this with the input; and finally adds together the grey-level values of the final image. At various points images are displayed for examination. In this language no data type assignments are required, and nesting of operations is allowed as well as loop-and-test constructs. The whole idea of this type of environment is to shield the user from every type of programming complexity. In particular, in this context, all references to parallelism are removed. The menu environment is particularly well suited to SIMD array processing, but implementations on, for example, programmable pipelines or graph reduction systems would be equally valid. It is likely that any implementation designed for MIMD systems would have to provide a syntax allowing for parallel and sequential components.

Most menu systems are associated with the familiar type of display in which a mouse or light pen is used to select items from a list appearing on a screen, which either executes the chosen function or generates a second menu, which is used in the same way. There is usually a separate screen area which displays any results or messages. The explosion in the use of personal computers by naive users made the use of such interfaces as alternatives to conventional languages imperative. Since almost everyone is a comparative novice in the area of parallel computing, it may be that a similar situation obtains, and that most users will start at this level of interaction.

The graphical interface associated with YAM, called Yamtool, is somewhat different, at least partly because it is specialised for image processing. A typical screen, shown in Figure 3.9, has basically four areas. At centre bottom is a set of miniature displays of current data files (images). To right

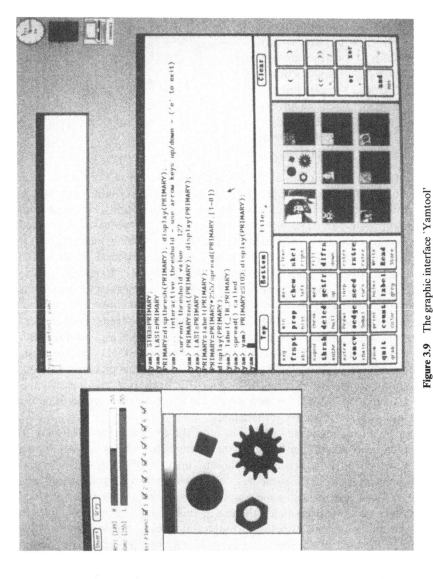

Figure 3.9 The graphic interface 'Yamtool'

and left of this are representations of sets of function buttons. Clicking the mouse on an image brings it up at full resolution in the active image area at top left. Clicking on a function button executes that function on the current active image. Each button in fact has three possible functions, of which only the centre function is active. Results are kept by clicking on 'Store' then on one of the miniature image areas, which is overwritten.

At the top of the interface is a text area where additional functions may be input, executed functions are echoed (along with any instructions as to interactive use of the keyboard if required) and names of files for data storage or retrieval may be input. The final major facility offered by the Yamtool system is session logging. A session, whether generated from the graphic interface or typed in from the keyboard, is stored as a *logfile* in the form of an executable program (which can be edited as required) under YAM. If appropriate, such programs can be passed through an optimising compiler to produce more efficient code.

Although the software systems used as examples here apply to SIMD array systems for use in image processing, the lessons to be learnt are of general application. First, in order to understand the significance of a particular piece of software, it is necessary to know what type of program it is. It is no good comparing the performance of microcode on one system with that of a graphical interface on another, for example. Second, the lower the level of software, the nearer to the parallel machine will the user be – more exposed to explicit parallelism, with more chance to write efficient programs (or faulty ones). Third, the higher the level of software, the less apparent to the user will be the parallel paradigm used. This implies that, once an appropriate choice of paradigm has been made, users may anticipate that they will be insulated from the more awkward consequences of their choice if a high enough level of software is used.

3.2 Parallel languages

These, then, are the fundamental aspects which characterise languages for parallel computing. How do they work in practice? It would be misleading to say that the following sections describe some of the more popular parallel languages, since the early stage of development of the field means that few have gained more than parochial acceptance. However, I have selected those which I believe have a reasonable chance of gaining wider acceptance, or those which are representative of a particular class. Unfortunately, limitations of space permit only the briefest overview of the most important aspects of each language. For a more complete understanding, students will need to consult the references suggested.

3.2.1   Fortran

The idea that 'faithful Fortran' is an example of a parallel language may be astonishing to some readers. However, it is important to note that the latest version has a figure '90' appended to the name. The basic Fortran language has evolved continually since its inception (from Fortran 66 through Fortran 77 and Fortran 8X to its latest embodiment) and will doubtless continue to do so. It has done so under pressure from users to incorporate additional features which they felt were required, whilst retaining compatibility with previous versions. The latest incarnation, agreed by a committee of the American National Standards Institute after a long and difficult gestation [15], incorporates a number of features which justify calling it a parallel language. However, the modifications to the language are not confined to these parallelising aspects, and it is not my purpose here to introduce the reader to unnecessary complications. Much of the relevant parallel syntax was borrowed from an earlier version, Fortran-Plus, within which its purpose is perhaps more clearly displayed. I shall therefore describe the features in terms of the latter language.

3.2.1.1   *Fortran-Plus*

Fortran-Plus is a language supplied by Active Memory Technology Ltd., who manufacture and market the DAP processor array systems [16]. The language is based on Fortran 77 with built-in extensions to exploit the characteristics of the target system. Foremost amongst these extensions is the capability to manipulate vectors and matrices as single parallel objects. This includes the following features:

(a) Declaration of the parallel entities (and indexed sets of them) in a manner similar to that of arrays of scalars in Fortran 77

(b) The application of operations to complete parallel objects (or subsets of them) without explicit looping

(c) The implementation of special functions (such as matrix operations) in ways which exploit the inherent parallel structure of the array

(d) The updating and accessing of parts of parallel objects by means of indexing

(e) Dynamic sizing of parallel constructs by means of arguments

(f) Parallel objects are differentiated from scalar arrays by means of the * notation, as follows

      INTEGER ARRAY(16,16)
      REAL VECTOR(*32)
      INTEGER MATRIX(*32,*64)

(g) To exploit the precision-dependent processing times of the single-bit DAP processing elements, a wide range of data precisions are permitted

– from three bytes to eight bytes for real data and from one byte to eight bytes for integers.Logical data is specified as one-bit per element.

The components of parallel objects are distributed over the processor elements of the DAP, with each component operated on by a single processor. The compiler organises objects which are larger than the host array so that processors operate on multiple components. This operation, together with any looping involved in manipulating such distributed objects, is transparent to the user. Arrays of parallel objects, usually called sets of vectors or matrices, are handled in the same way.

Just as in Fortran 77, the precision (in both senses) of the result of an operation on mixed data inputs is the precision of the largest object involved. Of course, such mixed operations are not always permitted.

An extremely important facility of Fortran-Plus is the variety of indexing mechanisms which are available. Use of these on the right hand side of an expression can result in the selection of more than one component from a parallel object, and they can be applied to expressions and the results of functions as well as to variables. Indexing can be used to extract a scalar from a scalar array, vector, vector set, matrix or matrix set; a vector from a vector set, matrix or matrix set; or a matrix from a matrix set.

These same techniques can also be used on the left hand side of assignment statements, in which case they specify the components of the object which are to be updated by the assignment. Thus scalar indexing updates a single component, while a logical matrix or vector index allows any subset of components to be updated. The following operation replaces those entries in ORIGINAL with the value 73, at points where MASK has the logical value *true*.

```
INTEGER ORIGINAL(*64,*128)      Assign original matrix
LOGICAL MASK(*64,*128)          Specify a logical matrix
ORIGINAL(MASK) = 73             Update original
```

Because of their frequent occurrence, built-in functions are provided to allow shifting of data in matrices. Thus the functions SHEP, SHWP, SHNP and SHSP shift matrices in the four directions East, West, North and South. These functions take an argument (which may be a scalar or a vector) which defines the amount of shifting required.

In addition to their use in simple expressions, vectors and matrices may be passed between subroutines, and may be the result of functions. When passed as arguments to subroutines, parallel objects may be declared within the subroutine with assumed dimensions, which allows generic routines to be developed.

A range of built-in subroutines, based upon but extending those of Fortran 77, is provided in Fortran-Plus. The additional functions include logical operators; routines for creating vectors and matrices from scalars or

Table 3.1 *The primitive processes of Occam*

Process	Syntax	Meaning
Assignment	$x := y + z$	The value of x is set to $y + z$
Input	$A ? x$	Input a value from channel A and assign it to variable x
Output	$C ! E$	Output the value of expression E to channel C

from components of other parallel constructs; functions which reduce the rank of their arguments by combining or selecting components, and routines for selecting subsets of parallel objects.

Fortran-Plus was developed using the Virtual Systems Architecture compiler methodology, which allows it to cater for a variety of host array sizes, and should permit easy updating in future.

3.2.2 Occam

Occam is the language which defines the programming model for transputers [17]. A program running on a transputer is formally equivalent to an Occam process, which means that a network of transputers can be described directly as an Occam program.

In Occam, processes are connected to form concurrent systems. Each process can be regarded as a black box with internal states, which can communicate with other processes via communication channels. Processes are finite – each starts, performs a series of actions and terminates. The actions may be sequential or parallel, which leads to the concept of processes with internal concurrency. All processes are constructed from three primitive processes – input and output, which are concerned with communication, and assignment, which computes the value of an expression and sets a variable to that value as shown in Table 3.1. A pair of concurrent processes communicate using a one-way channel. The key concept is that communication is synchronised and unbuffered. If a channel is used for input in one process and output in another, communication occurs when both processes are ready. Since processes may have internal concurrency, each may have many input and output channels performing communication at the same time.

A number of processes can be combined to form a construct, which is itself a process and can be used as a component of other constructs. There are four types of construct – sequential, parallel, conditional and alternative. A sequential construct is written thus:

```
SEQ
        chan1 ? x
        x := x + 2
        chan2 ! x
```

The effect of this segment of program is to execute each of the processes one-by-one, each process in turn being terminated before the next commences. The result would therefore be to input a variable x, increase its value by two and output it. The following parallel construct has a quite different effect:

```
PAR
        chan1 ? x
        y := y + 2
        chan2 ! z
```

These processes are executed concurrently – variable x is input on channel 1; y is increased by two and z is output on channel 2, all simultaneously. This construct therefore provides a straightforward way of expressing whatever concurrency is available in the program, and at the same time mapping it onto a parallel system. The conditional construct is used as follows:

```
IF
        condition a
                process 1
        condition b
                process 2
```

This means that process 1 is executed if condition a is true, process 2 is executed if condition b is true (and so on if there were more sections of the construct). Once one of the processes is executed, the construct terminates. The alternative construct is similar but different in effect:

```
ALT
        input 1
                process 1
        input 2
                process 2
```

This construct waits until one of the inputs is ready. When the first of them becomes ready, that input is performed followed by its own process, and the construct then terminates.

In addition to these somewhat unusual constructs, Occam includes facilities for looping, replicating operations, declaring a variety of data types, naming procedures and functions, and constructing expressions. Further, as a method of improving performance, processes can be forced to use individual transputers by means of the PLACED PAR construct, and may, in addition, have their relative priorities specified.

Since the transputer and Occam are merely different sides of the same coin, there is no doubt that Occam is a very efficient, functionally parallel, programming language for its target devices. Unfortunately, there is equally little doubt that its use is overly tedious for the majority of potential users.

3.2.3   Parlog

The word Parlog is an abbreviation of Parallel Logic, and is intended to emphasise the concepts of concurrency and declarative logic which are embodied in the language. Parlog syntax is based on that of Edinburgh Prolog, an earlier logic programming language which did not embody specific concurrency. I will illustrate the structure and use of the language with the aid of an example related to that in Chapter 1 of the secure entry system. We will postulate that all the preliminary parts of that problem, up to and including the identification of a caller, have been completed. Our problem now is to decide whether to admit the caller.

The first part of the program to handle this comprises *procedures* which have some aspects in common with small databases.

```
mode allow_in(?)

allow_in(Dave Doorman).
allow_in(Sally Secretary).
allow_in(Don Director).
allow_in(Mary Manager).
allow_in(Pete Programmer).
allow_in(Jim Janitor).
allow_in(Eliza Engineer).

mode call_police(?)

call_police(Diana Hacker);
call_police(Bill Bludgeon);
call_police(Mack the Knife);
```

This program consists of two procedures. The first defines a relation called allow_in which includes a mode declaration and a set of clauses. The second relation (call_police) has a similar form. The program is used (when a caller has been automatically identified) by a query in the following form:

```
<- allow_in(Mary Manager).
```

This will cause the procedure allow_in to see if Mary is part of its definition. Since she is, the procedure could then be made to activate the door mechanism. So much would be true for any declarative logic program. The parallel part of the operation is introduced by the full stop at the end of each clause. This syntax implies that all the clauses should be evaluated (compared with the query) in parallel.

However, imagine that our image analysis system has identified Bill Bludgeon. The first query would then be:

<- allow_in(Bill Bludgeon).

Which finds no match in the allow_in procedure. We therefore follow with:

<- call_police(Bill Bludgeon);

Note that, in this procedure, the clauses end with semi-colons. This tells the procedure to search its clauses sequentially.

The parallel searching which was initiated by the full stop was an example of OR-parallelism. As soon as any clause is matched the remaining active operations can cease. Now suppose that two individuals arrive at the door together, and that both are identified. The query will be of the form:

<- allow_in(Mary Manager), allow_in(Don Director).

This query instructs the procedure to search its clauses for two matches in parallel (AND-parallelism) and only return a positive answer if both are satisfied. An alternative to this would be to replace the comma between the two queries by &, in which case the queries would be evaluated in sequence, with any failure causing failure of the entire query.

The above example oversimplifies two aspects which require further consideration. First, what happens if a query could result in several possible matches (not possible, of course, in the above example)? Parlog embodies a strategy called *test-commit-output* which means that the first successful match which is made binds (fixes) the answer, and no further evaluations are attempted.

Second, the clauses only have one argument. It is perfectly possible, in Parlog, for clauses to have more than one argument, in which case queries can be used to discover associations between different characteristics. This enables variables to be used as one argument of a query, the process of evaluation leading to the assignment of a value to the variable.

Finally, in this very brief review of some of the facets of Parlog, variables can appear in more than one simultaneous query. If the output variable of one query is the same as the input variable of a second, then the second query will suspend until the first query has assigned a value to its output variable. The second query will then resume evaluation.

3.2.4 Dactl

Dactl, which was developed under the British Alvey computing initiative [18], is an example of the general class of compiler target languages. The basic idea of such languages, known as CTLs, is shown in Figure 3.10.

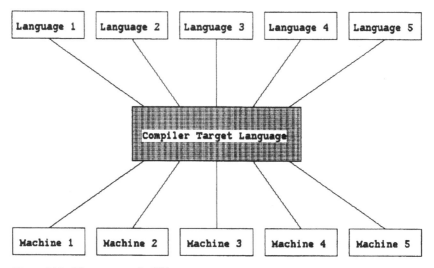

Figure 3.10   The purpose of a CTL

The notion is that there are many basic languages with which users are familiar and in which they would prefer to continue writing. Similarly, there are a plethora of machines (in our context, parallel machines), on which it might be desirable to run programs. The CTL is an intermediate level of code which is utilised in one of two ways. Programs can be written directly in the CTL language, and a suitable compiler is needed to transform the programs into machine level code. Such compilers are machine-specific, i.e. one is needed for each target machine.

Alternatively, programs are written in the desired source language, and a dedicated compiler transforms the program into CTL code. This CTL code is then compiled to machine language as before. The supposed advantage of such a system is that it separates the machine dependent aspects of compilation from the source language dependent facets. Thus, if we consider a system of N source languages and M machines, without a CTL we would require $N \times M$ compilers to achieve all-to-all mapping, whereas with the CTL only $M + N$ compilers are needed.

The Dactl language itself displays many of the characteristics typical of functionally parallel languages. Actions can be specified as sequential by the following construction:

```
SEQ_DO
                    FUNCTION1
                    FUNCTION2
                    FUNCTION3
    END_SEQ_DO
```

Whereas functions which may be executed in any order, and which may therefore be executed in parallel, are specified by:

DO

FUNCTION1
FUNCTION2
FUNCTION3

END_DO

Similarly, sections of program of the either/or type, which depend on the evaluation of external conditions, can be specified as having their conditions evaluated either sequentially or in any order (and therefore in parallel if required).

3.3 Cognitive training

We come now to the matter touched on at the beginning of this chapter, namely how is the training of a cognitive system equivalent to the programming of a more standard type of parallel computer? In general terms, this equivalence was described in the first chapter, but here we will consider it in more detail. Where necessary, the equivalence is extended to include aspects of hardware.

A cognitive computer is quite unlike its calculating counterpart, in that the physical entity can manipulate data without having been previously programmed by the user. In other words, a cogniser can be made to operate merely by applying data to the inputs (although the operation would be undefined under these circumstances). The function of operation is built-in to the hardware. Although it would be possible to construct normal computers which operated in this way, none, to my knowledge, does so. Any ordinary computer requires a program to tell it what to do. There is therefore not a complete equivalence between programming a calculator and training a cogniser.

Nevertheless, training a cogniser does (if carried out effectively) determine what function the system will perform, in the same way that the content of a program determines what function a calculator executes. In this sense, there is an equivalence between the two operations of training and programming. Of course, there is a significant difference between the physical effects of the two operations. At the lowest level, a calculator always carries out the same fixed set of operations – running a program merely affects the order in which functions are executed. Although the high-level function of a particular cogniser is always the same (classification, for example) the functions (or rather, the significance of the functions) at each node can alter, depending on the training which has been carried out.

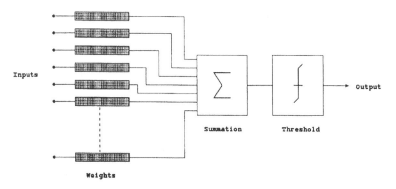

Figure 3.11   A typical cognitive node

Thus there is a partial, but not exact, equivalence between the operations of programming and training. It is therefore appropriate, in this chapter, to consider the methods and effects of the training procedure. Let us begin by reconsidering the typical cogniser node of Chapter 2, illustrated in Figure 3.11.

There are two ways in which the performance of the node can be affected – the values of the interconnection weights can be changed, and the thresholding level or mechanism can be altered. In Chapter 2, I suggested that a single node of this sort can only discriminate successfully between data sets that are linearly separable, and this contention can be demonstrated mathematically. (*An Introduction to Neural Computing*, by Aleksander and Morton, provides an excellent explanation of this and many of the other aspects which I touch on below.) Both the threshold and the set of weights are obtained by solving a set of linear algebraic equations which are defined by the required function of the node. However, two points need to be made clear. First, the solution tells us nothing about how the adjustments to the parameters should be implemented. This is an important point, since any real system is likely to comprise a large number of nodes, so that an automatic mechanism for adjustment is certain to be required. The second point starts from the same observation, that real systems comprise large numbers of interlinked nodes, so that the simplistic training rule outlined above – that is, the solution of sets of linear algebraic equations – will be, at best, tedious to implement because of its implied iterative nature and, at worst, impossible to apply because of the existence of internal (hidden) nodes whose functionality is not defined.

We therefore need to consider some of the more realistic approaches to training (i.e. to the definition of the weights and thresholds) which have been developed. The derivation of these approaches is considered in *An Introduction to Neural Computing* – here I will only attempt a brief summary of the methods themselves.

Training a cognitive system can be considered as a process of altering the internal states of the system in such a way that, when a particular set of input data is applied, a particular (desirable) set of outputs is produced. To reduce this to a logical sequence of events, we need to do the following:

(1) Define the set of input data
(2) Define the desired set of output states for each input
    Then, iteratively:

    (3) Apply the data set to the inputs
    (4) Modify the internal states of the system

until the desired outputs are achieved. Note that, at point (4), the required outputs for any particular input may not be achieved immediately.

If we compare this process with that of programming an ordinary computer, we can see that there are some equivalencies and some differences. Items (1) and (2) equate to the design of a program. Items (3) and (4) are as near as we come to programming the system, but the equivalence is not exact. The process itself is automatic (although it may be tedious) once we have defined a suitable method to implement item (4). This activity constitutes, therefore, the key point in 'programming' cognisers. Below, I consider two of the basic approaches to determining the eventual states of the weights in a system, and a significant modification to one of them.

3.3.1 Hebb's rule

This technique, described qualitatively by Hebb [11] in 1949, takes as its starting point a set of interconnected summing/thresholding nodes in which the connections between any pair of nodes are symmetrical. That is, for two nodes (i) and (j), there is a connection from (i) to (j) with weight W_{ij} and a connection from (j) to (i) with the same weight. Figure 3.12 illustrates an appropriate configuration – for the sake of simplicity, only the connections to node 3 are shown, and only the weights between nodes 3 and 4. W_{34} must equal W_{43} and, similarly, W_{13} must equal W_{31}, etc.

The approach is used in systems where minimisation is the aim, and is derived by considering a parameter of the system equivalent to the energy of (say) a group of atomic particles. In such a context, the energy (E) of a particle of mass (m) and velocity (v) can be defined as:

$$E = \frac{1}{2}mv^2$$

For one particular state of a system such as that shown in Figure 3.12, an equivalent expression exists:

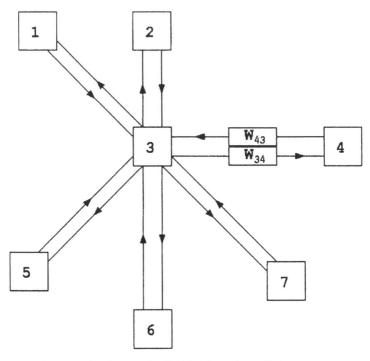

Figure 3.12   A system of nodes to which Hebb's rule can be applied

$$E = -\frac{1}{2}\sum_i\sum_j W_{ij}s_is_j$$

where s_i and s_j are the (binary) states of the ith and jth nodes respectively. In order to minimise this expression for a set of p independent system states $(\alpha_1 - \alpha_p)$ we find that:

$$W_{ij} = \sum_{\alpha=1}^{p} s_i^{\alpha}s_j^{\alpha}$$

Executing this manipulation on the set of system weights will effectively store in the system the set of training patterns. Provided that the training set satisfied a number of important criteria concerning their number and separability, any applied input pattern will then cause the system to settle into the nearest trained pattern.

This technique works well for small data sets which are *almost orthogonal*, that is where the components are significantly different. However, there are two sets of circumstances, still concerning systems involved in the process of minimisation, where some extra help is required.

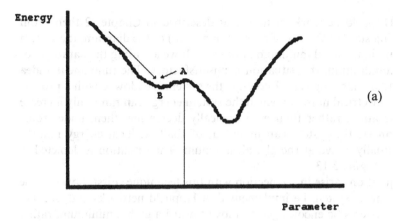

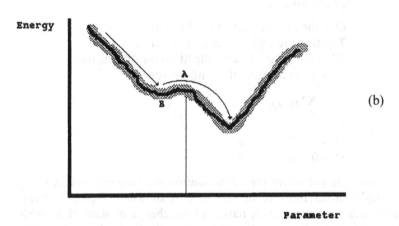

Figure 3.13 Avoiding local minima (a) The system ends in a local minimum
(b) A noisy system which finds the global minimum

First, with some sets of training data, systems can generate false minima in
their energy landscape. This can result in false answers being supplied for
some configurations of subsequent input. Second, when global minimisation is desired, systems can be trapped in undesirable local minima. Under
both these circumstances, the following technique can be of benefit.

3.3.2 Simulated annealing

It is perhaps easiest to approach this idea intuitively by considering Figure
3.13, which depicts a situation in which the energy of a system is plotted
against a single, arbitrary, parameter. If the system being represented is a

type of Hopfield network such as that described in Chapter 2 then, from any starting state to the left of point A in part (a) of the diagram, the system will end up in the local minimum at point B. If we are using the paradigm of global minimisation, this situation is unsatisfactory. The fundamental idea of simulated annealing is as follows. If the system is endowed with a property akin to electrical noise, in which the system energy can randomly increase at any iteration, rather than monotonically decreasing, then, under some circumstances, the system can jump out of shallow, local energy minima and eventually arrive at the global minimum. This situation is depicted in part (b) of Figure 3.13.

Two questions arise in connection with this technique. First, how can the idea of a noisy system be implemented in Hopfield networks and, second, how can systems be encouraged to move toward a global minimum, rather than just hopping about between whatever local minima are available?

The first question can be answered by expressing the state of a neuron in such a network mathematically.

If: O_i is the output state of the ith neuron
T_i is the threshold of the ith neuron
W_{ij} is the weight linking the ith to the jth neuron
A_i is the activation of the ith neuron

And if: $$A_i = \sum W_{ij} O_j - T_i$$

Then, for $i = j$: $O_i = 1$ if $A_i > 0$
and $O_i = 0$ if $A_i < 0$

We can associate the activation of the neuron with the probability of its output being in either the zero or one state as shown in Figure 3.14 (a), which illustrates the deterministic nature of the change of state. If we wish to implement a thermally excited system, a first step is to change the relationship to the situation shown in Figure 3.14 (b), where there is a certain (small) probability of a change in the output state from, say, zero to one, even though the activation remains slightly less than zero. The situation is, of course, symmetrical for the transition from one to zero.

It was suggested by Kirkpatrick [19] that a suitable probability function would be:

$$p(1) = \frac{1}{1 + e^{-A/T}}$$

This expression has two benefits. It certainly has the required general shape, and it introduces a parameter T (in the original formulation the temperature of a system of particles) which can be utilised to address the second part of our problem – how to make a system converge on the global mini-

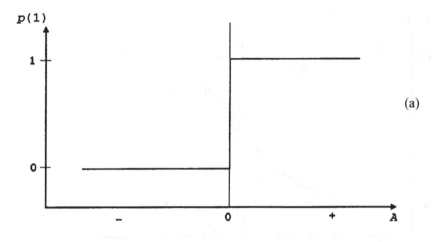

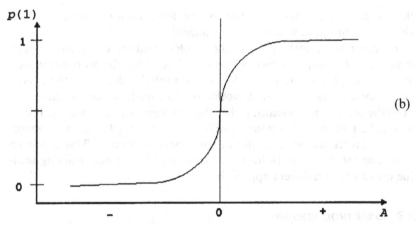

Figure 3.14 Activation probabilities for a neuron (a) Deterministic (b) Probabalistic

mum. It does this as follows. Figure 3.15 shows two curves, both derived from the suggested expression for $p(1)$, but with different values of T. When the value of T is large, there is a correspondingly high probability of change of state for values of A far from zero. When the value of T is small, the probability of transition for a given value of A is reduced.

This property of the function can be utilised to encourage convergence of the system to a global minimum. Iterations of the system state from its starting point are first performed with a large value of T. When no further consistent minimisation of system energy is obtained, the value of T is lowered and further iterations are carried out. This process is repeated until either no further benefit is obtained, or a satisfactory answer is achieved. It

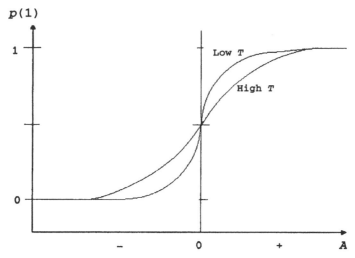

Figure 3.15   The effect of temperature on activation probability

is this process of gradual reduction of the temperature parameter which leads to the connection with the idea of annealing.

It is apparent, therefore, that the implementation of systems which embody these techniques provides one way of reducing the problems associated with the phenomenon of false, or unwanted, minima in the energy states of some types of neural networks. As described, this approach is relevant to the use of such systems, rather than to their original training. It can, however, be regarded as a training technique if the weights of interconnection are regarded as variables during an annealing process. This approach has been adopted for the Boltzmann machine [20]. The next training technique uses a rather different approach.

3.3.3 Back propagation

In this section, we consider the type of network shown in Figure 3.16. It comprises a layer of input nodes, an unspecified number of layers of internal nodes and a layer of output nodes. The general technique is as follows. First, the system weights, which are to be modified by the process known as back propagation of errors, are set at their initial (perhaps arbitrary) values. Next, a set of inputs are applied for which the desired outputs are known. The system state is then allowed to evolve, after which the actual outputs are compared with the desired outputs, generating an error value for each node. The weights of the output nodes are adjusted in such a way as to minimise the output errors. This in turn allows error functions to be calculated for the previous layer of nodes, which then allows their weights to be modified. This process is continued until the corrections generated by the

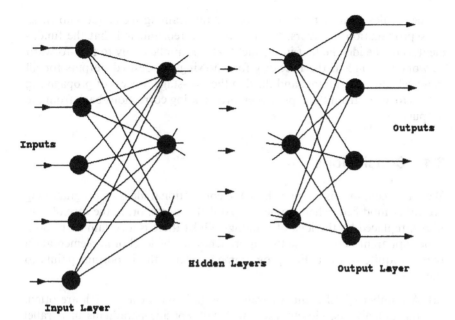

Figure 3.16 A feed-forward net

original errors are propagated back to the inputs. The whole procedure is then iterated as necessary.

We can express the method described above in mathematical terms. The object of the exercise is to define a way of altering weights for sets of neural nodes whose output is some general function of the activation states. A method of doing this has been set out by Rumelhart et al. [21] as follows.

During training, for the pth presentation of an input state, the necessary change in weight connecting the output of the ith unit to the input of the jth is given by:

$$\Delta_p W_{ij} = \beta \delta_{pj} O_{ip}$$

where O_{ip} is the output of the ith unit
      β is a constant related to the rate of learning
      δ_{pj} is some computed error

Then, if O_{ip} is defined by: $O_{ip} = \dfrac{1}{1 + e^{-A_n}}$

where, if T_{pj} are the target outputs, the errors can be stated as:

$$\delta_{pj} = (T_{pj} - O_{pj})O_{pj}(1 - O_{pj})$$
$$\delta_{pj} = O_{pj}(1 - O_{pj})\sum \delta_{pk} W_{pk}$$

for output and hidden nodes respectively.

These rules form a basis for applying the training technique known as back propagation of errors, but it should be remembered that the fundamentals of the idea lie first in the fact that it is applied only to feed-forward networks; second in the necessity for knowing the desired outputs for all input sets during training; and third in the two-stage process of propagating results forward from the inputs, then propagating corrections back from the outputs.

3.4 Conclusions

We have seen, in this chapter, how the conventional ideas of programming are either modified, when applied to parallel systems, or, in the case of cognisers, replaced by the idea of training. Whilst there is a certain correspondence apparent between the two approaches, at the level of implementation they are quite distinct. For programmed systems the important points to note are:

(a) A number of different programming paradigms exist which are often, but not always, closely associated with specific paradigms of parallel computing.

(b) There are significant differences between languages which utilise implicit and explicit parallelism.

(c) In general, programming data parallel systems is more closely similar to serial programming than is the case for function parallel systems. Languages for data parallel systems often simply add extended data types to conventional languages. Function parallel languages usually adopt quite different approaches.

(d) The level of abstraction of a language is an important parameter. The lower the level, the more efficient it is likely to be, but the harder to use, demanding greater understanding of the underlying system. Higher-level languages are easier to use but are, almost inevitably, less efficient.

(e) As yet, no parallel languages are widely accepted. The nearest to an accepted standard is the use of C as a base for a number of data parallel language implementations.

(f) The easiest way forward for the novice user of parallel systems will be through the increased use of suitable graphical interfaces.

The most important point to remember about training methods for cognitive systems is that the user (as opposed to the student of the subject) doesn't need to know anything about the details – they are built in to each specific system. The user only needs to consider whether a particular system is suited to the task – whether it requires repeated iteration of training procedures, if it is necessary to know the desired outputs while training, etc.

Having dealt with the question of how a user interacts with parallel systems, it is time to move on to consider some of the more technical aspects of the systems themselves. The most important of these is the question of how the various elements of a parallel system are connected together – after all, it is this aspect which differentiates such systems from a room full of separate computers.

3.5 Exercises

1. Explain the difference between *implicit* and *explicit* embodiment of parallelism in a programming language.

2. Using block diagrams, explain the programming models which are used for:
   (a) A pipeline system
   (b) A shared memory system
   (c) A message-passing system

3. Describe the structure of an imperative language. Illustrate your answer by showing how you might solve the following problem in Parlog:
   A crime has been committed in a known location, and you have a partial description of the perpetrator. You also have a database containing information about the appearance and whereabouts of a large number of known criminals. Devise a program to select suspects from your database.

4. List the different levels of software which can be used to program any computer. Discuss the advantages and disadvantages of each of the levels you have listed.

5. You are required to carry out the following matrix calculations in which each of the matrices is 100×100 floating-point numbers:

   $$X = AB$$
   $$Y = CB^{-1}$$
   $$Z = X + Y$$

   Indicate how you would program your solution on an appropriate parallel computer in each of the following languages:
   (a) Fortran-Plus
   (b) Occam

6. How does the control of a cogniser differ from that of a calculator (in programming terms)? What are the advantages and disadvantages of the two systems?

7. In what type of cognitive operation is it appropriate to apply Hebb's rule? Explain how the rule is applied to such a system, and suggest circumstances under which the technique will work effectively.
8. Explain the idea of simulated annealing in neural systems. Under what circumstances might its use be necessary?
9. What does *back propagation* mean in a system of neural nodes? Develop a set of rules which could form the basis for applying the technique.

4 Connectivity

Whilst the two issues of control (what are all these parallel processors going to do?) and programming (how is the user to tell them all what to do?) are perhaps the most difficult conceptual aspects of parallel computing, the question of the connections between all the many system components is probably the hardest technical problem. There are two main levels at which the problem must be considered. At the first level, the connections between major system components, such as CPU, controller, data input and output devices, must be given careful consideration to avoid introducing bottlenecks which might destroy hoped-for performance. At the second level, connections within these major components, particularly between processing units and their associated memories, will be the major controlling factor of overall system performance. Within this area, an important conceptual difference exists between two alternative approaches to inter-processor communication. Individual pairs of elements may be either externally synchronised, in which case a controller ensures that if data is input at one end of a line it is simultaneously accepted at the other, or unsynchronised. In this latter case, the donating element signals that data is available, but the data is not transferred until the receiving element is ready to accept it.

In addition to this, technical problems are present. The first is the position and purpose of memory in the general structure. As well as the usual computer design issues concerning such matters as cache memory or pipelining, additional questions arise as to whether processors or memory should communicate directly, and whether memory should be shared or localised.

The second problem, which is the subject of the major part of this chapter, concerns the design of the network by means of which elements communicate. The possibilities range from the simplest and most familiar – interfacing every element to a common bus structure – to the generally unattainable ideal wherein each element has a dedicated channel connecting it to every other. (To understand why this is unattainable except in the smallest assemblies, contemplate first the likely physical problems for a comparatively modest set of a few hundred elements, and then consider what the receiving element is going to do with all the – possibly simultaneous – input data.)

4.1 Synchronising communications

The philosophical divide, between those who would have their processors communicate synchronously when so ordered, and those who would allow their processors the freedom to communicate asynchronously at whim, is probably deeper than the conceptual difference between the two approaches warrants. There are, of course, significant differences in implementation between the two ideas.

The main conceptual difference between the two approaches lies mainly in the locality of control. Synchronous communication assumes that the situation shown in Figure 4.1 obtains – that any receiving element will automatically be in a state to accept whatever data is supplied to it. For this to be so, some external device must be in control of both elements – in other words, this technique is normally associated with the SIMD paradigm. The timing of the data transfer process can be guaranteed, so that the transfer is always effective. Conflicts can only occur (for example when two elements each wish to communicate with a third) when a system programmer error occurs.

Asynchronous communication is the necessary consequence of a certain degree of local autonomy in the processing elements of an assembly (considered fully in the next chapter). If processing elements are performing different tasks, with the timing of various operations determined only by their own sequencers, the interchange of data between them must be a matter of specific agreement. The simplest situation, shown in Figure 4.2(a), is conceptually almost as straightforward as that of synchronous exchange. The initiating element must signal to the potential receiver(s) that data is available, the signalling being carried out on a dedicated channel. When the receiver is ready, it signals either that data can now be sent, or that data has been latched, according to the detailed arrangements. So far, the only additional complication lies in the extra circuits and channels which must be

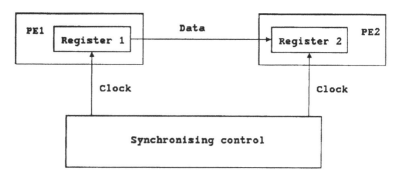

Figure 4.1   Synchronous communication

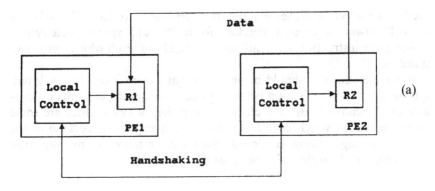

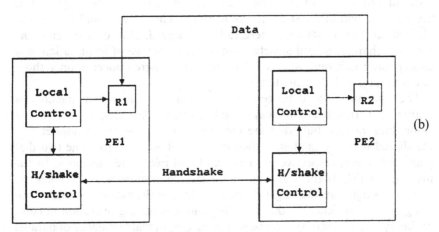

Figure 4.2 Asynchronous communications

supplied to deal with the exchange of signals, often called *handshaking*. However, a number of potential problems can arise. Suppose a receiver signals its readiness to accept data before a donor has it ready. Some provision must be made at the receiving end to delay the transfer. What if the donor is sending to a number of receivers, each of which becomes ready at a different time? Either multiple data transfers must be made, or the processes of all must be delayed until the most dilatory is ready. How about the situation where one receiver gets two simultaneous signals indicating that two donors want to send data? Clearly, some form of prioritisation of inputs must be provided.

There are two drawbacks to this. First, the resulting situation can become close to that shown in Figure 4.2(b) – a communications coprocessor is needed at each element. Second, the situation is akin to that which arises in normal software when error checking for faulty data types is implemented before every instruction – a significant overhead can result which slows data transfers.

From the above, it should be apparent that, where it can be employed, synchronous communication between parallel computing elements is desirable on grounds of cost and efficiency. Equally, however, there are some circumstances in which use of the technique is impossible because of the overall paradigm being employed. Such circumstances commonly arise when functional parallelism is being used.

4.2   The role of memory

A second overall factor in the design of parallel computing systems, which arises independently of the type of connection network to be employed, is the position, within the structure, of memory. There are a number of possible basic arrangements which need to be considered. (As we have seen in the previous chapter, neural structures implement storage of information in a conceptually different way, so that the debate here concerns only those devices I have called calculators.)

The first question to be considered is whether the system memory is shared or distributed. This was considered in the last chapter in terms of computing models, but what are the practical implications? Consider first the shared memory models, shown in Figure 4.3(a) and (b). The two diagrams represent, respectively, single- and multiple-ported memory. In the first case, which might well occur if the interconnection network takes the form of a single *bus*, the single physical channel to the memory forms a crippling system bottleneck – the most frequently occurring operation in computing systems is memory access, so the maximum viable number of parallel processing elements which could be used in such a system would be limited to something close to the ratio of the typical processing time to the memory access time, generally a rather small integer. Such arrangements are therefore likely to be confined to MIMD systems with small numbers of processors.

In the second case, the situation is improved, although probably not by quite the anticipated factor. The data bandwidth (the amount of data which can be simultaneously communicated) to memory is certainly increased by the number of parallel ports which are available (of course, it will be necessary for the interconnection network to support this increased bandwidth also), but a second factor must be considered. A certain number of simultaneous memory accesses are likely to be to the same memory address and, therefore, may represent logical conflicts. These usually occur in connection

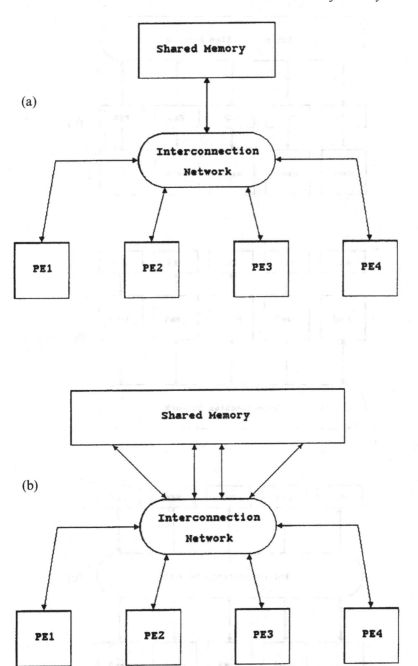

Figure 4.3 Shared memory systems (a) Single-ported memory (b) Multiple-ported memory

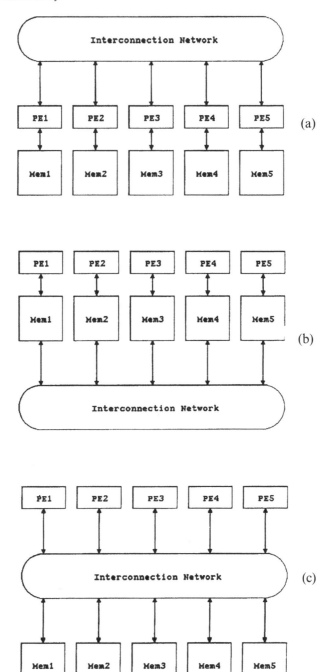

Figure 4.4 Distributed memory systems (a) Processors interconnected
(b) Memories interconnected (c) Symmetrical interconnections

with operations which write to the shared memory. Thus, for example, if one operation is writing to a particular location at the same time as a second is reading from that same location, the outcome of the second operation (the read) will be indeterminate. This may be acceptable in some circumstances, but is certain to be undesirable in others. Some provision must therefore be made to deal with such potential conflicts, and this is certain to impair the performance of the system in some cases.

There are also a number of alternative arrangements for the general case of distributed memory systems. The first is that shown in Figure 4.4(a), where the network connects the processors directly, with the distributed memory elements attached to the 'other side' of the processors. This arrangement, which is common amongst, for example, mesh connected SIMD arrays, has one advantage and one drawback. The advantage lies in the ready ability of such a system to carry out inter-processor communication simultaneously with processor-memory accesses during computation. This is significant if, as is often the case, communication is costly in terms of processor cycles, but occurs less frequently than computing cycles.

The disadvantage lies in the fact that a significant overhead is added to even the simplest data transfer, as compared to some alternative arrangements. One such alternative is shown in Figure 4.4(b), where the memories are directly connected to the data exchange network, and the processing elements are connected to the memories. This arrangement has the great advantage of conceptual consistency – all operations, whether data shifting or processing, are memory-to-memory functions. The drawback lies in the fact that either more costly dual-ported memories have to be used, or overlapping communication and processing is impossible. Even with dual-ported memories, this may sometimes be the case, since the same potential conflict over two operations accessing the same address exists as it did for the shared memory system.

A third type of arrangement is possible under this heading, shown in Figure 4.4(c). Here, the interconnection network is interposed between the set of processors and the set of memories. This is certainly the most flexible arrangement, although for this flexibility to be realised, the network needs twice the complexity of an equivalent for the alternative methods, because there are twice as many ports into the network. With the appropriate interconnections, it can even exhibit some of the benefits of a shared memory system (discussed in Section 3.1.2.2) although, like any other arrangement in which the memories are directly connected to the data exchange network, potential conflicts exist.

These, then, are general considerations which apply whatever network is employed to connect the elements of a parallel computing system. Some techniques are more appropriate to one design of network than another, and this will be emphasised in the following sections.

4.3   Network designs

I will begin this section by considering the general question of the degrees of flexibility which are available in physically connecting multiple processors. The first degree of freedom is the *bandwidth* of the connections. This may vary between a minimum corresponding to one bit per unit time (serial connection), up to a practical maximum corresponding to a complete data entity per unit time (parallel connection). If we consider these limits in terms of digital circuits, then a connection between any two processors might consist of anything between one and (say) 64 wires. Although this is, in one sense, a low-level technical problem, an improvement in data passing efficiency of nearly two orders of magnitude is likely to have an effect on performance as significant as differences in the form of interconnection network. A second factor which should be taken into account is whether communication is allowed in one or both directions simultaneously, effectively varying the bandwidth by a further factor of two.

Given that the bandwidth of any given connection may vary significantly, the next consideration must be the physical arrangement of connections, i.e. how to choose which elements to connect directly. Consider, first, the systems shown in Figure 4.5. In part (a), the only reasonable arrangement for connecting two elements is shown. Further complication could be added by allowing the elements to communicate through an external device (or two, or three,....) but, for the moment, I will exclude this possibility.

In part (b) of the figure, I show the potential arrangements for connecting three elements – there are just three (provided the elements are not distinguishable). On the single bus any pair of the three can communicate in one step – one data item can be passed in unit time. In the linear arrangement there are two connection channels (a maximum of two items in unit time), but the outer pair of elements can communicate only by passing data through the third – only one data item in two time units. In the triangular arrangement, three items can be passed in unit time, and any pair of elements can communicate in one step – the connectivity is completely symmetrical. Of course, in the case of only three elements, such differences in connectivity are unlikely to have significant effects on system performance, although an unsymmetrical arrangement might cause difficulties in programming the system.

In part (c) of Figure 4.5, I show some of the possibilities for connecting four processing elements, and already one can begin to see the opportunities for complexity and confusion which exist. The simplest (and least powerful) method is the bus, the most complex (and powerful) technique is the diagonally-connected square (a flattened tetrahedron). The relative properties of the arrangements shown are given in Table 4.1.

It is apparent that, even for only four processors, a significant variety of

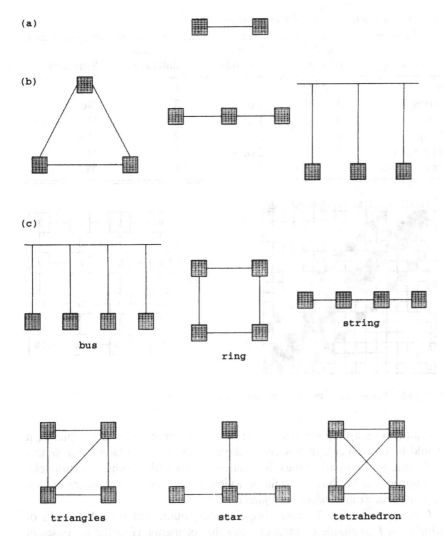

Figure 4.5 Connections for small numbers of elements (a) Connection scheme for two elements (b) Connection scheme for three elements (c) Connection scheme for four elements

alternative connection patterns can exist, each with its own combination of properties. Some of these are symmetrical, some not. It should also be easy to see that, as the number of processors increases, so does the number of alternative arrangements for connecting them. Figure 4.5 shows only the more regular arrangements possible for connecting four elements and, in general, this criterion of regularity has been used to select methods for use in assemblies comprising many processors. In the following sections, some of the most widely used and investigated of these networks are described.

Table 4.1 *Characteristics of different connectivities*

Arrangement	Number of wires	Inputs per node	Worst data shift time	Symmetry
Bus	1	1	1	Yes
String	3	1 or 2	3	No
Star	3	1 or 3	2	No
Ring	4	2	2	Yes
Triangles	5	2 or 3	2	No
Tetrahedron	6	3	1	Yes

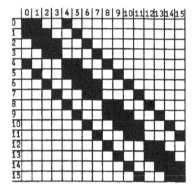
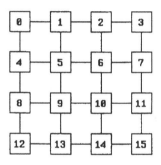

Figure 4.6   A first-stage connectivity matrix

Without pre-empting the discussion of performance given in Chapter 6, it would be convenient, in discussing these alternatives, to have some simple technique for comparing the effectiveness of one with another. Fortunately, an appropriate method is available which utilises the twin concepts of *connectivity matrix* and *adjacency matrix*.

Consider a set of N processing elements, numbered 0 to N-1, each of which has P available connections to other elements. (For the purposes of this discussion, each connection is assumed to be bi-directional. The bandwidth of the connections is irrelevant, so long as all are the same.) For any given arrangement of interconnections between these processors, we can construct an $N \times N$ element matrix in which a dot is placed at every location (i,j) where a direct connection is made between processing elements (i) and (j). This is the basic connectivity matrix, which shows those elements which can communicate in one step. Figure 4.6 shows a set of sixteen elements arranged as a two-dimensional grid, together with the corresponding basic connectivity matrix.

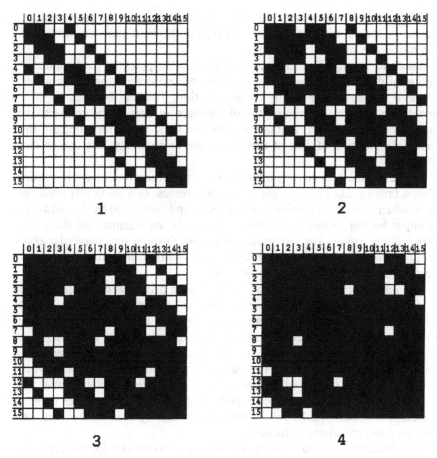

Figure 4.7 A set of connectivity matrices for a mesh

It is perhaps more useful, however, to consider the matrices which result when connections are permitted in two, three, etc. steps, i.e. between the specified processors (*i*) and (*j*) via other elements. These are shown, for the same set of 16 elements, in Figure 4.7, and it is here that the utility of the technique begins to become apparent. The object of the connection network between the processors is to facilitate transmission of data about the assembly. One convenient measure of how efficiently this is being done would be the number of steps required to permit any element to connect with any other. This situation corresponds to a completely filled connectivity matrix, so that the number of steps required to achieve such a state is one measure of effectiveness. Whilst the small number of processors considered in this example allows the reader to check the method of generating the matrix, it fails to give a true flavour of the pictorial nature of such matrices when applied to larger numbers of elements. However, this should become much clearer in the subsequent sections where, for the most part, assemblies of 256 processors are used as examples.

A second worthwhile measure of efficiency is the potential for even distribution of data throughout the set of elements, in less steps than the number required to permit any-to-any communication. This can be assessed, in a qualitative way, by examining the distribution of dots in the connectivity matrices corresponding to small numbers of steps. The more uniform the spatial distribution of dots at each stage, the more evenly data can be distributed.

Of course, the connectivity matrix does not tell the whole story. In particular, it fails to take any account of the effectiveness of a particular arrangement when more than one item of data is being transmitted by the network. It might be, for example, that in some specific arrangement all the paths which allow any-to-any communication pass through one particular connection. In such a case the efficiency of the network as indicated by the connectivity matrices might be completely illusory.

One method by which the probability of such problems occurring can be assessed is to construct the adjacency matrix for the network. (In fact, as with the previous technique, there are a set of such matrices, corresponding to one, two, etc., steps.) At each stage, the simple dot at any location (i,j) is replaced with a number which corresponds to the number of alternative paths which exist between the two elements. An optimally efficient network is indicated by a matrix which has an even distribution of values over the matrix – any great disparity between the highest and lowest values present indicates that some paths will be much more heavily used than others, i.e. that they will constitute bottlenecks.

With these tools to hand, then, we can begin to consider specific arrangements for interconnecting elements.

4.3.1   The bus

This is by far the most familiar of connectivity networks although, as we shall see later, by no means technically the simplest. Let us examine, first, a very simple manifestation, shown in Figure 4.8, to which a small number of (supposedly) identical processing elements are connected. The process of communication is as follows:

(1) One of the elements makes a request to use the bus. (This immediately raises the question – to whom is the request made? The answer, of course, is that one of the elements of the system must be designated as bus arbitrator – already the apparent symmetry is compromised.)
(2) If the bus is not busy, control is allocated to the requesting unit

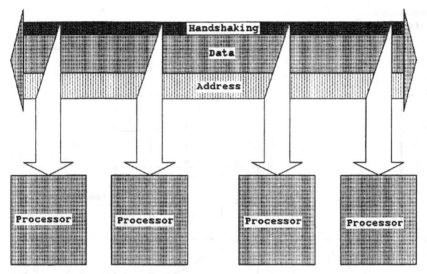

Figure 4.8 A simple bus-connected system

(3) This unit then calls the intended receiving units, usually by applying an address to the bus

(4) The receiving unit either issues a *wait* response (if busy) or a *ready* response

(5) The sender places data on the bus

(6) The receiver accepts the data and signals that the transaction is complete

(7) The sender relinquishes bus control

In terms of the operation of parallel systems, where significant quantities of data are likely to be exchanged between elements, this lengthy procedure raises a number of points. First, what happens if other bus usage requests are made while the process is taking place? Obviously, a suitable hardware/software arrangement must be implemented to allow queueing of requests. Second, what type of systems might be able to utilise the bus mechanism in spite of the undoubted bottleneck which it represents? The processing elements of the system certainly need to embody a high degree of autonomy, so that we are probably considering systems based on functional parallelism. Such systems typically employ relatively few elements, so that the bottleneck factor is reduced, and this reduction is further enhanced by the likely randomness of communications, and the relatively limited communication of data which is often a characteristic of programs running on such systems. Furthermore, the very feature which appears as a drawback, i.e. that only a single transaction can occur at any time, is, in fact, an advantage if the system embodies shared memory, since access conflicts are

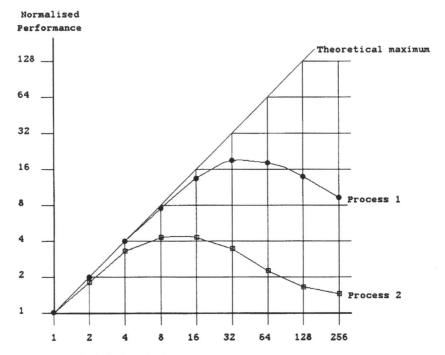

Figure 4.9   The limitation of a single bus system

automatically prevented. Finally, on the positive side, a bus is almost certain to be *bit-parallel*, i.e. a full word of data can be communicated in a single transaction. Very few other networks lend themselves to this arrangement at all easily.

Nevertheless, the bottleneck effect of a single bus does impose severe limitations on the amount of parallelism which can be incorporated in a system.
The effect is illustrated in Figure 4.9, which is based on research carried out
by Rubat du Merac et al. [3], and is itself a typical example of results
obtained by many other workers. The graph shows that not only is the
increase in effective power of the system not linear with increasing numbers
of processors, the power actually begins to decrease after a certain point
because of delays in communications. It is worth noting that this effect
intervenes long before the potential physical limits of the structure are
reached.

In order to mitigate this effect, some workers [22] have suggested that
multiple buses might be utilised. The idea is illustrated in Figure 4.10 and,
according to [22], is effective in extending the area where linear increase in
performance with increasing numbers of processors is observed. The physical drawbacks of such a system are, of course, significant, and it is difficult
to see how the idea could be extended to very large numbers of parallel

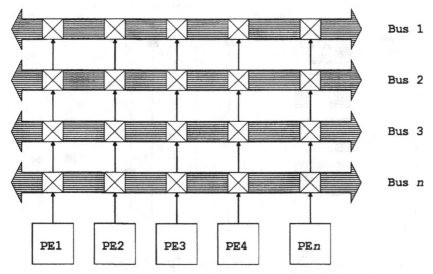

Figure 4.10 A multiple-bus system

buses. The originators of the idea suggest that there should be one bus for each processing element on the system and this renders the idea very similar to that of the *crossbar switch* (described in the next section), although this tends to be used in rather different contexts.

In summary, then, we might list the characteristics of bus connectivity as follows.

Familiarity	High
Conceptual complexity	Low
Technical complexity	High
Extensibility	Limited
Total bandwidth	Low
Processor complexity	High

Analysis of the bus systems by means of the connectivity and adjacency matrices is at best inappropriate and at worst misleading. A single bus offers any-to-any connectivity in a single step, so that the first stage connectivity matrix, for whatever size of system, would be completely filled. Unfortunately, this obscures the fact that, as soon as one connection is selected and made, the next such connection requires two steps, the next three steps, etc. It would thus be equally valid for the set of connection matrices to have one point at the first step, one at the second, one at the third and so on. Display of such a set would be uninformative (and tedious). The same arguments apply to the adjacency matrix.

In the case of multiple bus systems (and the same applies to the crossbar

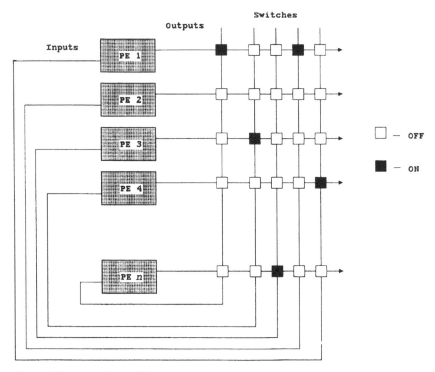

Figure 4.11   A crossbar switch

switch), one difference lies in the number of connections which can be made with each additional step – equal to the number of buses rather than equal to one. Beyond this, the matrix display technique is no more informative.

4.3.2   The crossbar switch

The principle of this arrangement, shown in Figure 4.11, is conceptually simple. Each processing element has one output channel and one input channel. Any pair – one input and one output – can be connected, but connections are constrained so that each input may be driven by only one output, whereas an output may drive any number of inputs. Figure 4.11 illustrates a permissible arrangement of connections (the solid squares are on).

This arrangement is obviously rather similar to that of the multiple bus scheme described above, but there are a number of significant differences. First, crossbar switch schemes are often conceived as subsets of, and substitutes for, all-to-all connectivity arrangements for large numbers of processors. There are always the same number of crossbars (which correspond to the buses in a multiple bus system) as processors, under the assumption that data communication will be a more commonplace operation. Second, communication on a crossbar system is often conceived as a synchronous operation, which is never the case for multiple buses. Finally, principally because crossbars are used in the context of larger numbers of processors, the data channels are often single lines.

It should be apparent, therefore, that the ideas of the multiple bus and the crossbar switch have much in common, with the choice of design details (and nomenclature) being determined by the context in which the arrangement is to be used.

4.3.3 Near neighbours

The idea of near-neighbour connectivity as a specific class of arrangement originally arose in the context of mapping spatially coherent data onto parallel processors. The importance of the arrangement comes about precisely because data in such sets is spatially correlated. This, in turn, implies that information needs to be assembled over spatially limited areas – in the limit, it is only passed between neighbouring processors.

Let us first examine how the idea can be implemented for processors arranged on a two-dimensional flat surface. In Chapters 1 and 2 I have already shown examples of sets of elements which are not arranged in this manner, but for the moment we will accept the constraints imposed by the original context in which this type of connectivity arose, namely image processing. Considering our two-dimensional plane to correspond to an image, there are only three regular polygons, multiples of which will completely cover the surface – the triangle, the hexagon and the square. Figure 4.12(a) shows how these fit together. Part (b) of the same diagram illustrates the basic idea of near-neighbour connectivity for each arrangement – elements (and, correspondingly, processors) are only connected to those other elements which they touch. In fact, such an arrangement could more properly be called nearest-neighbour connectivity, since near neighbour might imply connections to a more numerous, but still localised, subset of all processors. Even this term is not, however, strictly correct. Consider part (c) of Figure 4.12, which demonstrates that, for the system based on square elements, the distances between the centre of a given element and those of all the near neighbours are not the same. In some sense, the four which abut the faces of the square are nearer than those which connect across corners. A better term altogether might be immediate-neighbour connectivity, but this term does not have wide currency. Overall, the term near-neighbour connectivity is the one which most reliably communicates the essence of the idea to others, but the student should be aware of the possible confusion which may arise.

Given that we understand at least the present use of terminology, let us consider the three arrangements proposed in Figure 4.12. The system based

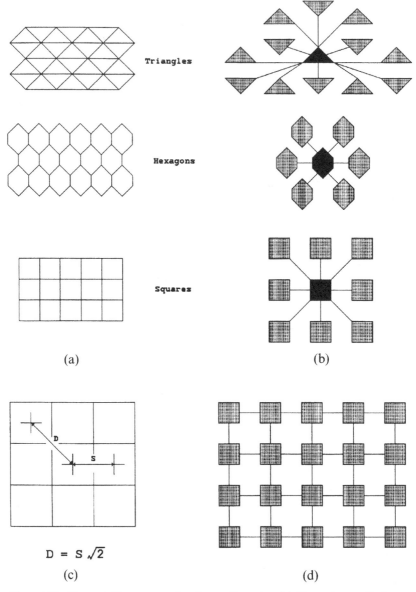

Triangles

Hexagons

Squares

(a)   (b)

$$D = S \sqrt{2}$$

(c)   (d)

Figure 4.12   Near-neighbour connections in two dimensions (a) Alternative tessellations (b) The corresponding connections (c) Variations in spacing (d) The four-connected mesh

on triangles is obviously the most complex – the elements are not even oriented the same way – and for this reason is almost never used. Of the others, hexagonal connectivity stands out as the most symmetrical system. In

(1)   (2)

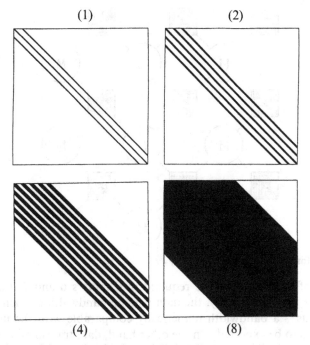

(4)   (8)

Figure 4.13   Connectivity matrices for the mesh (1, 2, 4, 8)

particular, each pair of elements is the same distance apart, and each pair communicates through the same interface – a face rather than an apex. Unfortunately, this system suffers an extremely serious perceived drawback – it does not allow a simple cartesian coordinate system to define processor locations in terms of integer grid units. So powerful a disincentive has this proved to be that the hexagonal system's advantage of symmetry over the square arrangement is almost universally ignored, and the system is almost never encountered.

We are left, then, with what I might describe as culturally the simplest system, that based on the subdivision of a plane surface into squares. Although some systems do provide the diagonal connections indicated in Figure 4.12, the most common arrangement is to limit the system to so-called fourfold connectivity, shown in part (d) of the same diagram. What are the properties of such a system?

First, we should note that near-neighbour networks are usually applied to massively parallel systems – those involving many thousands of processing elements. Where this is so, two properties follow naturally – communication is synchronous, and the connections are single-bit. Provision must therefore be made, within the processing elements, for dealing simultaneously with multiple inputs and for generating multiple outputs. We shall see in detail

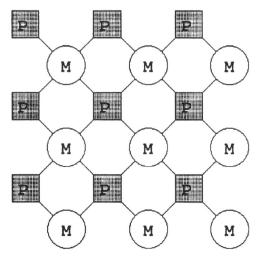

Figure 4.14   Interleaved memory in an array

what sort of arrangements are required in Chapters 6 and 7. Further we should note that, potentially, the data passing bandwidth of such a system is prodigious – a bandwidth numerically comparable with the number of processors is to be expected. On the other hand, data transmission is strictly local, and this can be a serious problem in some applications. Data transmission between distant processors can, of course, be achieved in a number of single steps, but this can be time-consuming. For this reason, many implemented two-dimensional networks have additional special arrangements superimposed, including orthogonal buses, locally controlled switches and added hypercubes [23] (see later sections of this chapter). The set of connectivity matrices shown in Figure 4.13 clearly demonstrates the point about poor long-range connectivity. The figure refers to a set of 256 processors in a square mesh, each with eightfold connectivity (this has been chosen rather than fourfold for the sake of consistency with results derived for other arrangements to be given later). The set of matrices illustrate the connections which can be made in one, two, four, and eight steps. A full matrix is not achieved until sixteen steps have been taken.

The next point to note about near-neighbour networks is their simplicity of implementation – all connections are short and uncomplicated. Of course, this only applies up to a certain maximum size where the planar arrangement can be physically maintained. Beyond this size, the folding of the plane which is required becomes a serious problem.

As was suggested in Section 4.2, connections are usually made, in systems of this sort, between the processing elements, rather than between the distributed elements of memory. Some workers [24] have suggested, however, that the arrangement shown in Figure 4.14 might be superior in some respects. In particular, it is suggested that the ability of each processor to access four blocks of local memory might confer some of the benefits of a shared memory system on the distributed memory of the array. The corresponding disadvantage of such a system would be the confusion arising over which programming model to employ of those described in Chapter 3.

Finally, we should consider near-neighbour connected networks of other dimensionality than two. A great many so-called linear arrays have been constructed in which each processing element is connected to only two others, forming a one-dimensional system. Naturally, the engineering problems involved in constructing such systems are rather simpler than for the two-dimensional array, but a number of other advantages are perhaps more important. First is the question of data mapping. The underlying assumption in a two-dimensional array intended for image processing is that one processor is mapped to each data item (pixel). For larger images (perhaps 4096×4096 pixels) this is presently quite impossible, so that less efficient stratagems have to be introduced to map the data set onto the available number of processors. In the case of the linear array, one column of pixels maps very naturally onto each processor, so that the necessary number of processors is reduced to the number of pixels in one row of the array. Such numbers are quite feasible in present-day engineering terms.

The second advantage of a linear array lies in the fact that, whilst it will map quite well onto two-dimensional data sets, it also maps onto such entities as vectors, lists and strings of data. In this sense, it is a less specialised architecture than the two-dimensional array.

It is also possible, of course, to construct near-neighbour connected arrays in three (and more) dimensions. This might be done in order to map onto data sets of correspondingly higher dimensionality, in particular physical volumes of data or time sequences of two-dimensional images. For three-dimensional, cubically divided space each processor has six neighbours. As far as the author is aware, connected sets of higher dimensionality are always treated in a rather different manner, discussed in Section 4.3.5.

4.3.4 Trees and graphs

Near-neighbour connected systems are variously specialised for data parallelism in general and image processing in particular. The general idea of graph-connected systems is perhaps as unspecialised as any idea can be. Each particular problem, frequently formulated in terms of functional parallelism, has a natural expression in the form of a *graph* which embodies the computational and communication requirements of the problem. A deliberately complex example which illustrates the technique (and which I have used previously [25]) is that of the computational model of a national econ-

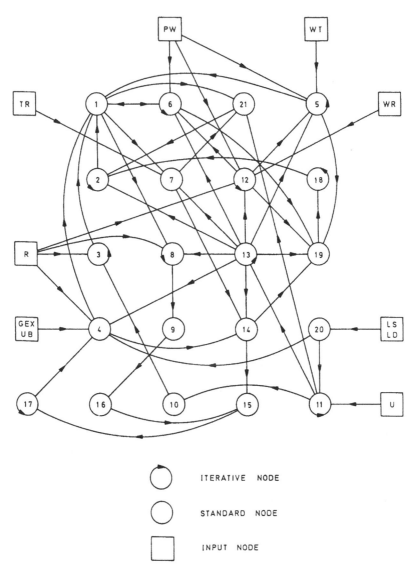

Figure 4.15   The dependency graph for a national economy, for a full explanation see [25]

omy. The model is written in terms of a set of relatively simple computations which are interdependent in the manner illustrated by Figure 4.15.

The main point of the illustration is that the connections required to permit the necessary dependencies are quite irregular – no mathematically definable regular structure implements these and only these connections between its nodes. Certainly a network could be constructed which would implement the computational graph which underlies Figure 4.15, but it would be completely specific to this one problem. The only general structures which would be useful in this context would be those embodying all-to-all connectivity (usually impractical) or *reconfigurability*. This last idea is one which I shall return to later, but for the moment I will consider what fixed structures might be of some use in this context.

The key to the problem is, as always, the mapping between problem domain and architecture. I noted earlier that my first example was deliberately complex. If we examine more general types of problems, it becomes apparent that many embody a hierarchical structure of some sort – database searching, model matching and expert systems are all types of problem which can be formulated in this way. This structure, in which many simultaneous processes are executed at a low level, then progressively fewer at higher levels, with the computation at these levels depending on results from lower levels, suggests the type of connectivity shown in Figure 4.16.

Part (a) of this figure shows a particular, arbitrary, case. Whilst this embodies the required hierarchical arrangement, it is still too irregular to be attractive in engineering or programming terms. Two of the most widely used regular alternatives are shown in parts (b) and (c) of the figure – the *binary tree* and the *quadtree*. The binary tree is particularly attractive in that it is the minimal implementation of the idea and is therefore likely to involve the least conceptual problems in use. The quadtree, and other tree structures of higher degree, are favoured because of their increased flexibility, particularly where the convergence of computations in the problem domain is likely to be faster than the repeated factor of two embodied in the binary tree.

The idea so far, then, is that these tree structures are particular examples of graphs which map well onto some classes of problem, whilst being sufficiently regular in structure to offer both generality of application and ease of programming. In particular, of course, the graph reduction paradigm finds its natural expression in such systems. However, without attempting in any sense a complete consideration of regular graph structures, two further matters require consideration. First, are there any simple enhancements to the basic tree which might improve efficiency without reducing generality? A number of workers, particularly Uhr in his book *Multi-Computer Architectures for Artificial Intelligence*, have considered this question, and one answer is illustrated in part (d) of Figure 4.16. Here, additional connections have been made within each level of the hierarchical structure. This immediately leads on to the second question we ought to consider – should data flow in tree structures be confined to the upward direction? The simple answer is that there are many reasons why it should not be so confined. Uhr's volume provides a useful introduction to a more detailed consideration of augmented tree structures, which I shall not attempt here.

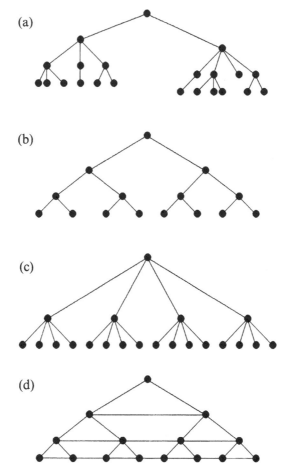

(a)

(b)

(c)

(d)

Figure 4.16   Alternative tree structures (a) An arbitrary tree (b) A binary tree (c) A quadtree (d) An augmented binary tree

Finally, we should examine the tree structure with the aid of connectivity matrices. I shall consider a quadtree structure with five levels, a total of 341 processors, with 256 processors in the lowest level. The matrices for one, two, three and four steps are shown in Figure 4.17. Just as in the case of the near-neighbour mesh, local connectivity is good, but some pairs of processors would require a total of eight steps to be connected. In view of the type of operations which are likely to be performed on such systems, this is almost certainly not a serious drawback.

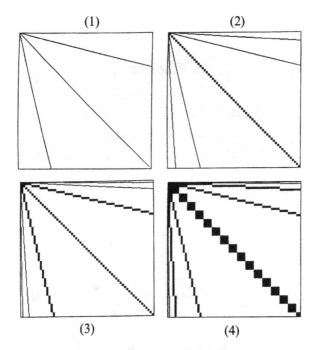

Figure 4.17 Connectivity matrices for the quadtree (1, 2, 3, 4)

4.3.5 The pyramid

The next type of interconnection scheme which I shall consider is perhaps best envisaged as being derived from two of the schemes already considered – the two-dimensional near-neighbour mesh and the tree (often, but not always, the quadtree). The basic architecture is that shown in Figure 4.18(a). Each level of the system (except the top layer) is a four-connected mesh. Connections between the layers are contrived so that every processor is connected to one element in the layer above and four elements in the layer below. (This obviously does not apply fully to elements in the top and bottom layers.) The local neighbour connections for one processor are shown in Figure 4.18(b).

The first question which needs to be addressed is that of the purpose of such an arrangement. There are, in fact, two quite separate purposes, which lead to two rather different styles of implementation of such systems. The first purpose concerns low-level image processing.

Mesh architectures have two undesirable properties from the image processing point of view – they are slow to pass data over large distances, and they do not lend themselves easily to the manipulation of data at different resolutions. One implementation of the pyramid is designed to overcome

(a)

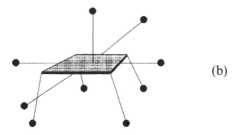

(b)

Figure 4.18   Connectivity in a pyramid (a) The basic architecture (b) Connections for one element

both these problems. Consider the question of data passing in an $N \times N$ mesh. As an example, to pass an item of data from one corner of the array to that diagonally opposite demands $2N$ shift operations. However, if the same array forms the base level of a pyramid, the operation can be performed with $2\log_2 N$ shifts, a considerably smaller number, by passing data to the peak of the pyramid and then back down. This level of analysis was, for a time, accepted as indicating that pyramid structures of this sort are generally better at passing data than equivalent meshes. However, Duff [26] has demonstrated that, if larger quantities of data are to be moved around the base array, passing the data via the pyramid connections is disadvantageous, as serious bottlenecks occur in the upper layers when the number of data items exceeds, for example, the number of processors in a given layer.

A second advantage does, however, remain. It is frequently advantageous in image processing to deal with a given image at a series of different resolutions. The pyramid architecture facilitates such operations by, for example, allowing each processor in a given layer to compute the average value of the image points held in the four processors directly connected to it in the next lower layer. These average values then constitute a new image, at lower resolution, which retains the same configuration as the previous image.

(1)   (2)

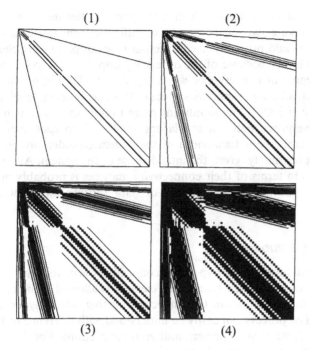

(3)   (4)

Figure 4.19   Connectivity matrices for a pyramid (1, 2, 3, 4)

As I suggested at the beginning of this section, it is probably best to consider such systems as combinations of meshes and quadtrees, and their data passing properties can be analysed by examining the connectivity matrices for these two arrangements separately. It is, however, possible to produce matrices which illustrate both types of connectivity simultaneously. For the sake of completeness, Figure 4.19 shows the matrices generated by allowing one, two, three and four steps for a system having a 16 × 16 mesh as the base layer (341 processors in total). The major significance of these matrices lies in their lack of symmetry, which indicates the inhomogeneity of the connectivity network in such a pyramid. This is almost certain to be reflected in undesirable algorithmic complexity. For this reason, and because of the demonstrable difficulty of moving large data sets through pyramids, work on systems of this sort has almost ceased.

Pyramid systems whose main purpose is that described above usually embody the same type of processing element at every point in the matrix. This is not, however, true for those pyramids which are intended to support the analysis of the complete vision problem. Such problems are often said to comprise three levels of analysis – iconic, symbolic and decisive. They are therefore thought to map well onto a structure having an image-sized mesh as the first level, a single processor as the top level, and a total of three levels. One homogeneous structure which corresponds to this might be a pyramid, but one having two properties quite different from those described above. First, it would probably need different types of processing elements at the different levels, because of the differing computational requirements. Second, the degree of convergence would need to be far higher than that offered by the quadtree pyramid. A system of this sort is being developed at Warwick University [27]. The significant point to note in this system is the degree of convergence between the layers – 64 to 1 in each case. This reduces the instantaneous bandwidth of the system considerably but, perhaps, not inappropriately, given the intended use of the system. An analysis of such systems in terms of their connectivity matrices is probably not significant because of the limited variety of data shifting modes which is employed.

4.3.6   The hypercube

The fundamental idea behind hypercube connectivity is as follows. If a system has 2^N processing elements, and each element is allowed N interconnection channels, the elements can be connected together into a hypercube of dimension N. The process can easily be understood with reference to Figure 4.20. For $N = 0$, we have 1 element and zero connections. For $N = 1$, the number of elements is 2, and only one wire is needed to connect them. This pair of elements is a first-order hypercube. When the number of connections per element is two, the number of elements is four, and the resulting structure (a second-order hypercube) can be visualised as either a square or a ring. Note that the total number of connections in the system is now also four. At the next stage, the number of processors is eight, each with three connections to neighbours, and the total number of channels in the system is twelve. The resulting arrangement (a three-dimensional hypercube – in fact, simply a cube) can be obtained by replicating the previous order of hypercube and connecting corresponding elements.

The final part of the figure shows a four-dimensional hypercube – which is as far as this author is prepared to attempt a representation of the architecture in this format. There is an alternative representation, shown in Figure 4.21, which demonstrates an interesting property of the hypercube, namely that it incorporates near-neighbour connectivity, with additional long-range channels. It is this combination of short- and long-range connections that makes the hypercube so interesting as a method of connecting many processors. The corresponding drawback is inevitable – to connect, for example, 4096 elements requires a twelfth-order hypercube and, therefore, twelve connections per element. For numbers of this order or larger, this represents a significant additional complexity for each processor. Furthermore, the incomplete symmetry of the arrangement means that

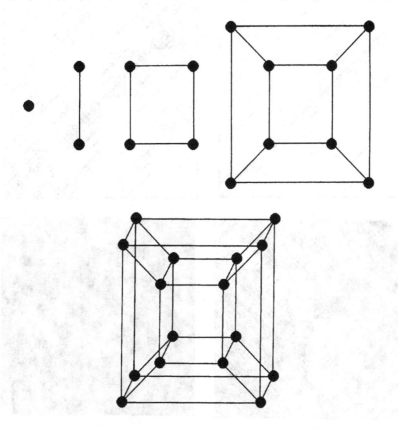

Figure 4.20   Hypercubes of increasing orders

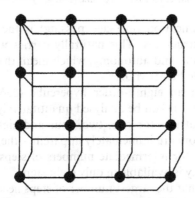

Figure 4.21   An alternative representation of a fourth-order hypercube

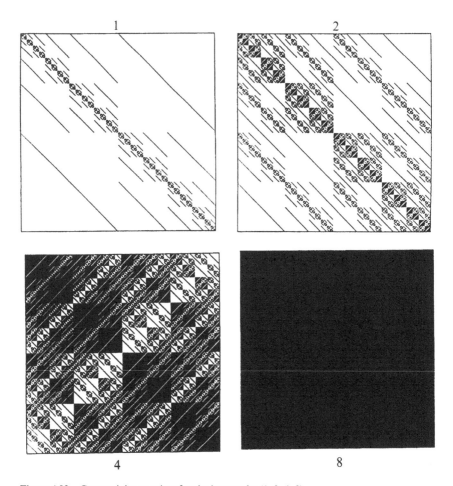

Figure 4.22   Connectivity matrices for the hypercube (1, 2, 4, 8)

asynchronous communication (message passing) is the most appropriate method within such structures. This naturally carries with it implications for processor complexity and autonomy, which mean that the paradigm on such systems is likely to be MIMD.

Connectivity within an eighth-order hypercube (256 processors, eight connections per processor) can be analysed quantitatively by examining the set of connectivity matrices for one, two, four and eight steps, shown in Figure 4.22. Two factors are immediately apparent – the evenness of distribution of connections for intermediate numbers of steps, and the fact that any-to-any connectivity is available in only eight steps.

It is generally true that the largest number of steps needed to connect two elements of an Nth-order hypercube is equal to N. At one time it was thought that this represented the optimum arrangement for the stated number of processors and connections, but Forshaw [28] demonstrated a number of more efficient alternatives, which I will describe in Section 4.3.8. Nevertheless the improved distribution of connections over, in particular, the near-neighbour arrangement is apparent. Of course, it is not to be supposed that this improvement is obtained at zero cost – the engineering difficulties of making long-range physical connections and the more complex communications algorithms needed are two of the drawbacks.

4.3.7 Multistage networks

One of the most difficult problems in considering networks of this sort concerns nomenclature. This is because a number of apparently different networks, separately discovered and named, subsequently proved to be topologically identical, or at least very similar. These networks included the shuffle-exchange, the butterfly, the omega, the binary n-cube and the SW-banyan. A full consideration of these (and many others) can be found in Siegel's book *Interconnection Networks for Large-Scale Parallel Processing*, but here I will merely attempt to present the essence of the method.

A good starting-point is the single-stage shuffle exchange network illustrated in Figure 4.23. The network is in two parts – the first part executes a so-called perfect shuffle, while the second part allows data from selected

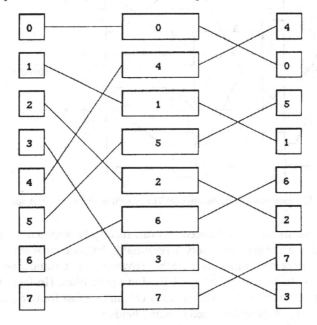

Figure 4.23   The single-stage shuffle exchange network

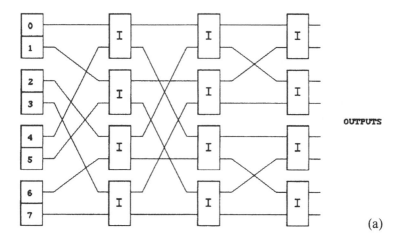

(a)

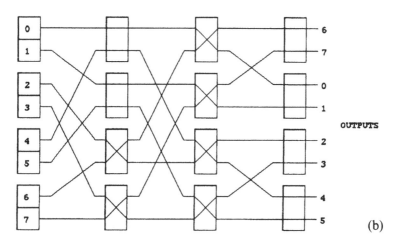

(b)

Figure 4.24   The generalised-cube network (a) The general arrangement (b) A specific case

pairs of elements to be exchanged. As can readily be appreciated from the diagram, this arrangement offers a reasonable balance between long- and short-range data communication paths. However, as it stands, such a network is likely to be somewhat specialised in application. (In fact, networks of this sort are excellently configured for calculating fast fourier transforms, which are themselves widely used in many fields.)

A more useful arrangement is known as the generalised-cube network, shown for eight processors in Figure 4.24. The network consists of alternating stages of links and interchange boxes. In general, a system with N inputs and N outputs will have $\log_2 N$ stages of each type. In Figure 4.24, with $N = 8$, there are therefore three sets of interchange boxes and three sets of links. This type of network is a switchable network, since each interchange box can be switched into one of four permissible states – straight through, swap, lower broadcast and upper broadcast. Thus, since the configuration of each box can be individually specified, any input can be connected to any output with the configuration shown.

In the second part of Figure 4.24, a particular selection of switches is shown which allows data to be shifted from each processor to the element with an address two higher than the original. This is an example of an achievable transform, but many desirable operations cannot be achieved without requiring some switches to be in two positions simultaneously. Such problems occur fairly frequently, particularly for networks with many processors. Even when such absolute blocking does not occur, working out a compatible set of routes for a given connectivity can demand a flexible and sophisticated algorithm.

In spite of this requirement, such networks are frequently implemented in MIMD systems having moderate numbers of processors (perhaps up to 512). There are three main reasons for this. In the first place, the network demands only one input and one output port per processor. Because of this, each connection channel can be multi-bit. Second, although the network is of moderate complexity, that complexity grows only slowly with increasing numbers of processors, and is in any case localised, i.e. the interconnection network can be isolated (in engineering terms) from the processor modules. Finally, a great variety of communication arrangements can be programmed into the network, which is therefore both flexible and easily controlled. These last factors are of great significance to system software engineers.

Because of the programmable nature of the network, it is extremely difficult to derive a meaningful series of connectivity matrices. In a sense, unblocked connections are always made in only one step, and each permissible arrangement generates its own connectivity matrix. There are therefore of the order of $4^{(N \log N)/2}$ matrices corresponding to N processors. It is neither practical nor beneficial to contemplate generating the near-infinity of matrices corresponding to 256 processors. The number of possibilities runs into millions even for eight elements.

4.3.8   Neural networks

So far, the types of network which I have described are those appropriate for the sort of computers I have categorised as calculators. Although some of these – notably, perhaps, enhanced versions of the three-dimensional near-neighbour net – can be pressed into use for neural computers, the requirements of suitable connectivity networks for such systems are sufficiently different to demand specialised solutions for optimised efficiency. If we take as our model the human neural system, then the requirements are easy to state but virtually impossible to achieve. First, we should need a network which, for the numbers of elements likely to comprise a practical system (of the order of a few thousands), approximates to all-to-all connectivity in a few steps – that is, a network where each processor is connected to about a thousand others. Second, we should require these connections to be randomly (dis)organised. Finally, the conductivity of each connection would need to be individually adjustable according to one of the training rules described in Chapter 3.

One way of implementing such an apparently impossible set of demands is to change the problem from the spatial to the temporal domain in the manner used in the WISARD system described in Chapter 7I. The method consists of streaming the complete input data set past a single point. At randomly-selected (but known) points in time, which correspond to certain physical positions within the data set, the data are recorded, and used to compose a state vector which is concatenated with the desired training state. This process, described more fully in Chapter 7I, effectively replaces spatial parallelism with temporal sequentiality – an undesirable process from the point of view of maximising parallelism. However, this does represent an extreme form of the technique more usually used within networks of the neural type – if the desirable connectivity cannot be achieved, for engineering reasons, within one time step, which feasible solutions will approximate the desired characteristics in the fewest number of steps?

An analysis of possible alternatives was developed by Forshaw [28] using the connectivity matrix technique explained above. For the sake of consistency, we will again limit our considerations to a set of 256 processing elements or nodes. It is also both consistent and feasible, from the engineering viewpoint, to limit the number of connections per node to eight. Modest improvements on this number are, of course, achievable, but these are likely to be limited. Bearing this potential improvement in mind, I will proceed with the analysis under the stated, consistent, set of constraints.

4.3.8.1   Pseudo-random

Figure 4.25 shows the distributions of connections which are obtained in one, two and four steps with connections between the set of nodes chosen at random. It is apparent that, with very minor massaging, such connections can simulate all-to-all connectivity in only four steps – an apparently very reasonable compromise. Two factors should be borne in mind, however. First, greater numbers of nodes are certain to require either more steps or more connections. Given that we can anticipate perhaps a fourfold

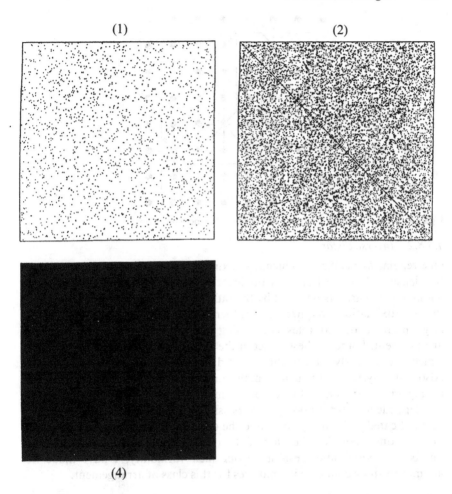

Figure 4.25   Connectivity matrices for random connections (1, 2, 4)

improvement in this latter factor, we might anticipate that networks of up to about a thousand elements could be connected with similar results. Second, and much more importantly, no general routing algorithm can be defined for such a network. Thus a given processor, wishing to send data to some other, would have no idea how to compute a route for that data – unless each processor carried a complete network definition. Even this might not be possible, if the connections had truly been made randomly. Similarly, modification of the conductivity of connections under training would be somewhat haphazard – typical of real neural nets but perhaps undesirable in their computing counterparts.

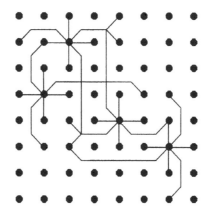

Figure 4.26   One possible arrangement of inverse distance connections

4.3.8.2   *Inverse distance*

One regular arrangement which approximates the natural model is to have the density of connections fall off inversely with distance. Unfortunately, within the constraints imposed by the rather small numbers I am using here, the approximations required are rather gross. Furthermore, there are a large number of variables concerning the detailed design of such an arrangement. Some of these concern the inverse distance dependence itself, which could clearly have a number of different starting points and slopes. Also, for a system with such a small number of connections per node, the arrangements are likely to be non-symmetrical, as well as approximating the dependence rather poorly. One possible arrangement of connections is that indicated in Figure 4.26, where the connections exhibit fourfold asymmetry – one example of each orientation is shown. Because of the large number of possibilities resulting from such variability, I have made no attempt to show connectivity matrices for this class of arrangement.

4.3.8.3   *Minimum diameter graphs*

By definition, a minimum diameter graph for a given number of processors is a network in which any two elements can communicate in the minimum number of steps. Perhaps the most impressive result of those networks examined here is displayed by what Forshaw calls the *hash* network. It is a particular example of a minimum diameter, low degree graph. The excellent apparent performance of the system is, however, obtained at the cost of added complexity. In this system, either a high proportion of the connecting wires are long-range, or the input multiplexing arrangements of each processor must be separated from that processor and remotely located. Under these conditions, for the number of processors considered here (256), the number of steps required to allow all-to-all connectivity is only three. The connection matrices for one, two and three steps are shown in Figure 4.27.

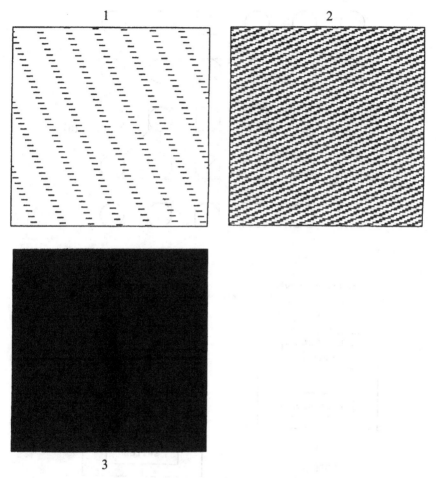

Figure 4.27 Connectivity matrices for a minimum diameter graph (1, 2, 3)

4.4 Reconfigurable networks

Some of the networks which I have described above are intrinsically recon-figurable – they embody sets of switches which can define a variety of con-figurations according to their settings. Examples of networks of this sort include the crossbar switch and the generalised cube network. In fact, the use of reconfigurability is more widespread than this, and *Reconfigurable Massively Parallel Computers*, edited by Li, collects together a number of examples of the technique. It is worth considering why so many examples do exist.

As ever, at the root of this technique lies the desirability of mapping

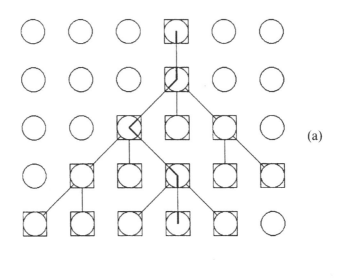

(a)

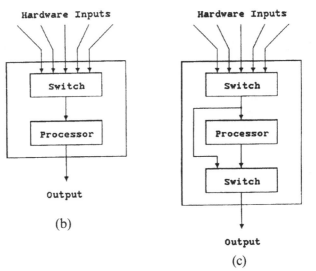

(b)

(c)

Figure 4.28 Techniques for reconfiguring connectivity (a) Local interconnection setting (b) Implementing local connections (c) Implementing element bypassing

problems onto architectures. For those arrangements which embody selectivity in a natural way, it is no real problem to map a variety of applications onto the common architecture since, in fact, the architecture is changed to fit the requirements of the new problem domain. In the case of architectures such as the near-neighbour mesh, however, the changing data structures which almost inevitably arise in the course of solving a problem cause considerable difficulties and, usually, inefficiency. Two ways around this problem exist, illustrated in Figure 4.28. In the first technique, a local switch allows a particular connection (or set of connections) to be chosen out of those which the hardware makes available. As the diagram shows, this permits, for example, a tree structure to be mapped onto a mesh.

The second technique is rather more general in action. Here, switches allow direct connections to be made between inputs to, and outputs from, individual elements (see Figure 4.28(c)). Using this technique, it is possible to bypass subsets of processors and, for instance, to map all the upper levels of a pyramid, simultaneously, onto a square mesh.

In general, then, it is apparent that allowing reconfigurable connections in otherwise fixed networks can considerably extend their field of efficient action.

4.5 System interconnections

So far, I have concentrated on the problems inherent in connecting a set of processing elements in a profitable and efficient way. There exists, of course, another dimension to the problem, that of connections between the naturally disparate units of a system, such as program sequencer and array in an SIMD mesh. This area of system design hardly exists for cognisers, although the question of data input can be important.

The general layout of a computer system is shown in Figure 4.29 but, in considering the significance of the various elements and the connections between them, we must bear in mind the likely parallel nature of each item. At a more basic level, of course, the required bandwidth of the various system connections (which is the important parameter) would be defined with reference to the data structures which each is likely to be handling. In practice, systems are often designed from their major components outwards. Let us consider a few of the specific areas of Figure 4.29.

First, the question of system control. The author knows from experience that it is quite easy to throw away an order of magnitude in system performance by poor design of the parallel processors control interface. From the point of view of connectivity, it is vitally important to achieve the maximum amount of horizontality in control microcode, and then to retain this level of parallelism throughout the distribution system. A second point in this connection is that skewing of control signals must be avoided at all cost.

The second major area concerns the input, output and storage of data. As discussed in earlier chapters, one of the main reasons for using parallelism in the first place is to deal quickly with very large data sets. It is of absolutely no use to execute any required computation or cognition at breathless speed, only to have the production of results delayed by communication

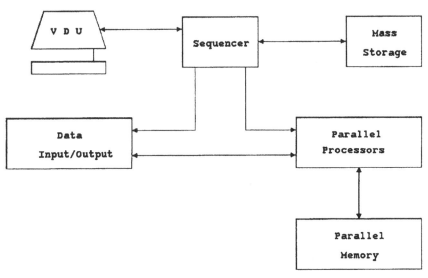

Figure 4.29   A typical parallel computer

bottlenecks with the outside world. When stated thus, this point seems trivially self-evident, but can easily be overlooked by developer or user in the sometimes blinkered enthusiasm generated by parallel computing.

4.6   Conclusions

There are clearly a number of points which should be noted concerning communication in parallel computers. First is the fact that some alternatives are closely associated with particular paradigms. Thus, for example, MIMD, buses and shared memory often go hand-in-hand. Similarly, SIMD two-dimensional near-neighbour connected networks with distributed memory are common. Many cognisers use techniques which approximate (or simulate) all-to-all connectivity.

In every case, however, there are alternatives which can logically be supported. The most important points are, perhaps, that systems should be coherent, and should map properly in all respects to the desired area of application. In the context of coherence, we should perhaps consider a further complication. Thus far, I have implicitly assumed that the subsidiary units which make up each system are homogeneous and that, therefore, connections between them are similarly uniform. It is worth noting now that this is not always true, and giving some thought to the consequences.

Three particular examples of inhomogeneous systems are worth considering briefly, all taken from the application area generally called machine, or computer, vision. As I suggested earlier, this area is particularly complex because of the changing data structures which appear at various stages. One way of dealing with this is the PUMPS system [29]. This design consists of a series of rather disparate parallel modules, each optimised for one part of the problem, connected by buses of somewhat *ad hoc* design. The drawbacks of this approach are obvious – lots of potential for data bottlenecks between modules, and rather complicated programming requirements.

An alternative approach is used in a system called the IUA (Image Understanding Architecture), being developed at the University of Massachusetts [30]. Here the overall architecture is harmonious – a pyramid – but each layer is made up of quite different processing elements. The consistent overall architecture is an advantage, but the different programming approaches required by the three layers, and the two-dimensional organisation of the middle layer may be disadvantages.

Finally, workers at University College London are considering the idea of a pipeline of more general purpose linear arrays [31]. Here the major difficulty lies in determining the optimum interconnection arrangements between the arrays.

These few examples illustrate the fact that a rational analysis of heterogeneous systems is extremely difficult. Even if we confine our analysis to homogeneous networks, the available tools, such as the connectivity matrix used above, are somewhat qualitative and uncertain in application. I shall return to the question of measurement of system performance in general in Chapter 6, but for the moment it is sufficient to note that the performance of a particular network is likely to depend heavily on the application, on the bandwidths of communication channels, on the total number of such channels, and on their average range.

One figure which can readily be estimated for the various alternative networks, and which will give at least a qualitative feel for their comparative efficiencies, is the minimum number of processor-to-processor steps required to span the distance between the most distantly separated elements. The figures are given in Table 4.2 in terms of an arbitrary network of N processors.

Having presented this table, it is of the utmost importance to stress that it does not tell the whole story – in particular it refers to the transfer of only a single data item. The analysis of the performance of networks under the more realistic assumption of multiple simultaneous data transfers is much more complex.

It should be apparent from the previous chapters that the details of interconnection design are inextricably interwoven with the design of the elements which are being connected. The next chapter considers this area of parallel systems.

Table 4.2 *Relative efficiencies of data transfers*

Network	Number of steps
Bus	1
Crossbar	1
Mesh	$2\sqrt{N}$
Tree	$2\log N$
Pyramid	$2\log\sqrt{N}$
Hypercube	$\log N$
Multistage	1
Hash	$\log(\log N)$

4.7 Exercises

1. Explain what is meant by handshaking in the context of communication between processors in a parallel computer.

2. Illustrate two methods by which memory could be distributed in a parallel computer. Explain the advantages and disadvantages of each, and suggest a context in which each method would be the more appropriate.

3. Illustrate the possible (non-redundant) modes for connecting a set of four computing elements. For each mode, calculate the highest number of steps required to shift an element of data between any two processors.

4. Calculate the first-stage connectivity matrix for the following configuration of processors:

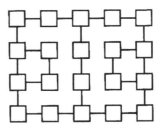

5. List the steps required to conduct a data transaction on a bus-based system. Suggest reasons why the performance of a bus-based system does not increase proportionately to the number of processors on the bus. What can be done to mitigate this effect?

6. Illustrate three methods for connecting a two-dimensional set of near-neighbour connected processors. Explain the advantages and disadvantages of each method. What is the most important drawback of any near-neighbour connected system?

7. Draw the first few levels of a ternary tree structure. Could such a structure be applied to pyramid connectivity? For a binary pyramid, derive the relationship between the number of levels and the maximum number of steps required to shift data between any two processors.

8. Draw a fourth-order hypercube in both two-dimensional and three-dimensional views.

9. Using diagrams of a system with eight inputs and eight outputs, illustrate how the generalised-cube network operates. What factor makes it difficult to generate the connectivity matrix of such a system, and why?

10. Give examples of two connection arrangements which might be suitable for a neural computer. Sketch the connectivity matrices for one of your examples.

11. Suggest appropriate connectivity schemes for the following types of parallel computer, and explain your choices:
    (a) A massively-parallel SIMD system
    (b) An MIMD system comprising 64 processors
    (c) A robot vision system using multi-resolution imaging

5 *Processor Design*

The second substantially technical issue in the design of parallel computers concerns the complexity of each of the processing elements. To a very significant extent this will reflect the target functionality of the system under consideration. If a parallel computer is intended for use in scientific calculations, then in all likelihood floating-point operations will be a *sine qua non* and appropriate units will be incorporated. On the other hand, a neural network might be most efficiently implemented with threshold logic units which don't compute normal arithmetic functions at all. Often, the only modifier on such a natural relationship will be an economic or technological one. Some desirable configurations may be too expensive for a particular application, and the performance penalty involved in a non-optimum solution may be acceptable. Alternatively, the benefits of a particularly compact implementation may outweigh those of optimum performance. There may even be cases where the generality of application of the system may not permit an optimum solution to be calculated at all. In such cases, a variety of solutions may be supportable.

We will begin our analysis of processor complexity by considering the variables which are involved, and the boundaries of those variables.

5.1 Analogue or digital?

Although almost all modern computers are built from digital circuits, this was not always, and need not necessarily be, so. The original, overwhelming reason for using digital circuits was because of the vastly improved noise immunity which could be obtained, particularly important when using high-precision numbers. In digital circuits, a signal-to-noise ratio of as low as $2:1$ can be tolerated with no loss of precision. If such a poor signal-to-noise ratio were present in, say, an analogue multiplier, the results would not be far removed from random numbers. Nevertheless, there are at least three reasons why the use of analogue circuits should not be dismissed out of hand in parallel computers.

First, many operations in parallel computers are inherently, as we shall see below, of low precision – indeed, many such systems employ one-bit processors. In such cases, analogue implementations of some circuit elements can be significantly more compact than their digital equivalents, whilst retaining suitable precision within acceptable signal-to-noise ratios.

Second, many parallel computers, particularly in the fields of vision and image processing, derive their original data directly from analogue sensors – a CCTV camera is a good example. The precision of such data is likely to be inherently limited by the effect of the prevailing noise environment, and it may therefore be appropriate to use further analogue manipulation. If so, maintaining a single regime of calculation (in this case analogue) may lead to a more compact and consistent engineering solution.

Finally, when considering the whole field of cognisers, it is possible to argue that a degree of approximation is actually desirable in the attempt to discover (and implement) qualities which might be equated with human intelligence. Human insight often appears to involve intuitive leaps of imagination which seem to be somewhat random in nature. Analogue circuits might have just the properties which are required to implement such functions naturally. Furthermore, as the complexity of pseudo-neural systems increases, it may be that the only way to deal with the required number of inputs to each node is by compact analogue methods – such techniques as current summing or charge accumulation might be appropriate. It is certainly true that the complexity of, for example, a 1000-input digital adder, such as might otherwise be required to add the values of 1000 inputs in one operation, is appalling to contemplate.

In spite of these, and similar, arguments, it is true that the vast majority of parallel computers are implemented in digital circuits. There are valid technical reasons for this – noise immunity is one – but there are significant commercial and cultural reasons too. Commercially, the use of off the shelf digital components unlocks access to an accumulation of technical expertise which represents a truly enormous investment. The analogy of the steam automobile is valid here – it might be that, with present day knowledge, a compact steam (or turbine, or rotary, or other) engine could be developed for use in personal transport, but the investment required would be very large, and the process would be fought tooth and nail by the manufacturers of the internal combustion engine, who could probably stay ahead of the opposition by applying a small fraction of the same investment. The same is true for analogue *vis-a-vis* digital computers – the manufacturers of digital circuits have all the heavy artillery (and a good many sound reasons) on their side.

The cultural advantages of digital computing are simply stated. The vast majority of users are familiar with digital computers, and the techniques of programming them make a host of hidden assumptions concerning the way digital circuitry works. Further, we are, for the most part, rather comfortable with the idea that computers are going to give us accurate answers –

even if most of us would be hard-put to justify our assumption of accuracy. The programming ethos of analogue computers would be very different and would therefore demand some difficult adjustments.

It is very likely, therefore, that in the near future most computers, perhaps with the exception of certain classes of cognisers, will be based on digital circuits. What, then, are the parameters which distinguish one digital circuit from another?

5.2   Precision

Let us first consider the precision of the circuits. I do not mean by this the precision of the answers any given circuit could calculate, given sufficient time. Alan Turing's famous work [32] demonstrated that a very simple computer can execute any required (computable) function. Here, I use the term to indicate the natural precision of data with which a given circuit works – we are all familiar with the concept of an 8-bit microprocessor, or a 32-bit multiplier.

The idea of parallelism tends, at one level, to minimise the complexity of the individual circuits, since a natural impulse is to attempt to increase the number of parallel computation units at (almost) any cost. This impulse led many developers, particularly in the field of data parallelism, to adopt minimal one-bit circuits as their processors [33]. In many cases, there were valid supporting reasons for this decision. SIMD arrays for image processing are required to act upon data sets of differing precision, and a single-bit processing element (PE) is maximally efficient in such an environment – the maximum possible number of circuit elements is always active. Parallel associative processor systems often need to execute bitwise comparisons – easily and efficiently achieved with one-bit processors. Systolic arrays frequently execute algorithms which depend for their validity on bit-by-bit operation.

A second type of reason supports the use of single-bit processors for data-parallel systems. The very large number of processors which can be used in the optimum arrangement means that cost per processor should be minimised – single-bit processors are certain to be cheaper than their multi-bit counterparts. Further, large numbers of processors means large numbers of interconnections. If the bitwise complexity of each interconnection can be reduced to a minimum, then engineering problems can be reduced.

Taken together, these reasons mean that, in some circumstances, a one-bit processor is a very valid choice. However, this is not always so and, when it is not, things become more complicated. One difficulty, mentioned above, which arises in considering the use of multi-bit processors in a parallel system, concerns efficiency. In a single-processor computer system, the cost of even the most complex CPU is likely to be small when compared with the costs arising from the rest of the system. It is therefore relatively unimportant if that processor is somewhat over specified. If, for example, a 32-bit processor is used in a system where most computation occurs on 16-bit numbers, no great cost penalty accrues from the (mostly unused) extra 16 bits. This argument does not hold in a parallel computer embodying perhaps thousands of such processors. It becomes much more important, in such systems, that the costly computing power should be distributed efficiently – after all, if each processor can be halved in complexity, twice as many processors can be deployed for the same cost.

There is therefore a very complex balance to be struck between the precision of each processor and its efficiency in executing calculations on a broad range of data types, and we shall consider this problem more fully in Chapter 6. Of the paradigms considered in Chapter 2, this dilemma is most likely to arise in MIMD systems and in linear SIMD arrays. In the former case the difficulty of the problem is mitigated by the necessity to incorporate a program sequencer at each node, since this has the effect of making the cost of the computation part of the circuit a smaller fraction of the total. Where a program sequencer is not a necessity but an option, as in some types of linear array, the whole situation becomes much more complicated. This particular analysis is so complex that it is rarely, if ever, attempted in any depth when systems are being designed.

Other options are available to the parallel system designer which can have similar effects on the system costs and efficiency. Thus, there is the possibility of incorporating either hard-wired multipliers or floating-point accelerators at each node of the parallel system, and these could be between 16- and 64-bit precision. Since some parallel computers are constructed in an attempt to obtain more sheer computing power than is otherwise available [34], such an approach is perfectly reasonable. However, it is usually the case, that the higher the precision of each individual processor, the lower the complexity of the interconnection network through which they communicate. The relationship between communication rates and computation rates is certainly not as simple as a reciprocal, but an increase in one usually implies a decrease in the other.

It is therefore the case that there are a variety of implementations which can validly employ processors having precisions between one and 64 bits. It was suggested above that one factor which might modify the efficiency of any particular choice was the presence or absence of a program sequencer. As we shall now see, this factor itself is more complex than it appears at first sight.

5.3   Autonomy

Flynn's classical taxonomy of computer architectures embodies the ideas of singular and multiple instruction and data streams and is widely used as the basis of a convenient shorthand method of classifying multi-processor architectures. From two of the principal categories of classification (SIMD and MIMD) it is usually assumed that only the two extreme modes of control – complete independence (autonomy) or complete synchronisation – are possible in an assembly of processors. The advantage of this viewpoint is its simplicity. The disadvantage is that physical implementations of the two extremes differ so enormously in complexity (and therefore cost) that consideration of the best level of autonomy for a particular application is often overwhelmed by the economic requirements. In fact, this degree of polarisation is unnecessary. Recent work [35] has developed a sequence of levels of autonomy which permit a much finer and more accurate choice to be made.

In the following sections a progression from pure SIMD to complete MIMD is presented which allows a variety of designs of increasing complexity to be developed. It is important to remember that, no matter how much independence each element in an assembly is allowed, some degree of global control will remain. In the following it is assumed that an appropriate global control is provided and that, usually, control of the locally-autonomous aspects can be either global or local as required. The available levels of local autonomy are as follows.

No local control: In order to develop a progression of autonomous processors, we should first define a starting-point. Although it ought to be rather easy to propose a processor which embodies no local autonomy, it is, in fact, more difficult than might have been supposed. One example which the author can adduce is that of a single-function systolic array, for example a convolution device [36]. Not only is no local autonomy permitted, but the global function cannot be changed.

Local activity control: Many so-called SIMD systems do in fact embody very simple local autonomy, namely the ability to locally determine whether or not each processor in the array is active. This can be easily achieved by a variety of means and leads to substantial improvements in performance.

Local data control: Processors which embody this type of autonomy allow the source and destination of the data used by a globally-determined process to be locally selected. This can be achieved either by calculating a local address (or offset) for the local memory, or by local control of the neighbourhood connectivity functions. In either case the processor function is under global control.

Local function control: The processing elements in a system can be regarded as consisting of two sections, one part concerned with movement of data around the processor, the other part executing some function upon that data. The function generator may be singular (a single-bit ALU) or multiple (ALU, barrel-shifter and multiplier). In either case this stage of local autonomy allows each processor to select which function is to be performed, data movement being under global control. This can be achieved either by storing a previous result and using that to control the function, or by local addressing of a lookup table of functions.

Local algorithm control: In this mode of local autonomy, each processor in the system is provided with a section of program control store. However, the sequencing of these stores is under global control, thereby ensuring synchronous operation of the system. The size of the program store may be small, in which case only a single algorithm is stored at each processor. The processors can have different algorithms and synchronous operation is ensured by appropriate padding, all algorithms comprising the same number of microinstructions. The same is true if the program store is large, but in this case a library of algorithms can be stored at each processor, selection being by local addressing.

Local sequencing control: Each processor in this type of system not only has local selection of algorithm, but is also able to sequence its own program memory. This in turn implies that synchronisation over the system is no longer automatic, but must be ensured by appropriate handshaking operations. At this level, only data needs to be passed between processors.

Local partitioning control: At this highest level of local autonomy, processors not only autonomously manipulate data which may be passed between them, but can alter the placing of program segments within the system, presumably on the basis of load equalisation or as a result of sequencing a complex program of the expert system sort.

5.3.1 Implementations of variously autonomous processors

In order to examine the implications of incorporating these various levels of autonomy in the processors intended for use in parallel computers, I present here results from a set of circuit designs which embody the various degrees of autonomy. Each processor incorporates:

(a) Programmable functions
(b) Local memory
(c) The ability to communicate with eight neighbours

(d) Global selection of local or global control
(e) A consistent set of design principles

Each processor embodies the level of complexity required by the relevant degree of autonomy, and the quantity of memory which is appropriate to the degree of complexity.

The purpose of this exercise is as follows. It is a truism that, once a computer has reached a certain minimal level of complexity, it can be programmed to perform operations of any degree of complication. The reason for introducing added complexity is to improve the efficiency of execution. In order to determine whether such an improvement is being obtained, it is necessary to determine the cost of increased complexity as well as the effects on performance. Efforts to measure the benefits of increased autonomy are considered in the next chapter, but it is possible to quantify the costs quite accurately.

The basis of this set of designs is the 16-bit circuit shown in Figure 5.1 (a), which embodies about 16 000 transistors. Table 5.1 shows the effects on circuit complexity of incorporating each of the levels of autonomy just described, and the circuit configuration required for the highest level of autonomy is shown in Figure 5.1(b).

It is evident from the figures in Table 5.1 that quite significant increases in autonomy can be achieved for rather small increases in costs (which are closely related to the number of transistors), but that, at a certain point, the costs increase steeply. This is the point at which it is necessary to store and sequence large programs at each processor, and the bulk of the increased costs is derived from the amount of memory needed at each site.

It is also apparent that, if we were to divide processor designs into SIMD and MIMD on the basis of the presence of a local program sequencer (however minimal), then the first three levels of local autonomy would fall into the SIMD category, whilst the remainder would be considered as MIMD. That this is a meaningful division is supported by the complexity of the circuits, which increases much more rapidly above the dividing line.

Table 5.1 *The costs of increasing autonomy*

Type of autonomy	Number of Transistors	% Increase in complexity over base level
Activity	16 200	1
Data	17 000	5
Function	17 500	8
Algorithm	38 000	140
Sequencing	45 000–150 000	180–850
Partitioning	270 000	1600

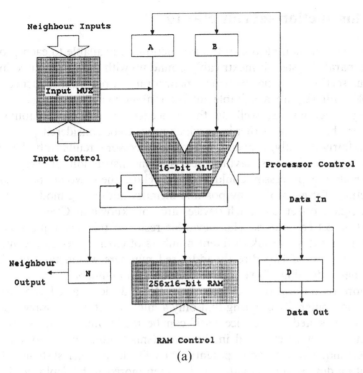

(a)

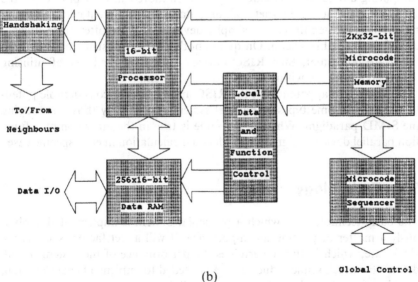

(b)

Figure 5.1 Variously-autonomous processor circuits (a) The basic 16-bit processor
(b) A fully-autonomous processor

5.4 Instruction set complexity

At one level, the complexity of the instruction set available to each processor in a parallel system is inextricably bound up with the issues raised in the previous section. Any device which incorporates a program sequencer, for example, will require a suitable instruction set including branching and stacking functions, as well as those needed to execute computation. However, there is one further issue which needs to be considered.

Until fairly recently, conventional microprocessor circuits embodied very complete instruction sets, having essentially one instruction for every operation which the processor could execute. Thus, there would be separate instructions for each of many possible memory addressing modes – direct, indirect, page offset, etc. Such devices are now known as CISC – complex instruction set computers. The inevitable result of this technique was that different instructions took different numbers of clock cycles to execute – a simple addition of two directly-addressed numbers would take far fewer cycles than a division of two indirectly-addressed numbers.

A more recent approach is that of the RISC device – a reduced instruction set computer. By ensuring that only a minimal set of necessary instructions are executed, the device itself can be made much simpler, and all instructions can be executed in the same (small) number of clock cycles. This technique has obvious potential benefits in parallel systems. If the computing device can be made simpler, then more can be deployed for the same cost. Further, if a variety of computations of different complexity are required, as is often the case, a simpler device is likely to offer more efficient use of the available silicon. On quite another tack, if instruction execution times are consistent, then RISC devices offer the possibility of utilising enhanced autonomy within a synchronised system.

It is therefore apparent that the RISC approach is of considerable potential benefit in some types of parallel system, particularly those embodying the SIMD paradigm. Whether the same is true in the more complex function parallel devices is a matter for detailed calculation in each specific case.

5.5 Technology

The basic technology in which a particular system is implemented is obviously a matter of paramount importance. It will affect factors such as the clock rate, which in turn determines the performance of the system. It will define how much semiconductor area is needed to implement each function, and therefore affect the system costs. It will determine how many such functions can be mapped onto a basic constructional unit, and will therefore affect system compactness. Within the context of this book it is clearly impossible to give a thorough grounding in this area – I shall attempt only to pick out some of the most important points. Readers who require a more complete treatment might begin with *Semiconductor Devices – Physics and Technology* by Sze which, although rather detailed, does cover most of the subject.

There are three fundamental factors which have to be taken into account – the basic material to be used, the type of devices to be fabricated from that material, and the scale of the fabrication. Let us consider them individually.

5.5.1   Basic materials

It would be natural to begin this section by considering semiconductor materials, but it is perhaps worth noting first that a number of researchers are investigating semi-biological systems in an attempt to emulate both the performance and construction of live neural networks [37]. All of this work is at a very early stage, but the reader should note that, even if it eventually comes to fruition, it will be applicable only to the cognitive class of computers.

Of the more conventional materials, there are, at present, only two realistic alternatives – silicon and gallium arsenide. Silicon technology is mature, well understood and widely available, and therefore relatively cheap. It can offer combinations of packing density and performance which appear to satisfy the great majority of requirements. From an engineering point of view, conventional devices fabricated from silicon place no untoward demands on the system engineer – clock rates are moderate (of the order of 10 MHz), power dissipation requirements are similarly undemanding (perhaps 1 μW per device) and noise immunity is good.

Gallium arsenide, on the other hand, offers an almost diametrically opposed set of properties. Because it is a relative newcomer, both ready to buy devices and manufacturing facilities are hard to find and costly. Because of its different energy band gap structure, it can be used to fabricate optical devices. Because of its higher carrier mobility, it can offer clock rates of the order of hundreds of megahertz. Because typical devices operate at lower supply voltage levels, however, signal-to-noise ratios tend to be lower. These last two factors mean that, if advantage is taken of the available performance, satisfactory system designs are much harder to develop – for example, all signals must be carried along properly terminated transmission lines. Finally, at least partly because of the relative immaturity of the technique, the number of devices available in a single circuit is still small.

It should be apparent, from this brief discussion, that the vast majority of computational devices will be fabricated from silicon. However, the ability of gallium arsenide to offer very high clock rates, combined with the possibility of constructing optical devices from the material, means that a number of research programs at the leading edge of technology are proposing to use this material in parallel systems [38].

5.5.2   Device types

Only a few years ago, the variety of device types available in silicon was quite wide – a buyer could choose between bipolar, PMOS, NMOS and CMOS. For all practical purposes, this has now been reduced to just one – CMOS. Complementary metal-oxide-silicon devices offer such enormous advantages in their combination of properties that the alternatives are only used in specialised applications where one particular property or another is of overwhelming importance. The main natural advantages of CMOS include very low power consumption – there is no low-impedance DC path between supply and earth – and very high packing density – devices with typical linear dimensions of one micron are now commonplace. Improvements in this last factor have even allowed makers to overcome the original CMOS limitation of speed (caused mainly by the low mobility of charge carriers in the p-type devices) to the point where clock rates approaching 100 MHz are available.

Because of the limited amount of work being done, it is not yet possible to make any such general statement about gallium arsenide devices. It is undoubtedly true, however, that the fabrication of optical and computing devices in the same circuit is going to be a major advantage of the material. Optical devices, such as LEDs, lasers and photodetectors, will be utilised for communication within circuits as well as with the outside world in the form of sensors and displays.

5.5.3   Scale of fabrication

The trend towards smaller devices, mentioned above, has meant that increasing numbers of logic gates can be implemented on a given area of silicon surface. At the moment, a good figure for an advanced computational circuit would be about a million devices (figures for memories are usually about a factor of four in advance of those for general circuits). This seems (and indeed is) impressive, but it is very far removed from the situation where a substantial parallel computer can be implemented on a single conventional integrated circuit. Consider two not untypical cases. A fairly small SIMD processor array might comprise 64×64 elements. If each element, including local memory, comprises approximately 35 000 devices, then the total count for the system is 140 million. Similarly, a modest MIMD system might include 128 processors, each comprising a million devices – a total of 128 million. Given figures like these, it is worth asking what can currently be achieved in developing compact systems.

As far as the MIMD system is concerned, we have a fairly well balanced situation. Each node of the system needs (basically) two packages – a powerful microprocessor and a large memory. For the SIMD system, the key point of design is to separate the memory from the processors. Advantage can then be taken of the commercial availability of large memories (in this case a 32 kbyte device would serve eight processors) while the largest possible number of processors can then be concentrated in a single chip. Device counts would indicate that up to a thousand processors could be integrated on a large chip but, unfortunately, the limiting factor is likely to be the number of connections which can be made to a single package rather than packing density, and this is liable to constrain the number of processors to no more than 128 per package. In any case, by this stage the number of memory packages for our imaginary system (512) is overwhelmingly larger than the number of processor chips (32), indicating that any further improvements would have minimal benefits for system costs.

At this point the question naturally arises – can anything be done to improve the compactness, and therefore perhaps reduce the cost, of such systems? The likely answer in the near future is yes, by utilising the technique known as *wafer scale integration* (WSI). The method should be self evident from the name – instead of creating a set of separate circuits on a semiconductor wafer and then slicing it up, we create a single circuit which remains connected. Parallel computers are ideal vehicles for this technique for two reasons. First, such systems consist of simple circuits, replicated many times – this fits in well with current manufacturing techniques. Second, implementation of the whole parallel computer as a single item means that the inter-processor connections, always the most difficult system engineering problem, can be handled as part of the circuit design.

Wafer scale integration is therefore likely to be the next substantial advance in the cost-effective implementation of parallel computers of all kinds, since it is equally applicable to analogue or digital, silicon or gallium arsenide, complex or simple circuits. For the moment, however, let us consider how the various technical factors currently affect the design of processors for particular types of system.

5.6   Three design studies

Having examined the technical alternatives which are available, we will now consider typical examples of each of the three main classes of parallel computer set out in Chapter 1, and determine which processor design might be appropriate for each, and why. In arriving at these designs, we shall have to make some assumptions about efficiency which will not be fully justified until the next chapter. It will also be necessary to consider the impact of inter-processor communication on the processor design, and the justification for any assumptions made here will be found in Chapter 4.

5.6.1 An MIMD computer for general scientific computing

The starting-point for our design should be, as always, the target application area – in this case scientific computing. The expectation is, therefore, that much of the processor's work will be carried out in a high-precision *milieu*, and that a floating-point calculation unit would be appropriate. Although the decision to use such a costly device as the heart of our processor might seem to be a substantial constraint on other parts of the design, in fact it frees us to take a number of decisions which might otherwise be more difficult. The reasoning is as follows. The presence of a high-cost computation unit – costly in terms of silicon area and, therefore, also in terms of cash – means that the overall processor cost is bound to be high. The incremental costs of any additional parts will, therefore, be relatively low, almost irrespective of their absolute cost. We are thus free to determine the configuration of these extra items on the grounds of maximum performance, rather than cost-effectiveness.

The first consideration is the nature of the program sequencer (we are working on the assumption that this will be an MIMD system but, even if we were not, the argument in the previous paragraph might lead us to include a sequencer, because the general-purpose nature of the system means that it might be useful under some circumstances). The alternatives are CISC and RISC and, although both are supportable, I believe the balance of arguments favours CISC in these circumstances. First, since we can afford a complex instruction set, and therefore a complex sequencer, we should use one, since it is bound to be quicker under some circumstances. Second, if there are floating-point units present, then instructions for these will be needed, so the processor cannot be truly RISC.

The next area of design to think about concerns memory, and there are a number of aspects to this. First, should the data and program memories be separated? I believe they should, since our system is likely to have to solve some problems which are data intensive, if not actually data parallel. This comment reflects the experience of many users, that MIMD systems are often used in an SIMD mode. Similarly, although there is an argument in favour of a substantial cache memory on our processor chip – many algorithms in this type of system use the same data repeatedly in iterative operations – the experience of users indicates that the main data memory should be separate. This allows us both to take advantage of the latest commercial developments in memory technology, and to increase the amount of memory should our first estimates prove insufficient.

Next, we come to the most specialised area of the design of any device intended for use in a parallel computer – the arrangements for communications. In this case some aspects are difficult, some are self-evident. Communications in such a system as this will inevitably be asynchronous – the disparate nature of the anticipated applications demands it. Since we have not defined a particular style of interconnection for our imagined system, there is some difficulty about determining how many neighbours should be allowed for. The first point to consider here is what is the ultimate bottleneck in inter-processor communication. In a system such as this, it is the rate at which any individual processor can absorb information – not the rate at which it can generate it, since if every processor were to attempt to broadcast information to all others, then the required reception rate is the generation rate multiplied by the number of processors. It follows, then, that each processor need only communicate data at a rate determined by its memory access rate, which in turn implies that only a single data port is needed to the outside world. However, this situation represents only a sort of average worst case. In most other operations it will be useful to connect this single port to a dedicated, multi-port message passer which incorporates input and output queueing. For ease of system connection, and for flexibility in different configurations, this should be a separate device.

At the level at which I intend to consider matters, we now have all the functional blocks of our processing element assembled. They are shown in Figure 5.2. There are a number of significant points to note about the overall design which are not depicted in the diagram. First, all the units are 32-bits wide and are connected by 32-bit buses. It could be argued that some scientific applications demand 64-bit precision, and that the organisation should reflect this. However, the design brief here is to produce a general-purpose system, in which such complexity would not be justified. Second, in the configuration which is depicted, whilst the pin count on the processor chip is not a limiting factor (less than 128 pins), that for the communications processor presents a serious difficulty. Even with the modest arrangement of eight neighbour ports, the pin count is approaching 300 – any real design exercise would have to consider carefully whether the maintenance of full 32-bit parallelism justified the inevitably high costs of the necessary package. Nevertheless, the separation of this part of the design into its own package does allow such decisions the maximum flexibility. Finally, I have shown 1 Mword of data memory, a reasonable figure given the current best levels of integration but one which would, at the time of writing, require at least four integrated circuit packages.

The only remaining question concerns the technology of implementation. If the project to design this device were a research one, we might consider using wafer scale integration to make a complete system, although this would have the disadvantage of having to implement examples of three different devices on the same wafer – the processor, the communicator and the

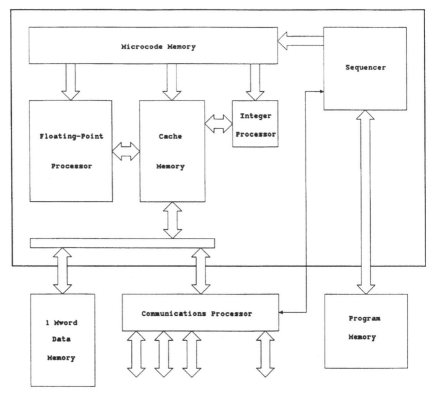

Figure 5.2   An MIMD processor design

memory. Gallium arsenide would not be a viable possibility with today's technology because of the large number of transistors required by the main processor chip – certainly of the order of a quarter of a million. A commercial project of this sort would certainly be implemented in something like 1 micron CMOS silicon, where the technical problems have all been solved and success can be guaranteed within a reasonable number of design iterations.

It is, perhaps, instructive to compare our design with some of those available on the market. One obvious example is the transputer [39], shown in Figure 5.3(a). It has some significant differences from our design, particularly in the area of neighbour communication, which is also the area where greatest criticisms have been levelled against an otherwise well received device. Each chip is provided with four data channels which are bit-serial in operation. The data transmission rates which these channels provide act as a serious bottleneck in system communications.

The second part of Figure 5.3 shows an Intel device, the i860 [40] which, when it was introduced, bid fair to take the world of parallel computing by

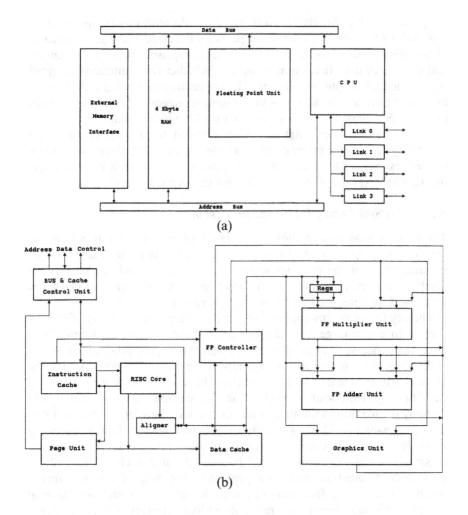

Figure 5.3 Examples of commercial MIMD processor designs (a) The transputer
(b) The Intel i860

storm. Although it has no special on-chip arrangements for communication
with neighbours, it was viewed as a replacement for the original series of
transputers by a number of manufacturers, not least because of its astonishing computational power – up to 80 MFLOPS (millions of floating-point
operations per second).

I believe that the question of interconnection to other devices is a crucial
one for success in this type of system, and is subject to the same considerations that apply to the provision of memory. No designer would consider
limiting the amount of local memory to that which could be provided on

the processor chip. Similarly, no designer should limit provisions for inter-connections to a specific number of ports on the chip. The logical outcome of this discussion is the idea of a chip set comprising processor, memory and communicator. It remains to be seen whether the limitations accepted by commercial suppliers in this area by concentrating on single-chip imple-mentations are as restricting as the argument suggests. There are certainly powerful economic factors in favour of the monolithic solution.

It is apparent, then, that a device intended for incorporation in an MIMD system shares many of the characteristics of general-purpose micro-processors, but with special emphasis placed on communication arrange-ments. The next type of device I will consider is very different.

5.6.2   An SIMD array for image processing

The most concise way to show how the design of a suitable processor for this type of system is arrived at would be to suggest that the reader turns all the arguments of the previous section on their heads and implements the results. Such an approach might, however, lack something in clarity of detail, so I shall instead begin from first principles.

The key factor of this application is the desire to map an array of proces-sors on to a very large, two-dimensional, data set. The ideal situation is to have one processor per pixel and, although this is presently impossible for really large data sets (which can comprise up to 4096×4096 pixels), the more nearly the ideal can be approached the more efficient the system will be. This argument leads directly to the conclusion that a system should embody the maximum number of processors and, therefore, to the idea that each processor should be minimally simple. The fact that image processing algorithms tend to operate on variable-precision data sets supports the con-clusion that the processors should be one-bit, since such devices will be maximally efficient at any data precision (but not, of course, equally speedy). There is, in fact, only one area in which the search for minimal complexity is abandoned – the provision of local memory. The performance of SIMD systems, in common with that of their MIMD brethren, depends crucially on avoiding any processor-to-memory bottleneck if at all possible. This means that the amount of local data memory provided must be as large as possible. There are, of course, a number of questions which need to be asked concerning the detailed design of the individual processor. They include:

(a) What local neighbourhood connectivity should be employed?
(b) Should an enhanced long-distance connectivity net be provided?
(c) How should the neighbour inputs be handled?
(d) What instruction set should the processor implement directly?
(e) What data I/O arrangements are needed?

Table 5.2 *Ranking of augmented connection networks*

Arrangement	Performance	Cost	Bandwidth	Distance
Buses	1	1	2	1
Propagation	4	2	3	1
Hypercube	3	2	1	4
Switches	2	4	3	1

Many of these questions impinge on the overall design philosophy of the system, but all concern the processor design. The first three have to be considered together.

In the first place, it is probably only necessary to consider the case of square tessellation – although hexagonal tessellation offers benefits of symmetry, the advantages of a cartesian coordinate system outweigh these. We therefore have to consider the relative merits of fourfold and eightfold connection. If the search for minimal complexity is to be carried out fully, then we should clearly opt for four-connection, although this will inevitably lead to some inefficiency in neighbour operations.

Next comes the question of longer range connections. First, we should ask whether any long-range connections should be provided at all? The answer to this must be a definite yes. The added complexity is minimal, whereas the improvement in performance can be better than a hundredfold for data shifting operations. In a previous publication [23], I examined a number of possibilities, including orthogonal buses, a fast, dedicated data propagation channel, a superimposed hypercube and locally controlled data diversion through switches and produced the figures of merit shown in Table 5.2, in which the four alternatives are ranked under a number of possible measures of efficiency, with 1 indicating the best and 4 indicating the worst.

The table indicates that, of the alternatives considered, the provision of orthogonal buses is likely to be the most cost-effective – it is ranked first (or equal first) on three measures and second only on bandwidth. It also has the lowest actual incremental complexity, which fits in well with our search for minimal complexity.

As far as the interconnections are concerned, there remains only the question of how they should be presented to the processor. The two realistic alternatives are via a simple multiplexor, or through a more flexible gating system which allows logical combinations of the inputs to be generated. Again, the minimal extra complexity of this second arrangement is warranted by improvements in performance of an order of magnitude in some cases. Figure 5.4 illustrates how the three aspects of interconnections are realised for a small section of the two-dimensional array. Part (a) shows the

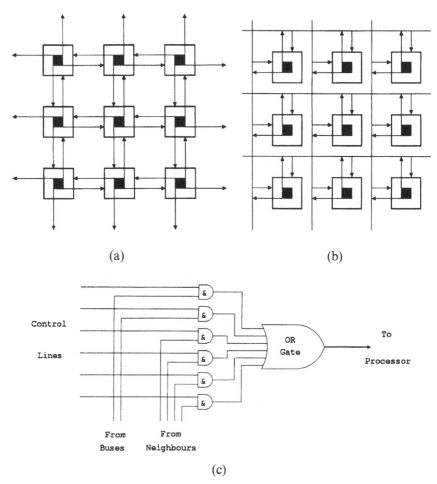

(a)   (b)

(c)

Figure 5.4 Aspects of interconnection in an SIMD array (a) Mesh connections (b) Orthogonal buses (c) Input gating arrangements

near-neighbour (mesh) connections, part (b) the orthogonal buses and part (c) the input gating arrangement for one processor.

It is relatively easy to define a suitable processing unit by specifying the necessary instruction set. This should include addition, logical combinations of two variables, and the ability to superimpose an activity mask. It only remains to decide that there should exist a dedicated I/O channel which can operate in parallel with processor functions, and we arrive at the design shown in Figure 5.5. The minimal nature of this processor can be gauged from an approximate count of transistors – about 200 would be needed to implement this design, given that the local memory is on a separate chip.

Having arrived at the design, we should now consider implementation.

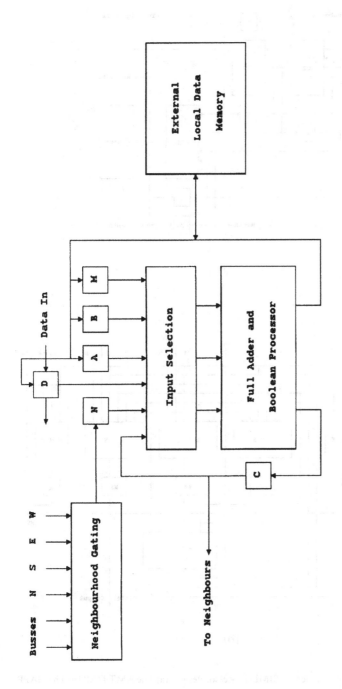

Figure 5.5 An SIMD processor design

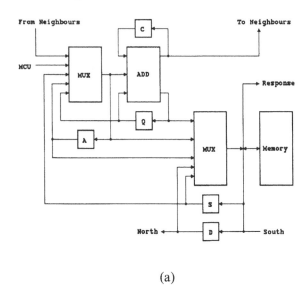

(a)

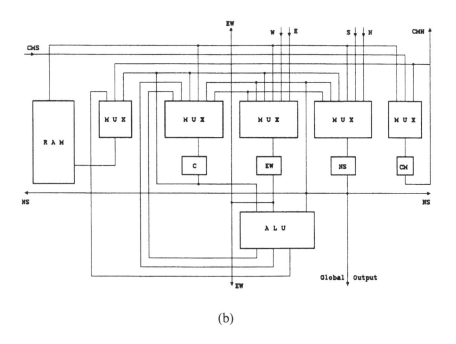

(b)

Figure 5.6   Examples of commercial SIMD processor designs (a) The AMT DAP (b) The GAPP

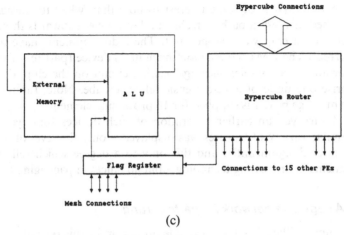

(c)

Figure 5.6 (*continued*)   (c) The CM1 device

Supposing, for a moment, that neither wafer scale integration nor the use of gallium arsenide are viable options (almost certainly the case for a current commercial project), what are the limiting factors to integration? It is perhaps unreasonable to aim for more than 100 000 transistors in a rather specialised custom design of this sort, but this would still give us the scope for a few hundred processors on a chip – perhaps an array of 16 × 16 would be reasonable in view of the manifest dislike of computer engineers for numbers other than powers of two. However, consider the implications of this for the chip connections. Every processor needs one channel to its local memory (256). Each processor on the periphery of the device needs an input and an output to neighbours (128). Data I/O demands 32 pins, and control of the system perhaps a further 16. The total so far is over 400 pins! At the time of writing this is not commercially viable (although it is just about technically feasible). A more sensible system would integrate 64 processors in an 8 × 8 array, demanding 160 connecting pins. It is certain that the yield of working chips from such a design would be better, too – an important commercial consideration.

In 1991, a special issue of the *Proceedings of IEEE* [41] surveyed the field of massively parallel computers (the editors' name for what I am calling SIMD arrays), and found six manufacturers who had developed devices such as that discussed above. The AMT device, shown in Figure 5.6(a) and further discussed in Chapter 7F, is fairly typical and exhibits many of the features incorporated in the design developed above, in particular the minimal processor complexity, external memory and integration of 64 processors on a chip. The GAPP device shown in part (b) of the figure is unusual in the way it implements the required instruction set, and in its provision of on-chip memory. (It is of some interest to note that, when the design was first published in 1984, a path of technical development towards thousands of elements on a chip was mapped out. These developments have not, so far, occurred.) The CM1 (connection machine 1) device (part (c) of the figure) incorporates a complex message-passing circuit on the chip, designed to comprise one node of a 12-dimensional hypercube. Note, though, that only one message passer is supplied for 16 processing elements.

When I surveyed an earlier generation of such devices some years ago [33], a similar variety of features was displayed – only the level of integration has altered significantly, and this only to a degree which reflects not improvements in processing technology, but advances in packaging.

5.6.3   A cognitive network for parts sorting

Before beginning the design of a suitable processor for this type of system, it is necessary to specify a set of design goals for the machine. The set which I propose to use here is the following:

(a) The system should be trained on acceptable parts by use of a technique akin to the Hebb's rule. Further, it should be retrainable
(b) The system will be required to sort parts, rather than check for correct manufacture or assembly
(c) There will be a relatively small set of categories of parts to be sorted, but a large total number of parts in unit time

Such a set of aims, of which the above is only one of many possible, goes a long way towards defining the structure of the cognitive elements. Consider the goals individually. The first tells us that the weights of the connections between elements will be externally programmed, rather than self-adjusted. The second indicates that the overall response of the system will not need to be highly precise – it will not be looking for tiny differences from predefined norms, and might even work better if it ignored such disparities. This, together with the highly connected nature of any cognitive system, suggests that an analogue approach may be appropriate. The final point tells us that decisions will have to be reached quickly, rather than by a lengthy process of iteration, implying that a multi-layer perceptron approach will be required, rather than a Hopfield net type of system.

Taken together, these points lead to the outline processor design shown in Figure 5.7. The elements include a set of inputs which are weighted by programmable resistors; current summation and thresholding units; and an interface to permit reprogramming of the weights. There are, however, a number of important technological aspects which need to be taken into account.

One major consideration concerns the number of connections to neighbours which are to be provided. Leaving aside, for the moment, difficulties

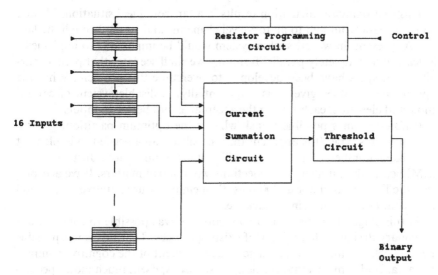

Figure 5.7 A possible cognitive element

with system implementation, it is desirable to maximise this factor to improve the flexibility of the system – remember that the system's knowledge about classification categories is embodied in the weights. The more weights, therefore, the more complete will be the knowledge. Since we have specified a low limit on the number of classification categories, there will be a corresponding limit on the necessary complexity of interconnection. However, practical factors such as the available package connections are likely to intervene before this theoretical maximum is reached.

A second consideration for system design, related in some ways to the problem of determining the number of interconnections, is that of the necessary number of cognitive elements (in this case, perceptrons). One way to analyse the network, which may offer an answer to both questions, is as follows. Let us suppose that our input data will be images of the various items, received from a TV camera at a resolution of 256×256 pixels. Further suppose that it will not be necessary to sample every pixel of each frame of data, but that only one point in 16 needs to be examined. (Although this figure is somewhat arbitrary, the principle is valid – in general, cognitive systems are able to work efficiently with partial data sets.) Lastly, suppose that our system will consist of three layers, the final layer comprising 16 elements (this would correspond to discriminating between 16 classes).

The analysis is then as follows. If each cognitive element has N inputs, there must be (of the order of) $16N$ elements in the middle layer, and (similarly approximately) $16N^2$ elements in the top layer. Finally, the total number of inputs from the data will equate to about N^3. Thus, N must be about 16.

This approximate calculation results in a far from ideal situation. Ideally, all input data would go to all top-level elements, and so on through the layers. At present, however, such a system would be impossible to implement, at least in a completely parallel fashion – we shall see later that pseudo-parallel techniques have been developed to overcome this problem. What the approximation does give us is a (potentially) realisable system of several thousand elements, each having the acceptable number of 16 inputs.

It now becomes possible to ask what is the optimum partitioning for a system of this type. It is apparent that the silicon area needed to implement any likely number of processors will not be a limitation. Just as in the SIMD case, the number of connections will control matters. If we accept a realistic limitation of about 200 pins, then eight of our cognitive units could be accommodated in a single package.

At this stage of the previous two sections, it was possible to compare our imaginary design with a variety of existing devices. That this is not possible here reflects the much earlier stage of development of the cognitive computing area. It also means that the design exercise is, itself, much more speculative than the same process in the other two cases. It is, nevertheless, worthwhile as an illustration of the type of factors which will need to be taken into account during the process of designing cognitive elements.

5.7   Conclusions

A number of general conclusions can be distilled from the above sections. First, processor designs for parallel systems tend to be heavily polarised – that is, the designs for different types of systems tend to be very dissimilar to one another. The point is illustrated by Table 5.3. The disparity between various implementations probably reinforces the validity of the idea that there are significantly different types of parallel computers, and that the process of attempting to find the best match for any particular application is a worthwhile one.

The second point of general interest is the overwhelming significance, in every type of design, of arrangements for connections to other elements. This is exactly what would be expected but, in an area such as this where intuition is perhaps an uncertain guide, it is satisfying to have expectation reinforced by analysis.

A final point is the pivotal role played by memory in the design of these elements. In the case of the cogniser, although the memory is hidden in the form of connectivity weights, it is still a controlling factor, in the guise of its effect on attempts to maximise connectivity. In the other two designs, the effect of the desire to maximise the amount of local memory is more straightforwardly obvious. For the MIMD system, this results in a process-

Table 5.3 *Parameters of parallel computer processors*

System	Precision	PEs per pack	Relative Complexity	Connectivity
MIMD	32-bit	1	250 000	8
SIMD	1-bit	64	250	4
Cogniser	analogue	8	5 000	16

ing unit which comprises six components rather than three. In the SIMD system, the provision of memory in the form of commercially available packages has the curious effect of limiting the level of processor integration which is worthwhile.

Many of the factors associated with processor design are modified or controlled by the question of cost-effectiveness. Whilst it is relatively easy to estimate the costs associated with particular implementations, the other side of the equation – performance – is a much more difficult problem. The next chapter considers some ways in which the problem can be approached.

5.8 Exercises

1. Name three advantages of binary over analogue computing. Explain the factors which affect the choice of processor precision in a highly parallel computer system.

2. List, and explain briefly, the various levels of processor autonomy which might be incorporated in the elements of a parallel computer. Suggest a possible use for each of the levels you describe.

3. Explain the main technological factors which affect the implementation of parallel computers. Wherever possible, give numerical values for the factors you consider.

4. Describe the main differences between a RISC element and a CISC element. Sketch a possible design for each.

5. Draw a block diagram of a specific commercial microprocessor-type computing element which would be suitable for incorporation in a general-purpose MIMD computer, and explain briefly how it works. List the advantages and disadvantages of the device you describe, and suggest how the design might be improved.

6. Explain fully why many massively parallel arrays intended for image processing have processors of minimal simplicity. In what area of the design of such systems is this philosophy most usually contradicted?

7. How would you set about deciding which long-range connectivity enhancement to implement for a mesh-connected processor?

8. You are required to design a cognitive network which will eventually control an autonomous vehicle. Draw up a set of design goals for the system, and explain how each of the goals you have set helps to define the implementation you need.

9. Draw up a table which specifies the parameters which define the differences between the three major types of processing element which are used in parallel systems. Explain and justify the numbers in your table.

6 System Performance

As was indicated in Chapter 1, there is a *prima facie* case for supposing that parallel computers can be both more powerful and more cost-effective than serial machines. The case rests upon the twin supports of increased amount of computing power and, just as importantly, improved structure in terms of mapping to specific classes of problems and in terms of such parameters as processor-to-memory bandwidth.

This chapter concerns what is probably the most contentious area of the field of parallel computing – how to quantify the performance of these allegedly superior machines. There are at least two significant reasons why this should be difficult. First, parallel computers, of whatever sort, are attempts to map structures more closely to some particular type of data or problem. This immediately invites the question – on what set of data and problems should their performance be measured? Should it be only the set for which a particular system was designed, in which case how can one machine be compared with another, or should a wider range of tasks be used, with the immediate corollary – which set? Contrast this with the accepted view of the general-purpose serial computer, where a few convenient acronyms such as MIPS and MFLOPS (see Section 6.1.3) purport to tell the whole story. (That they evidently do not do so casts an interesting sidelight on our own problem.)

The second reason concerns the economic performance, or cost-effectiveness, of parallel systems. For one thing, the true commercial cost of systems developed in research laboratories, often with government funding and other assistance, is nearly impossible to determine. For another, there are rather few companies successfully marketing parallel computers (by comparison with the numbers selling normal systems), so that very little statistical evidence of their commercial effectiveness exists.

Further, we should not forget the special difficulties of assessing the probable performance of cognitive computers. In their case, measures such as the number of instructions executed per second are completely meaningless – it may be that the only useful measures are the twin ones of training time and execution time for specific problems.

Nevertheless, the questions of performance and cost-effectiveness are of burning interest to at least three groups of people – those who are potential users, those who want to find out how to build something better, and those who want to prove they are king of the hill at any point in time. There was even, at one time, a prize, available to those who applied and were success-ful, for the most parallel system working in any one year, although how this was adjudicated and what was its significance are moot points. I shall take the view that there are three aspects of performance – structural, functional and algorithmic – each of which adds something to our understanding. Ideally, all three should be considered together to give the best idea of a computer's performance. It is an unfortunate truism that any single mea-sure, such as the number of MFLOPS, will at best give a very skeletal idea of performance and at worst will be totally misleading. A good starting point for a more rational, although unfortunately more complicated, approach is a brief review of the validity of some of the simpler measures used to quantify the likely performance of any type of computer.

6.1   Basic performance measures

6.1.1   Clock rate

This is the simplest and, except in certain specific circumstances, the least useful of all frequently quoted performance measures, principally because the figure says nothing about what operations occur in a single clock cycle. Thus, a processor with an on-board floating-point unit might take three clock cycles to execute a multiplication; one with a floating-point coproces-sor might require 10 cycles for the same operation, and a device with no dedicated hardware might need 20 clock cycles. The fact that each of these (supposed) units has the same nominal clock rate is not irrelevant in judging their performance, but it is certainly insufficient.

A second confusing factor is sometimes present. The transputer, for example, derives a faster on-chip clock from a relatively slow applied clock (which is used to ensure synchronisation of several devices). To assess the performance of the device, it is necessary to know the on-chip rate – but the off-chip rate is important too, since it might affect system design, and there-fore available performance.

The only circumstance where the clock rate, taken in isolation, is a useful measure of performance is when comparing processors from the same series – thus, a 20 MHz 68030 will run faster than a 12 MHz 68030.

The final point to note here is that clock rate almost always refers to processor performance – it says little about the performance of other aspects of a system (particularly a parallel system).

6.1.2   Instruction rate

This is a more useful measure of performance, although again it only refers to a processor (or processors), rather than to the system. Of course, the use of the word instruction immediately invites the question – which instruction? These can vary in complexity from incrementing a register to transferring a file of data – itself having an execution time dependent on the file size. It is true, however, that an unspoken convention is to use an instruction of the type *add together two integers* as the usual basis of such figures. This is indeed a useful measure of a processor's computation rate, and is usually somewhat indicative of performance in other areas at a similar level.

6.1.3   Computation rate

There is, at present, a *de facto* standard in existence for measuring the performance of single processors – the number of millions of floating-point operations carried out per second (MFLOPS). However, even here there is some confusion, since the operations do not always correspond to the relevant IEEE standard. Nevertheless, this frequently quoted figure does provide a fairly reliable basis for comparing the performance of one processor with another in the area of high-precision arithmetic. It has to be borne in mind, however, that this may have nothing to do with the rate at which other functions may be carried out. For this reason, the MFLOPS rate is a less general measure than the equivalent MIPS (millions of instructions per second) figure.

6.1.4   Data precision

The obvious question of data precision is sometimes overlooked in comparing performance. A rate of 10 MIPS may be less effective than one of 2 MIPS if the former refers to 1-bit additions and the latter to 16-bit operations. On the other hand, if a user expects the majority of the data to be in the form of logical (1-bit) entities, the first figure really will indicate better performance.

6.1.5   Memory size

In considering the size of a system's memory as a parameter of performance, we come to the first of those factors where the implication of the numbers involved is not straightforward. The problem is that the amount of directly accessible memory which a system incorporates will have a non-linear effect on the likely performance. For any programs where the combined memory required falls below the quoted figure, one rate of performance will be achieved. For larger problems where, for example, it is necessary to access blocks of data held on mass storage discs, the effective performance will certainly be different, but with a dependency which only a careful analysis of the program, its data structure, any parallelism of functions which the system will allow, and measures such as the disc access time, will reveal even approximately. The impact which the access time of discs has on program execution time can be catastrophic, quite overwhelming factors such as the MIPS rate. It is therefore of particular importance that a user who wishes to be able to predict the performance of a system should give considerable thought to the likely memory requirements of the programs, and should select a system containing sufficient memory. This factor is, perhaps, particularly significant for parallel systems, since the overheads involved in the use of secondary memory are likely to be particularly severe.

6.1.6 Addressing capability

This factor has similar implications to that considered above. A system may well be supplied with more main memory than can be immediately addressed by a single instruction. It is not uncommon for instruction address fields to be limited to, say, 16 bits (the equivalent of 64 kwords of memory), whereas the system may be physically supplied with many Mwords. This can have two effects. In the worst case, programs may have to be structured in blocks whose size does not exceed the address space, and this can have a significant effect on the efficiency of the programs involved. Even if this is not so, sections of program and blocks of data may have to be effectively swapped in and out of the available address field by some kind of paging mechanism, with consequent damaging effects on performance. These are unlikely to be as great as those occasioned by use of disc storage, but can easily extend execution times by a factor of two or more.

6.2   Measures of data communication

If we can agree that the above are reasonable measures of a computer system's performance, we still need to decide if any additional measures need to be considered for parallel systems. It is immediately apparent that communication of information is of paramount significance. In data parallel systems this information will be mainly in the form of data, but in function parallel systems both data and programs may need to be transmitted efficiently.

Because of the complexity of the structures involved, a number of different measures are required to give a valid picture of the likely performance of any parallel computing system. The first of these is concerned with the physical number of wires in the system which are dedicated to transporting information.

6.2.1 Transfer rate

In what follows, I shall define the *transfer rate* of a system to be the number of bytes of information which a system can transfer per second. Such a fig- ure is, of course, made up of a number of components – the relevant clock rate, the number and length (in clock cycles) of the instructions required to effect a transfer, and the number of transfer operations which can take place in parallel. In order to permit some degree of standardisation, I shall assume that all transfers will be memory-to-memory operations, although this may not be the most effective technique in some situations.

We can derive a mathematical formulation for the transfer rate.

Let t_c = time for one clock cycle
        B = bit-width of each channel
        I = number of instructions to execute transfer
        n_i = number of clocks for the ith instruction
        N = number of parallel transfers

Then the total time taken for one transfer operation is t_T, given by

$$t_T = t_c \sum_{i=1}^{i=I} n_i$$

The time to transfer one byte is t_b, given by

$$t_b = \frac{8t_T}{B}$$

and the transfer rate where N simultaneous transfers are possible is R_T, given by

$$R_T = \frac{N}{t_b} = \frac{BN}{8t_c \sum_{i=1}^{i=I} n_i}$$

Within this definition, there are two situations which we need to consider – operations where no inter-processor communications are involved, andthose where processor-to-processor communication is necessary. Even within a given system, the two parameters N and $\sum_{i=1}^{i=I} n$ are likely to be dif- ferent for the two types of operation. Figure 6.1 illustrates two possible cases.

The first, shown in part (a), is for a shared memory multiprocessor sys- tem. Obviously, the limiting factor here will be the parallelism of the con- nection between the memory and the interconnection network (assuming that this connection mirrors the degree of multi-porting of the memory). In

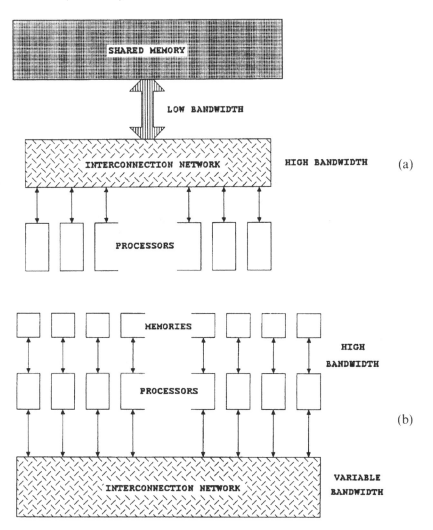

Figure 6.1   Two methods of distributing memory in a system

this case, there will be little difference between operations which do or do not involve inter-processor transfers, since the parallelism in the interconnection network is likely to be considerably higher than that between the network and memory. One situation where this assumption is untrue is for a bus-connected system, where transfers involving processor-to-processor operations are likely to take approximately 50% longer. Further, in such systems, the factor N is equal to one.

The second case shown in Figure 6.1(b) is a distributed memory system. In such systems, when we consider transfers simply between individual processors and their own dedicated memory, the multiplication factor N is the same as the number of processors in the system. However, when inter-processor communication is required, the parallelism available in the inter-connection network may dominate the situation, and certainly has to be considered. For many networks, such as the mesh, the hypercube or the crossbar switch, the number of simultaneous transfers possible is also the same as the number of processors in the system. (Within the definition of transfer rate which I have chosen, N can never be greater than the number of processors in the system since, in all realistic cases, each processor can only receive, and transmit to memory, one item of information at a time.)

6.2.2   Transfer distance

The second factor which we need to consider concerns not the bandwidth of the information transfer system, but its physical distribution. Consider the set of processing elements shown in Figure 6.2 – they are depicted as a ring in order to clarify the illustration. If each processor is allowed four (bi-directional) connections, these could be arranged in a number of different ways. Part (a) of the diagram illustrates what I might call the most localised arrangement, whereas part (b) includes some longer-range connections. If we measure distance through the network in terms of numbers of processors around the rim of the circle (and I will consider the validity of this approach shortly) then, although the total bandwidth of our system is the same in the two cases, the way in which data can be distributed in one transfer opera-tion is obviously significantly different.

However, for this difference to have significance in terms of system per-formance, we must assume that redistribution of data over the processors is a significant operation. Obviously, the degree to which this is so will depend on the particular application but, in general, any program in which data appears in different formats (lists, arrays, databases, etc.) will require some redistribution to take place. Further, for the use of number of processors as our distance measure to be valid, we have to assume that the physical arrangement we choose as the basis of the calculation has, itself, some sig-nificance in terms of the arrangement of data at some stage of the process. That this is so should follow from the original precept that an application should map accurately onto a system, but this circumstance, and therefore our assumption, is by no means guaranteed.

Again, we can formulate a measure, which I call *transfer distance*, which expresses this idea mathematically. I shall define the transfer distance for a given system as that distance, measured in processor-to-processor steps, over which the amount of data implied by the transfer rate can be moved in a single memory-to-memory shift operation. If the system is the linear array shown in Figure 6.3 part (a), with one connection to each nearest neigh-

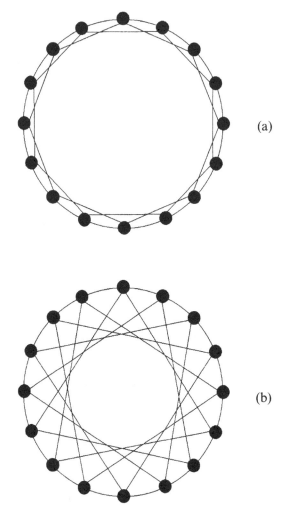

Figure 6.2   Two systems with different transfer distances (a) Localised connections (b) Long-range connections

bour, it is said to be in its base state. For an array of *M* elements, *M* items of data can be transferred memory-to-memory in unit time over one processor-to-processor distance – the transfer distance is one.

In part (b) of the diagram an extra set of wires allows each processor to receive data from a distance of two processor units away in unit time – the transfer distance is two. In part (c) the transfer distance is four, for the set of wires depicted as solid lines. However, in an MIMD system a combination of sets of wires may be used. For example, an extra connection could be introduced such as that shown as a dotted line on part (c) of the figure.

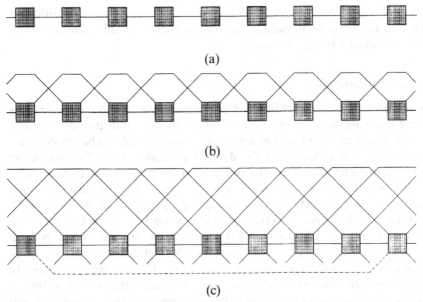

(a)

(b)

(c)

Figure 6.3 Alternative methods of interconnecting processors (a) Transfer distance 1 (b) Transfer distance 2 (c) Transfer distance 4 or 8

For this reason we need an averaging formula, so that the average transfer distance D_T is given by

$$D_T = \frac{\sum_{i=1}^{i=M} D_i}{M}$$

where the D_i are the individual transfer distances for the M channels involved. This averaging becomes even more necessary when considering structures such as meshes with superimposed partial hypercubes (the system used in the Connection Machine).

Although the transfer distance as calculated above is a valid measure of parallel computer structure, it suffers from two drawbacks. First, it is of second order importance in assessing the likely performance of a system. This is principally because the variations in transfer distance from one structure to another are fairly small – perhaps about one order of magnitude – in comparison with other factors. An additional reason is that the parameter is only of significance for a subset of parallel operations which is difficult to define in any particular case.

The second drawback lies in the difficulty of calculating the measure. Some systems allow a straightforward calculation, but for many it is necessary to make assumptions, which may not be justified, about the likely method of use. For these reasons, the typical intending user can probably ignore this parameter when deciding between alternative systems, although the student and perhaps, ultimately, the designer of parallel computers will need to consider its importance.

6.2.3 Bottlenecks

A problem that the potential user of parallel systems must consider concerns the possible presence of bottlenecks in data transmission arrangements. There are two levels at which the problem ought to be considered – the overall system level and the detailed processor level. Two particular problems which may arise at the system level are illustrated in Figure 6.4.

The two most likely areas where hidden bottlenecks may occur are in the data and control interfaces to the processor array. Each of these may arise in a way which appears, at first sight, to be beyond the control of the parallel system designer. Data may originate from a device whose output is naturally serial, such as a disc or TV camera. Control programs usually originate in a host – a conventional computer of moderate power and speed. In either case, the concept which is needed to overcome the problem is that of buffering. As an example, consider the case where a parallel computer needs to accept data from a device whose natural data set generation time is long. So long as data capture and processing can themselves proceed in parallel – often found to be the case – it is only necessary to minimise the time during

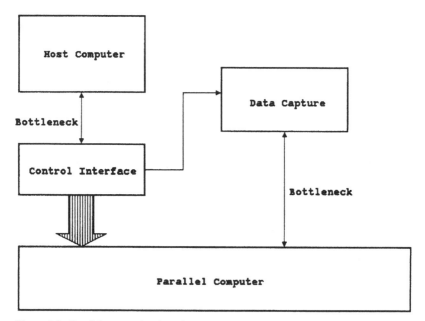

Figure 6.4 Possible system bottlenecks

which actual transfer to the computational elements is taking place. This is easily achieved by interposing a buffer between the two parts of the system which offers a high-bandwidth path to the processor.

Bottlenecks at the detailed processor level are not so easily dealt with. As I have observed previously, there are some applications where the comparatively low-bandwidth serial channels, by means of which assemblies of transputers communicate, seriously compromise the performance of the system. The serial links are there because of the near impossibility of providing sufficient package pins for parallel links. Such technical factors are frequently found to be the root cause of bottlenecks at the circuit level, and their mitigation is usually difficult, principally because of the complexity of the factors which result in any particular design compromise. We are still, apparently, at a stage of technical development where the architectural requirements of many parallel systems are not all simultaneously achievable, at least at an acceptable cost.

6.3   Multiplication factors

The next aspect which is uniquely relevant to the performance of parallel systems is, obviously, a consideration of whether the multiplicity of processors operating in parallel produces a commensurate increase in performance over that of a single device. Certainly numerical measures such as the number of MFLOPS will increase linearly with the number of processors but, equally certainly, a complete answer to this question is, as ever, not completely straightforward.

In order to illustrate this point, I will consider a number of possible scenarios. First, let us suppose that we are addressing a problem requiring the data parallel approach, in which we confront a two-dimensional square data set of fixed size with a variety of differently sized square processor arrays. When data set and array size match exactly, we will obtain a certain (let us call it unit) performance. Unless we can discover some aspect of functional parallelism, and unless our array can implement this, no increase in the number of processors will result in an improvement in performance. However, any reduction in the number of processors, down to one quarter of the original, will immediately reduce performance by a factor of four (since the processor array will have to take four bites at the data to process it). A similar variation is observed as the number of processors is further decreased. Thus, under these circumstances, improvement in performance with increasing number of processors will be very non-linear indeed, as illustrated in Figure 6.5.

Now, let us consider a functionally parallel problem and solution. Suppose that our problem has (effectively) an infinite degree of concurrency.

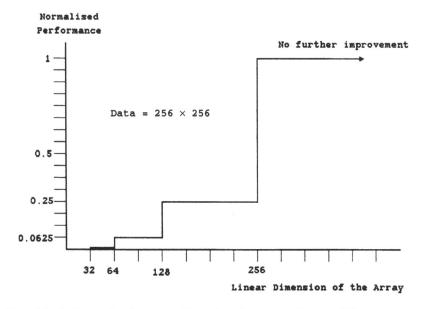

Figure 6.5   Variation of performance with number of processors (data parallel)

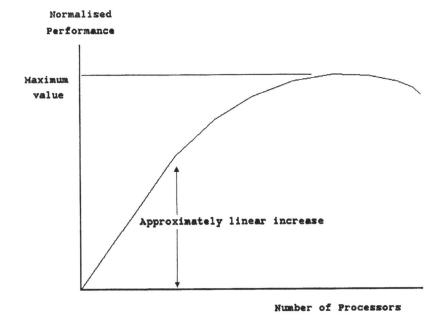

Figure 6.6   Variation of performance with number of processors (function parallel)

As we begin to increase the number of processing elements in our system, then the performance will increase linearly to a first approximation. However, as this number increases further, a secondary effect has to be considered, namely the ability of the inter-processor communication network to support any communications required by the program. We have already seen, in Chapter 4, that one network (the bus) can become saturated with a rather small number of processors. Although this effect does not appear so quickly with networks of greater bandwidth, it usually becomes apparent at some stage, so that a typical curve for increasing performance as the number of processors increases, under these circumstances, is that shown in Figure 6.6.

Every other type of system which we might consider has its own variation from the (perhaps anticipated) linear increase in performance with number of processors. This unfortunate fact is a result of one of the major reasons for using parallel computing in the first place – that parallel computers can map more effectively to parallel problems. If one particular size of system matches optimally to a given problem, larger systems may match less optimally, and so less efficiently.

6.4 The effects of software

In Chapter 3 I drew attention to the confusion which might arise if the performance delivered by two different systems, running different levels of software, were to be compared. It is worthwhile at this point reiterating the reasons why this is so.

The software which is used to control parallel (or any other) computing systems may be at any of the following levels:

(a) Microcode
(b) Assembly-level
(c) High-level
(d) Menu
(e) Graphical interface

We might reasonably suppose that no-one would attempt to benchmark a system using either a graphical interface or a menu system, but the use of any of the other alternatives would be supportable under different circumstances. It is therefore important to know what hidden factors might arise at each level.

It is perhaps simplest to begin with microcode, since this is the level which offers most immediate access to the raw hardware performance of a system. In some sense, therefore, performance figures derived under this regime will be the best that can be expected. However, a user should beware of such figures. As I indicated in Chapter 3, the difficulties of microcode programming are manifold, and it is therefore unlikely that a user will be able to exploit it in such a way as to obtain performance commensurate with the benchmark figures. The use of microcode demands a level of familiarity with the detailed system structure which the typical user is unlikely to achieve, even after buying a system. It is highly likely, however, that a manufacturer's figures for such performance measures as MIPS or MFLOPS will have been derived from microcode or its equivalent, hard-wired routines.

By far the most usual programming level for benchmarking a system will be a combination of a high-level language such as C with dedicated subroutines written in assembly-level code. This yields a much more representative guide to a system's likely performance in use, since it is the same technique as that by which application programs will be generated. Even here, however, a potential user should beware, since particular applications may require specific subroutines to be written, and the potential loss of performance caused by inexpert assembly-level code is unlikely to be less than a factor of two, and might be as much as an order of magnitude. Again, this is particularly so in the case of parallel systems, where the complexities of structure which can generate high performance are significantly greater than for a serial system.

In summary, then, the reader should be aware that certain levels of software can themselves have a serious (and always detrimental) effect on the performance of parallel computers. In particular, the relationship between performance estimates obtained from hand-crafted assembly-level routines, and attainable performance from typical application programs, can easily be an order of magnitude. It is also likely to be a function of the effort expended on code development, and this can correspond to a significant extra cost.

6.5 Cognitive systems

The analysis of the performance of cognitive systems requires a quite different approach to that used for calculators if anything other than task completion times are to be considered. Even at this level, it has to be remembered that two times have to be taken into account – that required for training a system and that required for subsequent operation. The time taken to train is made up of two factors – the time taken to learn each input pattern, and the number of such patterns which constitutes the training set. The first of these is system dependent, and is an easily measured parameter, the second is problem dependent, and is therefore difficult to determine beforehand. The latter part of this statement requires some clarification. To return to the example, used in Chapter 1, of a face recognition system, it might be thought that the number of patterns in the training set is the same as the number of permitted entrants. In fact this is not so, since faces may be presented to the data capture system in a variety of poses and expressions, and the system should recognise all of these. In this case, the problem is even worse, in that the size of the training set required for 100% accuracy can never be completely known. However, the size of the set required for acceptable performance will certainly be a significant multiple of the number of permitted entrants.

When considering the time required for operation of a network, there are two cases which have to be considered. Feed-forward networks of the multi-layer perceptron type will consistently produce answers in a time which is easily computed by considering the delay times of the circuits involved and which will be, in any case, short. Thus, cognisers which are implementing the classification paradigm are likely to be very fast in operation. Systems of the Hopfield net type, which embody feedback, are quite different in operation. Such devices routinely require many (sometimes many thousands) of iterations to produce a satisfactory result. It is extremely difficult to anticipate what this number of iterations is likely to be in any particular case, as it depends not only on the complexity of the system and of the data which has been stored therein, but on subtle factors such as the degree of difference between the alternative results, the exact configuration of the pseudo-energy landscape of the system and, in the case of systems following the Boltzmann approach (discussed in Section 3.3.2), the required annealing routine.

We may summarise the situation, then, by saying that cognitive system performance during the training phase is difficult to anticipate under all circumstances, but that this is the less important parameter of the two we must consider. In the case of classifiers, operational performance is likely to be good and reliably projected, but the performance of systems implementing minimisation is much worse, and much harder to anticipate.

6.6 Benchmarking

So far our considerations have been restricted to the simplest, most basic functions we could define. That these cannot tell the whole story is inherent in the complexity of the structures we are dealing with. The inevitable result of this realisation is that we are forced to consider the problem of benchmarking. This is the procedure whereby a computer is made to run a standard set of programs, its execution time then being a performance measure for the system. Perhaps the best known of these for serial computers is the Whetstone benchmark.

The problems of benchmarking parallel systems are compounded over and above those for serial machines. Particular attention must be paid to such questions as whether data input and output times should be included, how to deal with non-linear effects such as latency, and what to do about scaling results to allow for different sizes of otherwise similar systems. One way to demonstrate the difficulties of the procedure (or rather the difficulties of agreeing on the significance of the results) is to review some of the benchmarks which have been used in the recent past.

6.6.1   A brief survey of benchmarks

I am indebted to E. R. Brocklehurst of the National Physical Laboratory, UK, for permission to make use of material from his recent survey of benchmarks [42] in preparing this section. He categorises benchmarks as falling into four categories:

(a) Problem statement, in which the problem is specified but the method of solution is left to the solver to choose
(b) Solution method, which allows the specification to be precise and unbiased toward a particular category of architecture
(c) Data flow, in which the message passing of program and data are specified, which facilitates the specification of the detailed tasks to be carried out in the benchmark
(d) Source code, which specifies the benchmark at the lowest feasible level, ensuring that each system under test performs the same operations

Brocklehurst notes a number of factors concerning the benchmarks which he surveys. First, there are a variety of proprietary benchmarks whose makeup is, for commercial reasons, unpublished. In this section, I shall merely list these under a separate heading. Second, to date no benchmarks have been specified at the data flow level. Finally, most, if not all, benchmarks are specified at only one level. Brocklehurst makes the point that, in order to properly allow for efficient implementation on a variety of architectures, they should ideally be specified at all possible levels. Whilst agreeing with this point, I believe it can be argued that the less tightly specified the benchmark, the more potentially useful it is. I therefore list the categories here in what I believe to be increasing order of usefulness, particularly from the point of view of understanding the overall process involved.

6.6.1.1   Proprietary benchmarks

AIM: Available from AIM Technology, Palo Alto, USA.
Business benchmark: Office application benchmarks from Neal Nelson and Associates, Chicago, USA.
CUP: The standard Cray unit of performance.
RAMP/C: A transaction processing benchmark from IBM.

6.6.1.2 Source code benchmarks

Debit/Credit: Simple transactions of 25 Cobol statements developed by the Bank of America in 1973.

DFVLR Kernels: Ten primitive loops specified in Fortran and C, aimed at the determination of processor unit performance of parallel systems.

DODOC: A 5300-line Fortran program simulating operations in a nuclear reactor. Accurately tests instruction fetch bandwidth and floating-point performance.

EUROBEN: Three modules written in Fortran for assessing scientific computing on supercomputers and distributed memory machines.

GENESIS: Aimed at the evaluation of distributed memory MIMD machines, the suite includes a 1-D FFT, two Quantum Chromodynamic codes, a molecular modelling routine and a linear equation solver. It is written in Fortran.

IOBENCH: This synthetic C code was developed at Prime Computer Inc. and is claimed to be independent of operating system. It is a comprehensive test of data searching and reporting.

LANL: This suite comprises 13 pieces of Fortran which are said to represent the workload of the Los Alamos National Laboratory. Developed exclusively for Cray architectures, it covers particle transport, linear algebra, hydrodynamics and electromagnetics. Modest changes in the code are permitted to optimise performance.

NAS kernels: This is a set of seven complete Fortran linear algebra algorithms. The 1000 lines of code are intended to measure the vector performance of single-processor supercomputers.

PERFECT: This set of 13 benchmarks are drawn exclusively from the fields of science and engineering, and includes the SPICE benchmark (see later) as one of the set. Some attempt has been made to specify the problems at other than the code level, but this is not complete. The code comprises about 60 000 lines of Fortran.

SLALOM: This benchmark consists of the solution of a large system of linear equations, together with associated I/O functions. It measures the amount of work that can be completed in a fixed time.

SPEC: The Systems Performance Evaluation Cooperative is an independent company. Their set of 10 benchmarks is processor intensive, but is claimed to be independent of hardware or operating system. The tasks themselves include scientific applications, system software, device simulation and logic programming. The code consists of about 150 000 lines of C and Fortran.

SPICE: This is the most widely-used simulation program for integrated circuit design. The 20 000 lines of Fortran code were developed at the University of California at Berkeley.

6.6.1.3   *Solution level benchmarks*

HARTSTONE: This is a real-time benchmark written in Ada. It measures the ability of systems to handle multiple real-time tasks efficiently.

LINPACK: These routines, administered by the Argonne National Laboratory, USA, assess processors for the solution of linear equations. They can be easily vectorised, and can also make use of subroutine libraries which are more suitable for parallel systems.

LIVERMORE LOOPS: These are architectural and algorithmic benchmarks which are based on a typical Lawrence Livermore Laboratory, USA workload. There are 24 kernels written in Fortran.

PRESTON-SEIGART: These were produced to measure performance on image processing tasks. They were derived from the Abingdon Cross benchmark (see below), but are defined at the algorithm level.

6.6.1.4   *Problem level benchmarks*

Abingdon Cross: This image processing benchmark is covered in some detail in Section 6.6.2.2.

DARPA: This more comprehensive set of image understanding benchmarks is covered in detail in Section 6.6.2.3.

6.6.2   *Case studies*

It is apparent from the above survey that a great variety of approaches exist to the benchmarking problem, embodying both conceptual and detailed differences. At this stage it is worth studying a number of specific examples in greater depth. Because they are the most flexible, and therefore the most adaptable to various alternative parallel architectures, I shall describe both of the problem-level benchmarks listed above. However, to begin with, I examine a single, computationally expensive, task which is intrinsically of some interest, lends itself readily to parallelisation, and has been used as a readily perceived *de facto* standard of performance.

6.6.2.1   *Mandelbrot sets*

The field of fractal geometry is one of significant current interest to, in particular, workers in the area of computer-generated virtual reality environments who are concerned with simulating natural scenes. Because such scenes, and the computations associated with them, are of considerable complexity, this is another potential application area for parallel computers.

The founding father of modern studies in this area is generally accepted to be Benoit B. Mandelbrot, and it is the calculation of the Mandelbrot set associated with him which forms the basis of this particular benchmark. Readers who are interested in the subject of fractal geometry will find *The*

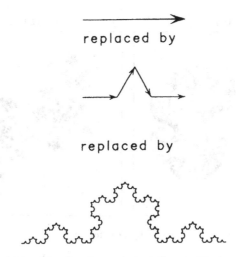

Figure 6.7   The von Koch snowflake curve

Science of Fractal Images, edited by Peitgen and Saupe, an illuminating text. However, it is rather easier to obtain a layman's feel for the underlying idea of fractal geometry by considering first the von Koch snowflake curve, which was demonstrated at the beginning of this century. The idea is illustrated in Figure 6.7. Beginning with a straight line, three units in length, the centre third of the line is replaced by two units as shown in the first part of the diagram. The process is then repeated iteratively as often as desired. The resulting curve exhibits the fractal property of self-similarity at different scales, that is, given that sufficient iterations have been carried out, a magnified version of the curve looks exactly like the original (full-scale) curve.

Although this is a one-dimensional example, whereas fractal geometry is usually thought of in connection with two-dimensional surfaces, it exhibits a number of typical properties – it has been generated by a very simple rule, the result is complex in a visually pleasing fashion, the total amount of computation required is large for a large number of iterations, and it exhibits self-similarity at different scales. These characteristics, which it shares with the Mandelbrot set, are exactly those which have led to the generation of such sets becoming a *de facto* benchmark for parallel computers. There is one other reason why this has come about – the implementation of the problem can be easily decomposed to run on parallel systems.

A Mandelbrot set is generated as follows. Consider a simple equation having the form:

$$z = z^2 + c$$

Where z is a variable, c is a constant and both are complex numbers. For a given value of c, we choose a particular starting value for z, and then iterate

(a)   (b)

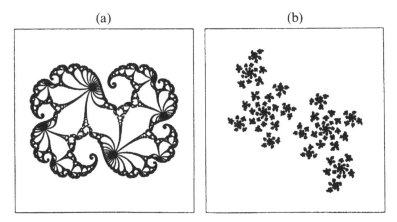

Figure 6.8   Julia sets (a) A closed contour (b) A Cantor set

the equation. It transpires that, depending on the starting value, the sequence of values of z which are computed will usually either converge to a bounded value or diverge to infinity.

If we plot, on the complex plane, starting points which converge as black points and those which diverge as white points, a figure such as that shown as Figure 6.8(a) is obtained. The shape of the interface between black and white areas depends on the value of c, and is a fractal contour. If a starting point on this contour is chosen, the value of z neither converges nor diverges, but moves around the contour. Such points form a Julia set. For any particular value of c the Julia set may be either a closed contour (as in this example) or a so-called Cantor set of separated contours, as shown in Figure 6.8(b).

A Mandelbrot set is obtained by plotting, in the complex plane, those values of c which generate closed Julia sets as black points, and other values of c as white. The Mandelbrot set is the set of black points, the boundary of which is another fractal contour. An example of such a set is shown in Figure 6.9.

Apart from its intrinsic interest, and the beauty of the resulting plots, why should such a process be suggested as a benchmark for parallel computers? There are three main reasons. First, the calculation is potentially of enormous magnitude. The greater the precision with which the values of z and c are specified and computed, the greater the magnitude of the task (and the more finely the fractal surfaces are plotted out). Further, in order to determine the convergence or otherwise of a particular calculation, many thousands of iterations may be necessary. The problem can therefore be sufficiently large to exercise any available level of parallelism. Second, the basic computation involved is extremely simple, so that no very great programming effort is required. Finally, the problem embodies enormous data parallelism, so that it is very easy to map onto parallel systems.

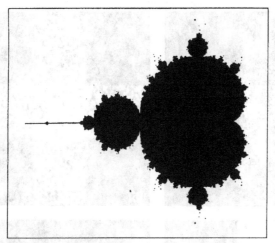

Figure 6.9 A Mandelbrot set

Given these great advantages, are there any corresponding disadvantages? Of course there are, and they are exactly those which we might suppose. Because the problem is data parallel, it offers no opportunity for exercising any functionally parallel techniques which a given system might offer. Because the basic calculation is very simple, it is also very specific – only high-precision arithmetic calculation is exercised, and there is little or no requirement for inter-processor communication. We may therefore conclude that the use of benchmarks of this type offers a very narrow interpretation of system performance which may be valid under some circumstances but that, usually, something more general is needed.

6.6.2.2 The Abingdon cross

During the early 1980s, a series of workshops were held at various locations in Europe and America at which a group of like-minded researchers in the fields of image processing and parallel architectures considered, amongst other topics, the question of benchmarking image processing systems. For reasons which I have already indicated, this proved to be a rather complex problem, but the final result of the process was notably simple. The chosen task was to find the medial axis of an image of a cross in a noisy background. Figure 6.10 shows a typical input image and the result obtained by one particular system. Any algorithm or set of algorithms could be used to solve the problem and the parameter by which performance was measured was simply the completion time of the processing.

This approach to benchmarking proved appealing on a number of counts. First, the task itself was conceptually simple and well-defined. Second, the rules of the benchmark allowed the task to be undertaken at whatever spatial resolution seemed desirable, with a simple proportionality

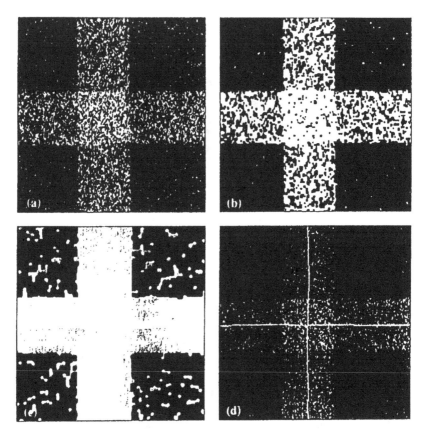

Figure 6.10   The Abingdon cross (a) The input data (b) After thresholding (c) After filtering (d) The result superimposed on the input

factor applied to the results afterwards to determine the final measure of performance. This allowed systems which operated at a natural best resolution to do so, but also allowed larger systems to yield proportionally better results than small ones. Third, the detailed programming of the benchmark was not defined, so that all the participants were able to apply their systems in the most efficient way. Because of these factors, Professor Kendall Preston Jr., who pursued this idea most determinedly, was able to persuade a large number of groups to participate in the exercise. The most recent results were published in 1989 [43], and Table 6.1 summarises some of those for parallel systems. The figures quoted in the table are obtained as follows:

If   Image resolution $= N \times N$ (pixels)
      Processing time $= T$ (seconds)
      System cost $= C$ (US dollars)

Table 6.1 *Results of the Abingdon cross benchmark*

System	Paradigm	Quality factor	Price factor
MPP	SIMD	50 000	0.8
CLIP4	SIMD	7 500	P
WARP	Systolic	500	P
DAP-510	SIMD	8 000	20
GAPP	SIMD	10 000	60
CM-1	SIMD	60 000	4
AIS5000	SIMD	40 000	200
PICAP-3	MIMD	7 500	P
CAAPP	SIMD	130 000	P

then

$$\text{Quality factor} = \frac{N}{T}$$

$$\text{Price factor} = \frac{N^2}{TC}$$

A price factor is only quoted for commercial systems – those in the table having a 'P' in this column are prototypes for which no realistic price could be estimated.

In spite of its apparent wide acceptance within the image processing community, a number of points have to be borne in mind concerning this benchmark. First, it is designed to measure the performance of image processing systems only. Therefore, although the general approach may have much to commend it, the particular task of the benchmark is hardly appropriate for assessing general-purpose machines. Second, the question of *a priori* knowledge is a problem. Since the technique of solution is left open to individuals to determine, and the input data is well defined, it might be thought reasonable to precompute the result and merely access it when the problem was presented. (Such a technique is not, after all, very different from that used in table lookup operations.) At the other extreme, it would be possible to ignore the arrangement of input data as an image, and therefore make the solution of the problem much more difficult. If comparability of results is required from a benchmarking process such as this, it is obviously necessary that the same degree of *a priori* knowledge should be used in each case, and that this should be defined as part of the benchmark. Third, even in the limited context of image processing, the defined task is confined to so-called low-level operations. Lastly, a number of important factors such as data input time are ignored.

Nevertheless, the overall approach is not without merit. The specification of task without technique gives operators the important freedom to try their best shot, whilst clearly defining the start and end points of the problem. This is an important benefit, on the two counts of realism – in the real world of applications, completion time is the only significant performance parameter – and popularity – operators will only willingly attempt benchmarking tasks where their ingenuity is rewarded. These facets provide a basis for devising a more general benchmark. The following attempts have been made to do so.

6.6.2.3   The DARPA benchmarks

The first attempt sponsored by the Defense Advanced Research Projects Agency, USA, to develop a vision benchmark, which culminated in 1986 [44], was not an unqualified success. It comprised a set of ten independent vision tasks, including gaussian convolution, connected component labelling and derivation of a minimal spanning tree, but the reported results were confusing because both the required input data and the tasks themselves were insufficiently specified. This resulted in a lack of comparability between the results.

However, out of this work developed a second, integrated, vision benchmark which I shall be considering here. In their proposal for this benchmark [45], Weems, Rosenfeld et al. suggested the importance of remembering that:

> the benchmark scenario is not an end in itself, but rather it is a framework for testing machine performance on a variety of common vision operations and algorithms, both individually and in an integrated form that requires communication and control across algorithms and representations.

With the deletion of the word *vision* from this statement, we could take it as a guiding principle for any more general benchmark. In spite of its concentration on vision operations, therefore, it is worth considering this second DARPA benchmark in some detail.

The first point addressed by the designers was that of whether the techniques, as well as the tasks, should be defined. They resolved this conflict by specifying a preferred technique (or algorithm) at each stage of the benchmark, whilst allowing alternatives to be used provided that full explanations were included with the results. If an alternative was used at any point, then the preferred technique should also be used, and results presented for both. In this way the designers hoped to satisfy the demands of both comparability and ingenuity.

The second general point concerned the input data to be used. The designers moved beyond the idea of specifying input data in mathematical terms, to supplying the data themselves in whatever format was required. They thereby hoped to avoid one potential area of confusion.

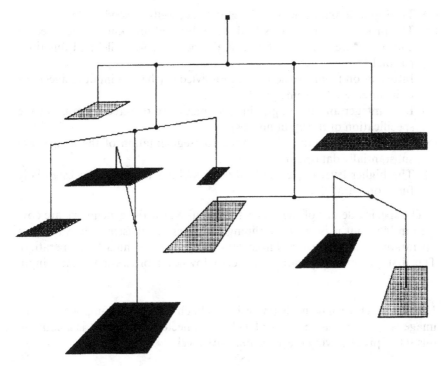

Figure 6.11   A typical DARPA benchmark 'mobile'

The overall task defined by the benchmark suite is that of recognising an approximately specified three-dimensional object from two images of the object, one of intensity and one of depth. The object to be recognised is a mobile sculpture consisting of a collection of rectangles of varying size, brightness, orientation and depth. An example of such a sculpture is shown in Figure 6.11. The recognition of the object from the images provided is in terms of a number of model objects, whose definitions are provided as part of the benchmark program. The input images are images of one of these target models, but are modified in a variety of ways. Only a part of the target may be present. Additional rectangles may have been inserted into the scene. The relative positions, sizes, orientations and depths of the rectangles may have been modified from their model values within some known tolerance. Rectangles may not be completely visible in either image. The overall goal of the process is to determine which of the target models is present in the input data.

The benchmark was designed so that no stage of the computation should be particularly difficult or challenging, but so that each stage would exercise a variety of operations. The main features of the process are:

(a) The input domain consists of well-defined, well-behaved objects
(b) The processing involved is both data-directed and knowledge-directed and, by inference, at least potentially both data-parallel and function-parallel
(c) Information from two sources of knowledge (the two input images) has to be integrated at some point
(d) Both integer and floating-point arithmetic are required (because of the specification of the input images)
(e) The low-level operations required for segmentation of the images are substantially data-parallel
(f) The higher-level object and model matching functions are essentially function-parallel

The specific details of the processing required for the benchmark are covered in [45], but it is worth outlining them here to illustrate the variety of operations that were deemed necessary for a valid benchmarking operation. The first group of operations concern low-level processing of the input images:

Label connected components (intensity):   Each connected component in the image is given a unique integer label. A connected component is a contiguous set of pixels having the same intensity level.

Determine corners of components (intensity):   For each connected component, the spatial curvature of the boundary of the component is calculated. Points of high curvature are detected by thresholding, and points of maximum local curvature are detected by differentiation. Corners are points which pass both tests.

Find component edges (depth):   The depth image is smoothed by applying a 3×3 median filter. The result is convolved with a standard 3×3 Sobel mask to create a gradient image which is then thresholded to obtain a binary edge image.

The next group of operations are higher-level functions concerned with matching the processed input data to the models provided, and with checking the input data for confirmation of hypotheses:

Rectangle hypothesis generation: Good quality rectangles with three or four corners visible in the intensity image are extracted. Components are declared to be candidates if there are at least three contiguous right angles on the convex hull. The centre of the rectangle, length of the major axis and orientation are computed from the corner coordinates.

Table 6.2 *Some results of the DARPA benchmark*

System	Cost (US$)	Completion Time (ms)
ASP*	(Simulation)	131
IUA [30]	(Simulation)	174
CM-2 [46]	10M	>350
Warp[47]	(Prototype)	63 700
Alliant FX/80	500k	436 000
Sequent S81	500k	251 000

* See Chapter 7H

Rectangle matching: The calculated rectangle parameters are matched to those of the set of rectangles contained in the models. Only size and intensity values are used at this stage.

Model matching: Pairs of image rectangles are matched to pairs in the target models. When all the possible pairs have been matched, the matching is extended to triplets, and so on.

Directed checking: The validity of the proposed matches is checked by directly probing the original intensity and smoothed depth data. The Hough transform is used within a window defined by the calculated parameters of the hypothetical rectangle, to check the original data for plausibility.

It should be apparent from the above that a great variety of sub-tasks have been included in this benchmark. From one point of view this must be an advantage, since it obviously gives a more valid measure of performance than a single operation. On the other hand, it does mean that any group wishing to attempt the benchmark has a considerable amount of work to do, and it might be thought that this mitigates against such attempts. What has happened in practice?

The results of a number of attempts at the DARPA benchmark program are presented in Table 6.2. It is apparent from this that the complexity of the task has not deterred a significant number of groups from the exercise. However, it must be borne in mind that DARPA is a funding agency of considerable significance, particularly in the USA, and this has an understandable influence on potential clients of the agency. This point, in fact, is an important one – benchmarking is a sterile exercise unless it has some external purpose. That purpose might legitimately be financial, scientific or egotistical but it must exist to lend the exercise point. This leads on to a further question – what is the significance of cost in exercises of this kind? The reader will already have noted that system cost is one parameter in both the sets of benchmarking results quoted so far, although a reasonable value for the parameter may not always be available.

6.7   Defining and measuring costs

It is very often the case that absolute performance is not the sole criterion for selection of a computing system – cost-effectiveness is also usually of significance in any real application. It is reasonable, therefore, to consider the question of costing parallel computer systems here.

6.7.1   Hardware

It is a peculiar fact of commercial life that the true hardware costs of a typical single-processor workstation are a rather small fraction of the overall costs, and that the processor cost of such a system is an almost vanishingly small fraction of the total. This implies that, as long as single processors of increasing power become available, increasing performance can be offered at minimal incremental cost. The same situation is not true for most parallel computers.

First, a parallel computer contains, by definition, more – often orders of magnitude more – processing hardware than a serial computer. Thus, an incremental cost of US$100 for a serial system might become an increment of US$10 000 in a parallel system. Second, the development costs for both processors and systems, which are always measured in millions of dollars, can usually be amortised over a far greater number of units for serial machines than for parallel systems. Where this is not so, as in the case of supercomputers, costs are disproportionately high.

These two factors conspire to make true hardware costs a far greater proportion of the overall cost of a parallel computer. However, this is likely to have a beneficial influence on cost-effectiveness rather than the opposite, since the proportion of final system cost devoted to unproductive (for the purchaser) elements such as marketing or profits is likely to be less.

6.7.2   Software

Somewhat similar arguments to those used above are likely to hold true for the costs of software, but with rather less force. The direct costs of providing software for computers are always minimal – it is the cost of developing software which, at present, dominates the eventual overall cost of most systems. This is equally true for serial and parallel computers, but the problems, and therefore the costs, of parallel software are likely to be rather greater. This is a disadvantage as far as the cost-effectiveness of parallel systems is concerned, since the end result is likely to be no more proportionally productive for a parallel system than for a serial one.

6.7.3 Prototyping and development

One further factor needs to be considered in assessing the costs of parallel computers. As I implied above, the development costs of complex systems are always an important factor in their eventual commercial cost. Many parallel systems have had the benefit that their development costs have been substantially funded by government agencies, either in the university or military sectors, so that these costs do not have to be recovered in full from customers. As commercial developments become more mature, of course, this effect becomes gradually diluted.

6.8 Summary and conclusions

At the beginning of this chapter, I suggested that the assessment of performance (in all senses) of parallel systems was a contentious area. It should have become apparent by now that this is principally because of the complexity of the problem of measuring performance and assessing costs. I have demonstrated above that, whilst there are a number of fairly simple and basic measures of performance which can be devised, these are more numerous but no more informative for a potential user than those applied to serial computers. The problem is further compounded by confusion over the appropriate level of software in each case. In the case of cognisers, any basic measures which are available are potentially confusing for the potential user, rather than being enlightening.

The approach known as benchmarking is rather more promising, but is itself fraught with problems. First, to be of any value, a benchmark has to be very carefully designed in terms of the functions which it exercises and any constraints on input data. Second, there is a fundamental conflict between the desire to specify a benchmark precisely (so as to ensure comparability) and the variety of approaches which parallel computing often implies. This conflict is sometimes resolved by confining the benchmark to a particular field of application, and sometimes by confining any comparisons of results to a particular class of system. In either case, universality is lost. The final problem is that, although a great number of different benchmarks have been proposed, there is little general agreement over their validity, leading to poor generality of results. The work involved in benchmarking is so great that substantial motivation is needed before the effort is undertaken.

These factors have resulted in a dearth of widely implemented benchmark programs. The only one to which I have been able to give (qualified) approval here is the second DARPA benchmark, and even this suffers the serious disadvantage of being confined to the vision application area. The situation is, however, improving somewhat. Substantial research programmes are in train at CalTech in the USA and at Southampton University in the UK which are seeking to address this problem. At the date of writing, however, there is no universally agreed standard against which the performance of parallel computers may be judged.

We are left, then, in the following situation. A student (or potential designer) of parallel systems can make a series of measurements or estimates of performance and cost at a detailed level which, taken together, will give a fairly good overall picture. Potential users would be ill-advised to adopt such an approach, but have few alternatives open to them. If none of the available benchmarks is suitable to their problem, they are thrown onto the willingness of potential system suppliers to demonstrate the suitability of their systems for the particular application. The user can be guided towards appropriate possibilities by the principles expounded in this book but, in the end, there is no substitute for measured, overall, performance.

Students and potential users alike do, however, have an enormous advantage over their counterparts of as little as ten years ago – there are now an increasing number of parallel computing systems of many types on the market. This increased competition inevitably means that vendors are willing to provide valid performance measures for their systems. The next chapter is devoted to descriptions of a number of such systems.

6.9   Exercises

1. Why is an assessment of the performance of a parallel computer difficult? List and explain as many reasons as you can, noting any which are specific to particular classes of parallel system.

2. State the definition of the *transfer rate* of a parallel computer. Derive a mathematical formula for the transfer rate. Which of the factors in your formula may vary for different operations in the same system?

3. Define, and derive a formula for, the *transfer distance* in a parallel system. For a set of 10 elements, sketch two systems having different transfer distances but the same number of connections per element.

4. Sketch a complete parallel computer *system*, and explain where bottlenecks might occur in the system.

5. Sketch the relationship between performance and number of elements for two systems:
   (a) A fixed-size processor array operating in data-parallel mode on various sizes of data sets
   (b) A functionally-parallel system applied to a problem of (effectively) infinite degree of concurrency
   Explain the curves which you have drawn.

6. Explain how software can affect the performance of a parallel computer.

7. Describe the various types of benchmark which might be applied to a parallel computer, and explain the advantages and disadvantages of each approach.

8. Describe and explain the main elements of either:
   (a) The Abingdon Cross benchmark, or
   (b) The DARPA benchmark
   Discuss the drawbacks of the benchmark you have chosen.

9. What elements of cost need to be assessed when benchmarking a parallel computer?

10. What do you regard as the most valid method for defining the performance of a parallel computer? Justify your answer.

7 Some Case Studies

Up to this point we have considered the subject of parallel computing as a series of almost separated facets – paradigms, languages, processor design, etc. – each of which can be examined in isolation. Of course, in arriving at the design of any real system, be it commercial or prototype, this approach is very far from the true manner of proceeding. In real system design, the watchword is usually compromise – compromise between specific and general applicability, compromise between user friendliness and efficiency in programming, compromise between the demands of high performance and low cost. No imaginary design exercise can do justice to the complexity or difficulty of this process, because the constraints in imaginary exercises are too flexible. In order to see how the various design facets interact, we need to examine real cases. This is the purpose of this chapter.

In it, I present a series of short articles concerning specific machines, each of which has been contributed by an author intimately concerned with the system in question. The brevity has been occasioned by the limited space available in a book of this sort, but it has had the beneficial effect of ensuring that the authors have concentrated on those areas which they consider to be important. Again, because of limited space I have curtailed the number of these contributions, although this has meant that some aspects of the subject remain unconsidered.

It is perhaps appropriate to note that, in this chapter, the reader will encounter for the first time some differences of interpretation concerning parallel computing, compared with those expressed earlier. I believe that this is entirely proper and is, indeed, an additional benefit of the chapter. I suggested earlier that the reader should be aware of just such differences of opinion, and you should be prepared to exercise your own critical abilities in order to form your own view. Here is an opportunity to do so. However, let me assure the reader that there are no unbridgeable schisms within the field. Few of the facts are in dispute, although discussions of the comparative value of alternative approaches may occasion some lively debate. I am most grateful to all the contributing authors for putting forward their ideas in this context. It should also be borne in mind that material of this sort quickly becomes, in strictly commercial terms, out of date. The pace of development is very fast, and manufacturers (and researchers) are constantly striving to improve their products. However, the principles, both of parallel computing and of design, which underly the work do not become invalidated with time.

Let us proceed without further ado to the individual contributions. I present them (as far as possible) in the order in which the paradigms they embody appeared in Chapter 2. In each case I precede the contribution with a short consideration of the system's relation to previous chapters, and a listing of systems which share some of its characteristics. In the system characterisation, *parallelism* means the maximum number of processing elements which operate in parallel, while *technology* refers to the level of chip integration used in the system.

7A   Datacube:
using DSP techniques to do real-time
image processing

David Simmons
Datacube, Inc.
Peabody, Massachusetts
USA

The Datacube company has achieved very significant market presence in the field of (in particular) image processing by concentrating on a relatively simple implementation – a high-speed bus connecting dedicated devices which may be linked in either pipeline or MIMD fashion. The characterisation of the system in the terms of this book is:

Basic idea	FPC
Paradigms	MIMD, pipeline
Language	C
Connectivity	Bus
Processors	Dedicated functions
Parallelism	16
Technology	LSI

In view of the importance which I have attached to matching application and architecture earlier in this book, it is perhaps appropriate that the author of this first contribution has chosen to concentrate on a particular application, and explain how the system is configured to solve that specific problem. Given the simplicity of the system itself, this approach offers some valuable insights. It is also of some interest to note that one of the dedicated units used in this pipeline system is, itself, a systolic array. A number of similar systems exist, based on the pipelining paradigm, including:

iWARP	Intel Scientific
	Cornell Oaks
	Beaverton
	Oregon
	USA
Cytocomputer	Machine Vision International
	Ann Arbor
	Michigan
	USA

7A.1 Introduction

When digital signal processing (DSP) chips were first introduced in the mid 1980s, they were designed to operate on data in a batched fashion. They did this by first copying the input data into their on-chip memory from external memory, and then executing the required computations on the stored data. When the computations were complete, they copied the results back out to external memory. By keeping the data on the same chip as the processor, these devices were able to minimise memory access times, and could provide about 10 Mmacs/s of processing power. (A *mac* is a multiply/accumulate operation, often used in DSP computations, which is used as a measure of performance for DSP chips.) The basic hardware unit in a traditional DSP processor consists of an 8-bit multiplier and a 16-bit ALU, arranged as shown in Figure 7.1.

To show how this simple hardware unit can be used to solve a practical problem, suppose you have an incoming signal that is tainted with noise which prevents you from seeing the fine detail of the signal waveshape. If the signal waveform is periodic, you can sample it every time the waveform repeats. If you then average the samples, you will gradually cancel out the random noise, and begin to see the waveform in finer and finer detail. This process of repeatedly sampling and averaging is called infinite impulse response (IIR) filtering. In theory, you could accomplish this average by simply adding the sample values from several successive cycles of the waveform, and then dividing by the number of cycles. However, if you're averaging a large number of cycles, the sum will eventually grow too large to store conveniently. To avoid this, you can calculate a running average, which is quite simple with the basic multiplier/adder unit described above, as illustrated in Figure 7.2.

First, the number of cycles being averaged is stored in the constant register. Next, as each of the running averages is read from memory, it is multiplied by the number of cycles. The resulting product is then routed to the input of the ALU, where it is added to the corresponding sample value. Finally, division by the number of cycles is accomplished by the ALU's

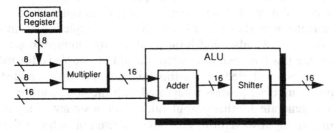

Figure 7.1 The basic DSP architecture

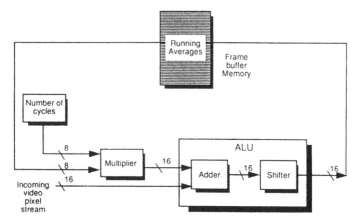

Figure 7.2   Using DSP devices for IIR filtering

shifter (in order to do this, the number of cycles has to be an integer power of two). The new running average is returned to the memory.

7A.2   Filtering in image processing

Video images are typically represented by continuous video signals, which can be digitised to produce a stream of pixel values. As long as the image is not changing, the video waveform is periodic at the frame rate. This allows you to use an IIR filter to average the pixels from successive frames. As the averages accumulate, random noise cancels out and finer and finer details become visible.

7A.2.1   Linear convolutions

One very useful DSP operation is called linear convolution, which allows you to take an incoming waveform and filter out unwanted frequency components. Linear convolution is an example of finite impulse response (FIR) filtering. It is used so much in DSP systems that the speed with which it can be carried out typically determines overall performance.

A linear convolution is done using a stream of samples taken from an incoming waveform as shown in Figure 7.3. Each sample is first multiplied by a constant $K_1, \ldots, K_8$, after which the products are summed to get an output value. Once this has been calculated, the oldest sample is discarded, all the other samples are shifted one position and a new sample is added. Then the multiply/accumulate process is repeated with the same constants on the new string to generate another output value. Thus a stream of input values (representing an input waveform) generates a stream of output values (representing a convolved waveform).

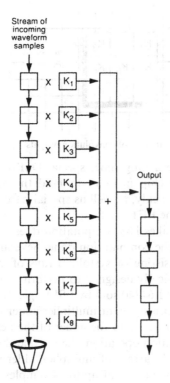

Figure 7.3   Linear convolution

The problem with doing linear convolutions this way is that you need to take a lot of samples to distinguish between similar input waveforms. Since you need to do a multiply and an addition for every sample used, the amount of computation rises rapidly as the number of samples increases. Because of this, most DSP systems do convolutions indirectly, by the following three-step process:

(1) They use the discrete samples of an incoming waveform to calculate a fast fourier transform (FFT), which is a set of complex numbers
(2) They multiply each complex number of the FFT by a corresponding complex number representing the transfer function
(3) They then calculate the inverse FFT of the set of complex number products, to produce values that describe the convolved waveform

The main advantage to the FFT approach is that it requires much less computation than doing a direct convolution. The main disadvantage is that the system must have a considerable amount of memory – perhaps two to four times as much as that required for direct convolution. Because computation of the FFT on general-purpose machines (even those with maths

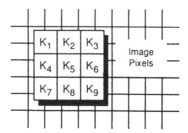

Figure 7.4   A two-dimensional array of convolution weights

coprocessors) can take a long time, special DSP devices were developed. They have enough on-chip memory to hold the array of sample values required to do FFTs quickly, as well as special hardware to access external storage and compute the FFT itself.

But just because it takes less computation doesn't necessarily mean it is the fastest way to get the computation done. Several chip vendors are now selling DSP chips consisting of systolic arrays of multipliers and adders, which have been specifically designed to perform convolutions. One example of such a chip is the L64240 sold by LSI Logic. It incorporates eight systolic arrays, each comprising eight multiplier/adder units. Since the output of each adder is fed directly into the adder of the next unit of the string, it can easily do a convolution operation like the one shown in Figure 7.3. The chip also allows the eight arrays of multiplier/adder units to be concatenated, to allow linear convolutions of up to 64 samples. The tremendous computing power of all this silicon hardware greatly speeds up the computation of convolutions.

7A.2.2   Using convolution in image processing

A special two-dimensional form of convolution, called spatial convolution, can be used to do image processing. To do a spatial convolution, you start with a two-dimensional array of constant multipliers, such as that shown in Figure 7.4.

This array of multipliers can be used as a template, which is to be centred over each pixel in the image being convolved. After centring, each pixel under the template is multiplied by the value on the template above it. Then, all of the products are summed to get an output value, which is stored as one value of a new (convolved) image. The template is then moved on to the next pixel to generate the next value of the output.

Most people use 8-bit pixels. The simplest convolution on 8-bit pixels is a $3 \times 3 \times 8$ convolution. This is fairly simple to calculate, and the hardware required is not too elaborate, but it really isn't very useful. Most people want to use at least a 16×16 array of values to represent the pattern they are looking for.

In the past, it has not been practical to do a 16×16 convolution directly – it has been faster to use FFTs. However, chips like the L64240, with its eight arrays of multiply/accumulators, can be configured to do $8 \times 8 \times 8$ convolutions directly. When four of these chips are used together, you can do a $16 \times 16 \times 8$ convolution faster than any chip using FFTs. In fact, you can do convolutions in real time, as a sequence of video images is received from its source, but in order to do that, you need to use a pipelined architecture.

7A.3   Pipelined image processing

Many common image processing algorithms consist of a simple sequence of arithmetic operations, repeated for each pixel of the image. A very basic set of pipelined hardware, configured to accept pixel values from a simple frame grabber, can accelerate many image processing algorithms. One simple example of this is the IIR filter described earlier. The sample values from an incoming video waveform (and the corresponding running averages from a frame buffer) can be 'piped' through a multiplier/adder unit to generate a stream of new running averages, which are piped back to a frame buffer for storage. In the same way, a pixel stream can be piped through an L64240 chip to generate a stream of convolved image pixels which can then be piped back to memory.

When interconnected properly, chips like the L64240 provide enormous processing bandwidths. By using private data paths to interconnect these specialised DSP chips, you can construct many different algorithms in hardware. However, to make this kind of architecture work, you need to have a very flexible interconnect scheme – one which allows connection of computing units in a manner appropriate to the data flow through the system. One good way to provide these connections is to build each computing unit as a modular printed circuit board, and then interconnect them with a standardised ribbon cable bus. This approach has another advantage – as old boards become obsolete, you can update your system by replacing them with newer ones.

This factor is very important when you consider the pace of technical advance. Figure 7.5 compares the performance and cost of three different VMEbus-based Datacube image processing boards, according to their year of introduction. The performance of each board is representative of the DSP integrated circuits that were available when each was designed.

7A.3.1   The MAXbus architecture

Datacube developed the MAXbus digital video interconnect standard to provide system architects with a high-bandwidth, skew-tolerant open data bus. The skew tolerance is important at high data rates because the sender

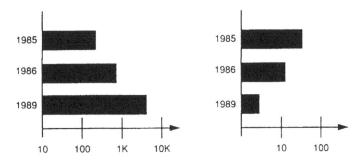

Figure 7.5   How performance and cost have improved with time

and receiver might be several slots apart in the card frame. To avoid skew problems, the sender generates a strobe with each byte of data which follows the same path as the data. This ensures that the two are synchronised at the receiver.

The MAXbus transfers data synchronously at a 10 MHz rate between the boards in a VMEbus system. A common 40 MHz clock ensures synchronisation between boards, and allows individual boards in the pipeline to run their internal hardware at 10, 20 or 40 MHz. All data is transferred over standard ribbon cables, allowing the user flexibility to connect boards in a customised pipeline. The width of the data transfers can be doubled simply by adding another ribbon cable.

The MAXbus technical specifications are available to designers wishing to incorporate it into their designs. Its flexibility supports a wide variety of user-designed pipeline architectures. Any combination of straight pipeline, parallel pipeline or recirculating pipeline can be easily implemented. To date, the following North American and European vendors have announced MAXbus compatible board products:

> Datacube
> Applied Memory Technology
> Interactive Circuits and Systems
> Southern Research Technologies
> SRI International
> Storage Concepts
> Vision Securities
> Chess Engineering
> Future Digital Systems
> Qualiplus

Many designers have experienced the frustration when new technology makes a current design partially or completely obsolete. This can occur often in the rapidly developing DSP marketplace. The Datacube MAXbus

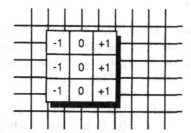

Figure 7.6 One multiplier template for the Sobel filter

interconnect allows you to incorporate new technology in your existing system.

7A.3.2   Designing a Sobel filter

To illustrate how important a flexible interconnect can be, suppose you want to construct a real-time Sobel edge extraction filter, which is used in image processing to enhance edges. The filter yields two outputs – an edge magnitude image and an edge orientation image. Each pixel in the edge magnitude image indicates how rapidly the original image's intensity varies at the same point. This is obtained by calculating separately the rates of change of intensity in the x and y directions, and then combining these to give the overall result by taking the square root of the sum of the squares of the two individual values. Each pixel value in the edge orientation image is proportional to the angle of any edge that passes through that same pixel in the original image. The value is calculated by taking the arctan of the ratio between the values of the rates of change of intensity in the x and y directions.

You can use two-dimensional spatial convolvers to calculate the x and y derivatives at each pixel of an image. For example, to calculate the gradient in the x direction, you might use a 3×3 template of multipliers like the one shown in Figure 7.6.

If the two-dimensional convolution described earlier is carried out using this template, the result is the gradient in the x direction. If there's no intensity change in that direction, the gradient will be zero but, if there is an intensity change, the output will be either positive or negative. The higher the rate of change, the greater the magnitude of the gradient. The gradient in the y direction is calculated in the same way, then both values are used to compute the edge magnitude and edge orientation values, as indicated above.

7A.3.3   The VFIR III

One of the most recent additions to the MAXbus family is the VFIR III (video rate finite impulse response filter, third generation). It is a single VMEbus board that provides eight times the performance and one quarter the per-point cost of previous products. The performance is 10^{10} arithmetic operations per second, or 5×10^9 8-bit macs/s.

The VFIR comprises a delay line, a convolver, a shifter, an adder and a formatter. The delay line is useful in pipelined architectures because data streams passing through different operations in a multipath line may suffer differing delays. When two of these data streams are then fed into another computational unit they may need to be synchronised. This is accomplished by delaying one or the other data stream.

The convolver can do $16 \times 16 \times 8$ convolutions in 50 ns on images up to 4000 pixels per scan, and up to 4000 scans per frame. The data and the multipliers can be independently programmed to be unsigned or 2s complement numbers. The shifter is used to normalise the results as they exit the convolver unit. The adder sums the shifted convolution result with data from the auxiliary input or with a programmable constant.

The formatter provides another shifter, which may be needed to normalise the output of the summer just ahead of it. It also allows you to store the summer's output in unsigned or 2s complement format. When the data cannot be represented in the prescribed format (because of overflow or underflow) the format element detects this and outputs a prescribed value instead of the invalid result. In some cases, you may only want the absolute value of the convolution. The format element also takes care of that.

The most important functional units on the board are the four L64240 convolution units. Each of these can handle ten million samples per second. Each includes a shifter, a summer, an auxiliary input multiplexor and a logic formatter.

The configurable pipeline concept is carried through the entire design of VFIR III. The four $8 \times 8 \times 8$ convolver units can be interconnected in almost any pipelined configuration by a crosspoint switch. This configuration is done by a host processor over the VMEbus. The crosspoint switch also allows you to pair up two of the $8 \times 8 \times 8$ convolvers to operate as a team on the same data. In this paired configuration, they can handle data rates up to 20 million samples per second. The same switch also allows each of the $8 \times 8 \times 8$ convolvers to be used independently. This flexibility allows you to make very effective use of the convolution hardware for a wide variety of applications. The crosspoint switch allows you to configure the four units into the $16 \times 16 \times 8$ convolver shown in Figure 7.7. The most common operating mode of VFIR III is expected to be 16×16 FIR filtering with 8-bit multipliers and data. In this configuration, the board is capable of 20 million output samples per second.

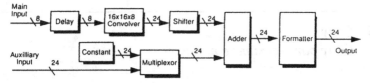

Figure 7.7   A 16 × 16 × 8 convolver

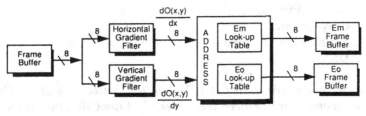

Figure 7.8   A Sobel filter design

7A.3.4   A Sobel filter using VFIR III

By using different multiplier templates, you can use the VFIR III to do a great variety of operations, such as high pass filtering, low pass filtering, convolution and pattern matching. For example, the Sobel filter discussed earlier can easily be implemented as shown in Figure 7.8.

The input stream is routed (via MAXbus) from a frame buffer into the VFIR III, where the crosspoint switch routes it to an 8 × 8 convolution unit, which is configured to work as two separate 4 × 4 convolvers. The first of these generates the horizontal gradient and the second the vertical gradient. The gradient values are each routed (again via the crosspoint switch) to a 64 kbyte RAM lookup table. The locations of the two RAMs are preloaded with values corresponding to magnitude and gradient respectively. The small number of possible input combinations (64k) makes the use of a lookup table practical, and the speed of the table makes it possible to do the calculations in real-time. As shown in Figure 7.8, the real-time Sobel filter requires five separate 8-bit busses.

7A.4   Conclusion

This article has shown how the MAXbus architecture can be exploited to implement some typical image processing operations. Some algorithms may require even more computational elements for real-time operation. In that case, the number of data paths you need will be even larger. In addition, for many image processing algorithms, you may need to maintain greater precision throughout the system, requiring 16-bit or even 32-bit busses. The flexibility of the MAXbus architecture allows you to do this when necessary, but doesn't commit you to it where you don't need it.

7B   Cray:
Cray parallel supercomputers

John G. Fleming
Cray Research
Minneapolis, Minnesota
USA

The supercomputer era started in 1976 with the first delivery of the Cray-1 vector computer system. Fifteen years later, the Cray C90 system is over 150 times more powerful although the clock is only three times faster. The other factor of more than 50 is derived from parallelism in one guise or another. Cray systems can be characterised by the following:

Basic idea	FPC
Paradigms	MIMD, pipeline, SIMD
Language	C, Fortran, Ada
Connectivity	Bus
Processors	Vector, scalar
Parallelism	16
Technology	VLSI

Cray computers are examples of vector supercomputers. It is arguable that vectorisation should itself be considered as a parallel paradigm, but it is only one of the many techniques which Cray systems deploy to obtain their formidable performance. Similar systems are produced by the major league players of the computing world such as IBM, Fujitsu and CDC.

7B.1   Introduction

This contribution shows the influence of parallelism in developing the family of Cray high-performance computer systems and indicates the promising future for both vector parallel and massively parallel units within general-purpose numerically intensive systems of the nineties.

The history of high-performance computers is an exciting story of searching out the bottlenecks in existing systems and producing innovations which eliminate them. During the 1960s, the availability of integrated circuits allowed for the first time the construction of reliable systems from large numbers of components. It began to be possible to conceive of increasing

Table 7.1 *Performance of four generations of Cray systems*

System	CPUs	Clock (MHz)	FP Results per clock per CPU	Words moved per clock per CPU	MFLOP rate at 1 data word per clock
Cray-1	1	80	2	1	80
X-MP	4	105	2	3	840
Y-MP	8	166	2	3	2667
C90	16	240	4	6	15360

the complexity of systems where this would yield higher performance. Thus, alongside improvements to component speed came approaches involving parallel operation of different parts of the system. Early techniques included pipelining and vector processing within the CPU and the movement of some system functions to separate processors.

Since 1976, each new generation of Cray supercomputer has been the performance leader for numerically intensive computing. By incorporating technological innovation and increasing parallelism, each generation has extended the capabilities available to scientists and engineers, as shown in Table 7.1.

The key innovation was the concept of vector processing which overcame the instruction issue bottleneck by permitting one instruction to indicate action on a series of data elements. The success of the Cray-1 system came from combining vector instructions with the use of vector registers, which allowed the processing of data within the CPU independently of the traffic of data between memory and processor logic. In addition, pipelining was used both in the instruction issue process and within the arithmetic units. Multiple independent functional units, each of which was a pipeline segmented at every clock period, further increased parallelism.

The Cray X-MP system became the first multiprocessor supercomputer by the addition of synchronisation logic between the processors in such a way that all processors could be coordinated on one task. It also introduced multiple parallel paths to memory from each CPU, thereby improving the performance for memory-intensive programs.

The Cray Y-MP system increased the number of processors to eight and reduced the clock cycle time. Packaging improvements and the use of higher levels of integration allowed the construction of a processor on a single physical module.

The Cray C90 doubled the number of processors and further reduced the clock period. The architecture was also modified to employ double-size vector registers and duplicated functional units allowing two results from each logical pipeline in each clock cycle.

7B.2   Architecture

In this section I describe the parallel features of Cray C90 systems in some detail. Whilst the range of systems includes physical frames which can accommodate 2, 4, 8 and 16 processors, I shall focus here on the largest, the C916 system, which has the following major characteristics:

* Up to 16 CPUs
* Up to 8192 Mbytes of high-speed central memory uniformly accessible to each CPU
* Up to 256 I/O channels providing up to 13.6 Gbytes/s bandwidth to peripheral devices and networks
* Connectivity to closely couple the C916 system to a massively parallel Cray T3D
* Optional SSD (solid-state storage) device containing up to 32 Gbytes of storage with a maximum bandwidth of 13.6 Gbytes/s

The C90 system offers a balanced approach to vector and scalar processing. Vector processing, the performance of iterative operations on sets of ordered data, provides results at rates greatly exceeding those of conventional scalar processing. Each CPU has two independent vector processing segments. Scalar operations complement the vector capability by providing solutions to problems not readily adaptable to vector techniques.

The system's central memory is shared by all of the system's CPUs, any one of which can access all of the central memory. Each CPU has four double-width ports to central memory, as shown in Figure 7.9. The central memory is organised as follows so that multiple data transfers may proceed in parallel:

* Eight independent sections
* Eight subsections per section
* Two bank groups per subsection
* Eight banks in a bank group
* 1024 total banks

Each CPU is connected by an independent access path to each of the sections, allowing up to 128 64-bit memory references per clock period.

The central memory contains program code for the CPUs, as well as data for problem solution. Memory is available in sizes from 128 to 1024 Mwords and is shared by the CPUs and the I/O section. Each word comprises 80 bits (64 data bits and 16 bits for error detection and correction).

An independent I/O subsystem (IOS) matches the processing rates of the CPUs with high I/O transfer rates for communication with mass storage units, other peripheral devices and a wide variety of other computer systems and networks. It also supports a number of 200 Mbyte/s high-speed chan-

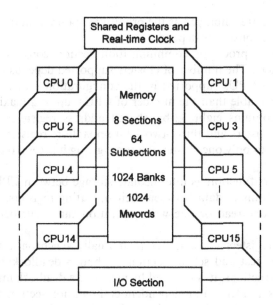

Figure 7.9 C916 Block diagram

nels for connection to the massively parallel T3D system and to the SSD. The IOS is connected to central memory with up to 16 high-speed communication channels. The SSD is connected to central memory with up to four 1800 Mbyte/s channels.

Each CPU is connected to central memory through ports A, B, C and D. Data transfer to and from the operating registers and instruction fetches to the instruction buffers take place through these memory ports. Ports A, B and C are used for register transfers, port D for I/O and instruction fetches. Once an instruction is issued to a port, that port is reserved until all references are made for that instruction. If an instruction requires a port that is busy, issue is blocked.

Each port is made up of two independent pipes, each capable of making one memory reference per clock period. The references for all the elements of a block transfer are made through the two pipes of a port. Concurrent block reads and writes are not examined for memory overlap hazard conditions so the software must detect the cases where this hazard occurs. Instructions are provided to resolve these cases and assure sequential operation.

The inter-processor communication section of the mainframe has three features to pass data and control information between CPUs:

* Shared registers to pass data
* Semaphore registers to synchronise programs
* Inter-processor interrupts to initiate exchange sequences

These features are employed as the primitives upon which the higher level parallel software constructs depend.

The CPU inter-processor communication section consists of identical groups of clusters. The number of clusters supported depends on the maximum number of CPUs supported in the configuration – there will be one more cluster available than the number of CPUs, up to a maximum of 17. Each cluster contains eight 32-bit shared address registers, eight 64-bit shared scalar registers and thirty-two 1-bit semaphore registers. Each CPU can be assigned to only one cluster at a time, giving it access to that cluster's registers.

These registers function as intermediate storage between CPUs and provide a way to transfer data between their operating registers. For register transfers, only one read or one write operation can occur per instruction issued.

Semaphore registers allow CPUs to mutually synchronise their operations, using the test and set instruction. Although deadlocking can occur using these instructions, it is resolved by means of a deadlock interrupt.

Each CPU is an identical, independent computation section consisting of operating registers, functional units and an instruction control network. Most functional units are fully independent; any number of functional units can process instructions concurrently. The operating registers and functional units are associated with three types of processing: address, scalar and vector.

Address processing is used on internal control information such as addresses and indices, and on control information related to vector length and shift count. It employs two integer ALUs.

Scalar processing is the application of arithmetic operations to single numbers or pairs of numbers. Five functional units are dedicated solely to scalar processing, and three floating-point units are shared with vector operations. Scalar and vector processing can execute concurrently except during floating-point operations.

A functional unit receives operands from registers, performs a specific operation on them, and delivers the result to a register when the operation is completed. Functional units usually operate in three-address mode with source and destination addressing limited to register designators. Functional units are fully segmented – a new set of operands for unrelated computation can enter a functional unit each clock period, even though the function unit time can be more than one clock period.

Most vector functional units perform operations on operands obtained from two vector registers or from a vector and a scalar register. Results from a vector functional unit are delivered to a vector register.

There are two parallel sets of floating-point (f-p) functional units with each set containing three functional units. These units perform f-p arithmetic for both scalar and vector operations. The vector registers use both sets of functional units, with one set processing the even-numbered elements and the other set processing the odd-numbered elements. For an operation involving only scalar operands, only one set of f-p units is used.

Vector processing is performed on ordered sets of elements, eliminating instruction issue time for all but the first operand. A vector instruction operates on a series of elements, repeating the same function with each, and producing a series of results. In the C916, vector processing employs a set of 128-element registers, where each element is 64 bits, which feed two independent vector processing segments. Each vector pipeline has six dedicated functional units and three shared f-p units.

The major computational registers of a CPU are the eight dedicated V registers, each containing 128 elements of 64-bits. The elements are divided into two groups, called pipes, one of which processes even-numbered elements and the other odd-numbered elements. Each pipe is supported by an identical set of functional units.

A vector is an ordered set of elements. Examples of structures in Fortran that can be represented as vectors are one-dimensional arrays; and rows, columns and diagonals of multi-dimensional arrays. A long vector is processed as one or more 128-element segments and a possible shorter remainder. The processing of long vectors in Fortran is handled by the compiler and is transparent to the programmer.

In vector processing, two successive pairs of elements are processed each clock period. The dual vector pipes and the dual sets of vector functional units allow two pairs of elements to be processed during the same clock period. As each pair of operations is completed, the results are delivered to appropriate elements of the result register. The operation continues until the number of elements processed is equal to the count specified by the vector length register.

Parallel vector operations allow the generation of more than two results per clock period. They occur automatically in the following situations.

* When successive vector instructions use different functional units and different vector registers
* When successive vector instructions use the result stream from one vector register as the operand of another operation using a different functional unit. This process is known as chaining

In general, vector processing is faster and more efficient than scalar processing. Vector processing reduces the overhead associated with maintenance of the loop-control variables (e.g. incrementing and checking the count). In many cases, loops processed as vectors are reduced to a simple sequence of instructions without branching backwards. Central memory access conflicts are reduced and, finally, functional unit segmentation is optimally exploited. Vectorisation typically speeds up a code segment by a factor of about ten.

The contents of a V register are transferred to or from central memory through a block transfer. This is accomplished by specifying a first-word address in central memory, an increment or decrement value for the address, and a vector length. The transfer proceeds at a maximum transfer rate of two words per clock period, although this can be degraded by central memory conflicts.

7B.3 Technology

In any significant engineering project there are trade-offs to be made in the choice of technologies used. In the case of vector parallel designs, the basic technology chosen is dictated by switching speed in conjunction with the level of integration available. For this reason the current choice is to implement in emitter-coupled logic (ECL) for the most powerful systems. It is, however, interesting to note that the same architecture has also been implemented in CMOS technology for the Cray EL98 entry-level system, which is air-cooled and significantly lower priced.

In each generation ambition is bounded by practical concerns related to the availability of components which can be used to construct a robust and reliable product. Figure 7.10 shows the increase in complexity of the processors in four generations of Cray systems. The progression in basic component technology is what makes possible the increasing trend per processor – the overall complexity of the processor part of the system is obviously increasing even faster. Table 7.2 shows the logic component level of integration for each range of systems.

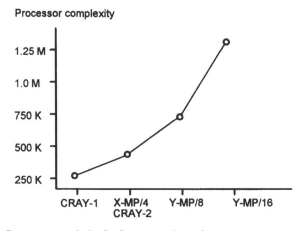

Figure 7.10 Processor complexity for four generations of systems

Table 7.2 *Integration density for four generations of system*

System	Gates/chip
Cray-1	2
Cray X-MP	16
Cray Y-MP	2 500
Cray C90	10 000

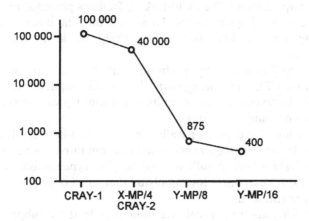

Figure 7.11   Numbers of integrated circuits per processor

The resulting physical construction of the systems, in terms of the numbers of circuits required to build a processor, is shown in Figure 7.11.

As the number of processors rises, an increasing proportion of logic has to be devoted to ensuring the ability of the memory subsystem to deliver data to the CPUs at high rates and low latency. In the case of the C916 system approximately half of the logic within the system is allocated to this task.

7B.4   Software

Parallel operation of hardware is to no avail unless it can be harnessed by applications software. Cray Research software offers a consistent user interface to the functionality and architectural features of the Cray systems. The system software enhances productivity through easy-to-use and flexible interfaces which enable users to introduce, debug and verify large and complex application programs.

The operating system UNICOS is based on UNIX System V, and provides interactive, local batch and remote batch interfaces. Several functions of the Fourth Berkeley Software Distribution (4.3 BSD), along with significant Cray Research extensions, provide additional performance and operational enhancements. UNICOS provides multi-programming and multi-processing facilities, and supports the application of multiple CPUs to a single process (multi-tasking). Multi-tasking is most effective when it is used on programs that embody a high degree of parallelism.

From the point of view of the programmer seeking performance, specific arrangements are required to support the use of multiple processors to execute a single application. The multi-tasking facilities provided result in substantial throughput improvements. To achieve this, the three techniques of auto-tasking, micro-tasking and macro-tasking can all be utilised in the same program.

Auto-tasking automatically partitions parallel Fortran and C codes across multiple CPUs, exploiting parallelism at the loop level. It requires no programmer intervention, but permits experienced programmers to tune programs for optimum performance.

Micro-tasking also exploits parallelism at the DO-loop level in Fortran and C code. It does not require code modification; rather, users insert directives to indicate where parallelism exists. The synchronisation costs of micro-tasking are extremely low, implying that small code segments can be successfully partitioned.

Macro-tasking allows parallel execution of code at the subprogram level on multiple processors. The user interface is a set of subroutines that explicitly define and synchronise tasks at the subprogram level for Fortran, C or Ada code. The user inserts calls to these subroutines.

7B.5   Massively parallel systems (T3D)

As levels of integration increase, new possibilities have emerged for the construction of parallel computers. The technological, architectural and integration concepts embodied in numerous research programmes offer the potential for defining a new dimension to the science of supercomputing – *scalability*. However, such systems have distributed memories and therefore exhibit non-uniform memory access times. Whilst some applications can tolerate this variability, most are structured to take advantage of the uniform access inherent in shared memory systems.

The Cray Research strategy is to extend the existing computational and programming models discussed earlier, by integrating selected distributed memory and processing features. The extended computational model supports a logically shared but physically distributed memory system. Design attention is focused on the memory-to-memory interconnect and management scheme that provides a single address space for all processors and thus eliminates many network programming problems. Distributed memory and shared memory capabilities are closely coupled, permitting applications to be optimally distributed across the architecture.

The distributed memory element of the system will implement a globally addressable, distributed memory MIMD massively parallel processor constructed from up to 2048 Digital Alpha microprocessors, each with peak performance capability of 150 MFLOPS. This component will be integrated with a vectorising component of the C90 family.

The extended programming model will allow for data parallel, message passing and worksharing (control parallel) modes. Suitable access, analysis and debugging tools are provided within the UNICOS environment. This approach maximises programmer productivity by allowing users to concentrate on the task of algorithm selection and implementation.

The composite systems will be of use in numerically intensive application areas where the highest possible performance is demanded. For the present, this performance will only be attained at the cost of additional algorithm development involving careful optimisation of memory usage.

7B.6   Future trends

Continued advances in semiconductor technology will result in further rapid advances in the capabilities of large computer systems. In all of these parallelism will play a crucial role, since improvements in raw clock speed will not suffice. Processor performance will continue to improve, but in most contemporary systems memory access is the significant determinator of system performance – few systems today are compute-bound. Memory capacity has increased steadily but access times have not kept pace, so the introduction of usable additional parallelism into memory components will be a key breakthrough.

Most programming today is based on the single processor model of computation, which explains the success of systems based on the vectorisation paradigm which conceal much of the parallelism from the programmer. Industry agreement on the standardisation of language constructs will be needed before rapid progress is made in implementing parallelism in widely-used applications. As yet it is not clear which programming paradigm will prevail for distributed memory systems.

The sustained performance of large parallel systems will also depend on advances in the understanding of suitable parallel algorithms and their successful implementation in commonly available languages. Significant investment in the appropriate restructuring of applications is only just beginning.

7C nCUBE:
the nCUBE 2 supercomputer

R. S. Wilson
nCUBE Inc.
Beaverton, Oregon
USA

The nCUBE company is a relatively recent player in the supercomputer game, and was perhaps the first to offer true supercomputing performance based principally on a high degree of parallelism. Their chosen architecture is scalable over the range 32 – 8192 processors, and the largest system can claim to be the most powerful commercially available (at the time of writing). The basic characteristics are:

Basic idea	FPC
Paradigm	MIMD
Language	C, Fortran
Connectivity	Hypercube
Processors	64-bit f-p
Parallelism	8192
Technology	VLSI

The hypercube approach to connecting moderate numbers of powerful computing elements has proved quite popular. Two other well-known systems which use the same technique are:

Connection Machine 2	Thinking Machines Corp.
	Cambridge
	Massachusetts
	USA
Touchstone	Intel Scientific
	Cornell Oaks
	Beaverton
	Oregon
	USA

7C.1 Introduction

The nCUBE 2's hardware architecture represents a unique synthesis of features, each designed to increase the computer's performance and reliability. The architecture centres on a hypercube data network of custom VLSI 64-bit processors, each with independent memory. This network is a modular, scalable system that allows multiple users to perform distributed computing. The hypercube design accommodates a variety of applications, from scientific modelling programs to relational databases. The inexpensive but powerful processors give the system its high speed and price/performance ratio.

7C.2 Hardware architecture

The custom-designed silicon chip used in the nCUBE integrates all the system's logic on a single device, allowing from 32 to 8192 processors to be supported. Each processor is an entire computer system on a chip containing 500 000 transistors, on which all the elements of a parallel computing system are consolidated. This chip, coupled with DRAM memory, constitutes a computing element, illustrated in Figure 7.12. Due to its greatly reduced number of components, nCUBE's custom VLSI provides faster and more reliable performance than large logic boards.

The processor uses state-of-the-art dual metal, one micron CMOS technology. It features a 64-bit CPU, a 64-bit IEEE standard floating-point unit, an error correcting memory management interface with a 39-bit data path, a proprietary message routing unit, and 28 uni-directional direct memory access (DMA) channels. These are divided into fourteen pairs of bi-directional communication lines that form the hypercube network with other computing elements and connect to the I/O subsystem. Running at a modest clock rate of 20 MHz, the processor is conservatively rated at 7.5 MIPS and 2.4 MFLOPS (64-bit). The 64-bit processor includes a four-

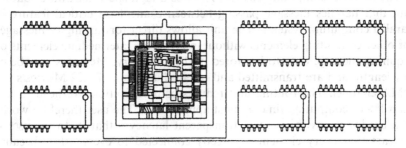

Figure 7.12 One computing element

instruction pipeline, a data cache of eight operands and an instruction cache of 128 bytes.

The system's distributed memory architecture places virtually no physical limitations on the speed of memory operations, because computing elements are not competing for available memory bandwidth. Adding a computing element increases the total system memory bandwidth and improves performance linearly. Local memory makes it easy to link thousands of computing elements together and scale systems to users' needs. Users can select local DRAM memory in increments ranging from 1 to 64 Mbytes per computing element. In the largest configuration – 8192 elements with 4 Mbytes each – the user has access to 32 Gbytes of memory. The maximum memory capacity of nCUBE 2 is 512 Gbytes.

Each nCUBE 2 computer comprises a compact network of computing elements. Up to 64 of these can be mounted on one 40 cm × 50 cm board, sixteen of which can be mounted in a single chassis to produce a 1024-processor system. Up to eight of these units can be connected together for a total of 8192 computing elements in a configuration with a footprint smaller than 5 square meters. Grouping processors in this way offers several benefits to users. First, the number of processors provides high performance. Second, the use of an inexpensive component as the basic building block results in a low cost for the whole system. Finally, because the same processor is used in all nCUBE 2 computers, software written for a small configuration runs on a large one, and vice-versa.

In the system's MIMD data networks, each computing element executes its own programmed sequence of instructions and can function independently. The computing element array resembles a group of mainframes connected together in an extremely high bandwidth network. This design provides a straightforward and familiar programming environment. It accommodates multiple users by allocating subarrays, which allows many different programs and a variety of operations to execute simultaneously. Through subarrays, the data networks achieve high efficiency in a large range of applications.

The nCUBE computing element features a high-speed hardware routing unit that handles message passing between elements, a critical feature in parallel computing systems. The unit allows direct forwarding of messages for other computing elements without interrupting intermediate elements or requiring message data to be stored in their memory. Messages may be of any length, and are transmitted and received at a rate of 2.22 Mbytes/s per DMA channel. The routing unit reduces communication overhead to less than 1% of computing time in most applications. The user therefore works in a hardware environment of transparent latency – that is, to the user it appears that every element is directly connected to every other, because message passing occurs so swiftly.

The low number of system parts and efficient network construction give nCUBE systems a calculated mean time between failures in excess of twelve months, much longer than most other high-performance systems. All nCUBE machines provide hardware error detection and correction capabilities on both memory and I/O systems. Distributed memory systems can easily be reconfigured around failed elements. If any processor or its memory fails, the user can isolate the faulty element and map around it. The rest of the system continues operation, ensuring graceful degradation.

7C.3 The hypercube network

The main distinguishing features of different parallel processing systems are the amount of memory available and the scheme by which processors are linked together. This section describes nCUBE's interconnection technology.

A hypercube network provides high performance without incurring architectural overhead. The sophisticated routing unit described above lets message passing take place between thousands of computing elements without user-directed route planning. The network is organised so that the connections between computing elements form cubes. As more elements are added, the cube grows to larger dimensions. Joining two hypercubes of the same dimension forms a hypercube of the next dimension. The number of computing elements in any size of hypercube is written as 2^N, where N is the order of the hypercube. A ten-dimensional hypercube has 1024 computing elements. The hypercube is scalable to thousands of computing elements because the logic for its implementation is highly integrated into a very small package.

One measure of a network's efficiency is the number of steps required to move data between the furthest computing elements in a system. In the hypercube topology, the greatest number of steps between computing elements is the same as the cube's dimension. This means that the user can double the number of computing elements in a system while adding only one additional step for communications between all computing elements. At the same time, communication occurs so fast, due to nCUBE's high-speed hardware message routing, that the number of steps is less of a performance limiting factor than it is in systems using store-and-forward message routing techniques.

It should be noted that although the largest dimension nCUBE available is of order 13, 14 communications channels are available on each computing element. The 14th channel is reserved for data I/O. To provide balanced system performance at all configuration levels, nCUBE has anticipated real-life applications requirements for I/O as well as for computing power and memory. Including a built-in I/O channel with each computing element allows users to increase I/O bandwidth automatically as processing power and memory are upgraded. The hypercube's inherent efficiency, together with the speed of the message routing hardware, create a streamlined, high-performance interconnect topology. The 8192 element nCUBE system has an inter-processor transfer rate of 236 million bytes/s.

The hypercube's large number of connections between computing elements offers a high inter-processor communications bandwidth. At the same time, its density of connections approaches the performance of a network in which every computing element is connected to all others. The hypercube provides a large number of data paths while keeping computing elements close together in a compact design that facilitates the rapid transfer of data. Network density is a critical factor in parallel computations, because the pattern of communication varies greatly between applications.

7C.4   Subcube allocation

Since the hypercube is defined inductively, hypercubes of varying dimensions are logically equivalent, and a hypercube can be allocated in subsets, or subcubes. This means that nCUBE computers are multi-user, multi-tasking systems. Each is built to accommodate many users without reducing performance. Multiple computing elements provide an ideal resource for the simultaneous execution of disparate tasks; more importantly, they give each user true autonomy. Subcube allocation is performed on hardware, where users designate physical hypercubes. Each subcube is a private computer for as long as the user requires it; there is no paging and no roll-in/roll-out, so response time is inherently fast. Further efficiency can be gained by scaling cube size to problem size.

Programs may be written to determine the hypercube dimensions just before executing. When executing, the program may allocate subcubes, which are released at the user's command. Subcubes can run programs interchangeably, with performance proportionate to the size of the subcube.

The allocation of computing elements is as straightforward as the allocation of memory, with simple parameters and calls. Because each computing element balances computing power with memory, users can easily determine the number of elements a problem will require by noting the amount of memory used to store the problem data.

Efficient allocation of resources is a key factor, because every program reaches a point where adding computing elements no longer improves performance. Beyond this point, computing power is wasted. The nCUBE operating system lets users maximise available resources by requesting subcubes of appropriate size, while additional computing elements remain available for others.

Subcube allocation allows nCUBE systems to be expanded in small increments. Without subcube allocation, then for any expansion to take place it would be necessary to double the number of computing elements in a system to take it from one order of hypercube to the next.

7C.5   I/O systems

The massive computation power of the nCUBE 2 is balanced by an equally powerful I/O system. This balance is achieved through the I/O system's use of the VLSI processor which was designed to act as either a computing element or an I/O element. Identical communication links can function either to connect the computing elements in a hypercube or to serve as data I/O paths.

The same programming environment exists in the I/O element and the computing element. Using a separate I/O element with its own 64-bit processor allows I/O execution time and overhead – in managing a disc drive for example – to occur in parallel with the operation of processing elements. In a large system, where as many as 8192 computing elements and 1024 I/O elements are operating, the extra computational power available for I/O overhead increases performance substantially.

High-performance computing commonly demands a fast, flexible I/O system. The nCUBE 2 provides users with a variety of powerful I/O interfaces, ensuring that users can connect to devices their applications need. These interfaces include the parallel I/O subsystem (PIOS), the open systems board and the peripheral board. Each of these boards has specialised features to connect to different types of I/O devices.

7C.5.1   The parallel I/O subsystem

PIOS is a high-performance system that provides I/O channels directly to the hypercube array. It allows users to balance high computational power with high-performance mass storage or other I/O systems, as shown in Figure 7.13.

The subsystem uses one of the computer's 560 Mbyte/s I/O channels. Each channel has up to 256 DMA links into the main processor array, and each link operates at 2.22 Mbytes/s. The subsystem has 16 independent peripheral connections, each of which can drive a different type of peripheral if required. This system answers the need of compute-intensive applications that require the attachment of a large number of devices. These can include:

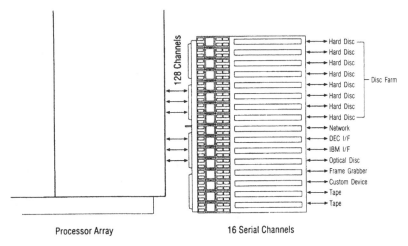

Figure 7.13   The parallel I/O subsystem

Disc drives
Tape drives
Networks
Cameras and frame grabbers
The DR11W 16-bit VAX connection
The DRB32 32-bit VAX connection
Terminal multiplexors
Remote graphics devices

Each of the 16 peripheral connections on the subsystem transfers data at 20 Mbytes/s. The subsystem's extremely high bandwidth allows the nCUBE 2 to make remote I/O connections without sacrificing its high data transfer rates. A fully configured model 80 nCUBE 2 can connect to as many as 448 I/O controllers. The peripheral controller chassis contains the peripheral devices and can be located up to 15 m from the nCUBE system, connected by cable. Optionally, a fibre-optic cable may be used to communicate with peripherals at a distance of up to 500 m. The peripheral chassis contains a cardcage with a generic peripheral controller card for each channel, and a specific I/O device controller for each type of peripheral.

7C.5.2   A parallel disc subsystem

A parallel disc subsystem, supported by PIOS, allows mass storage for nCUBE systems and provides an indispensable resource for many high-performance applications. In a parallel disc application, each peripheral connection supports a single ESMD disc controller, which in turn supports from one to four disc drives. A single subsystem therefore supports up to 64 disc drives; a fully configured nCUBE system supports as many as 1792 drives. Because the I/O rate of each channel of PIOS is 10 Mbytes/s (several times faster than the disc drive itself), it never limits the performance of the drive. The I/O subsystem uses each disc controller's local memory to optimise the disc transfers through double buffering and disc sector caching.

With the large number of I/O elements and disc drives available, discs may be configured in various ways to accommodate the needs of virtually any system. To achieve the fastest I/O performance, users can configure a system with a single drive for each I/O element, enabling all channels to be accessed simultaneously. For maximum data storage, 28 I/O subsystems, each configured with the maximum number of the highest density drives, will support up to 1800 Gbytes of data. The speed and size of this mass storage system make it well-suited for the management of large databases.

Running on each of the processors on the PIOS is an operating system that supports a hierarchical file system associated with the discs attached to that channel. The user can access the files from any given file system by making calls to the operating system on the processors. Any file system can be accessed from any processor on the hypercube array. In addition, there are support libraries for Fortran and C. The performance of the file systems is optimised by the use of caching in the I/O elements on the PIOS, and by using the local memory on the disc controller.

7C.5.3 Open system board

The open system board provides 128 links between the processor array and a variety of user-defined interfaces for custom devices. The interfaces are independent of the operating system. The boards contain up to 16 processors; each processor can have up to 64 Mbytes of memory.

7C.5.4 Peripheral board

The peripheral board is an interface for peripheral systems that reside on one board that plugs into the nCUBE and the I/O device. Examples of these single board subsystems are graphics controllers and video input boards.

7C.6 The operating environment

The nCUBE 2 supercomputer may be accessed through a Sun workstation front end. The nCUBE operating environment is seamlessly integrated with its front end, allowing users to control the entire system from a familiar platform. The operating environment is a multi-user environment in which every user acts independently and exercises complete control over the execution of their programs. The environment includes standard programming languages and high-level utilities to aid software development.

The system supports Fortran 77 and C with standard compile-time and run-time constructs. A complete suite of cross-compilers and cross-development tools is available for use on Sun workstations. Users do not need to know special or non-standard language constructs to set up communications between Fortran programs running on different computing elements.

Program loading and execution on subcubes, as well as message passing and other communication between subcubes, is handled with subroutine calls from the run-time environment library. Subroutines such as NWrite, NRead and NTest allow computing elements to send, receive and test messages from other elements. Other subroutines are available from the Express toolkit. This provides a run-time environment that automates program communication between computing elements.

nCUBE provides a range of tools to help users achieve maximum performance on their applications. Porting and conversion of sequential programs, as well as new program development, are facilitated by resources from nCUBE and other pioneers in the development of parallel processing systems.

The Parallel Source-Level Debugger: is a symbolic source and assembly-level debugger for parallel computers. It allows users to set break-points and to single-step through their code. Users can review variables, data, message queues, processor state and registers on any, all, or any set of processors at the same time. Data can be displayed in various formats: 8-, 16- or 32-bit ASCII, binary, decimal, octal and hexadecimal. All debugging information is presented in a single window, even on 1000-processor systems.

The Parallel Performance Monitor: is an evaluation tool to help users achieve maximum speed from parallel applications. Through a graphical interface, users see a timeline of occurrences to evaluate load imbalances and other flaws. The monitor provides three categories of information; time spent in individual routines, time spent in communications and I/O, and interaction between processors.

The Express Parallel Operating Environment: runs under the host's standard operating system. It provides the tools to parallelise C and Fortran code, making the writing very similar to writing serial code. Code written under Express is portable between parallel machines, and between sequential and parallel machines. The parallel toolkit features scalable software, dynamic load balancing, semi-automatic decomposition of data, and multitasking or single process operations.

7C.6.1   The nCUBE/Sun development system

The nCUBE 2 can be interfaced and networked with Sun-3 or Sun-4 work-stations. The interface allows the user to develop parallel programs for nCUBE systems in the Sun UNIX software environment. Parallel programs can be started, controlled and debugged from the Sun workstation. Multiple users can simultaneously access and use the nCUBE system by utilising the appropriate subcube allocation capabilities. If multiple work-stations are networked together, one is designated the host. Any remote login to the host gives the user access to the nCUBE system. The number of workstations in a network is limited only by the Ethernet.

The nCUBE/Sun development system provides C and Fortran 77 cross-compilers that generate code for the nCUBE processors. The library includes routines for allocating a hypercube and for sending programs and data to and from the hypercube. A parallel symbolic cross-debugger resident on the Sun provides complete capabilities for diagnosing a running parallel program. Also included are utilities for initialising and diagnosing the nCUBE system. Support for dividing the array into subcubes is available from the Sun system.

The hardware interface from the nCUBE to the Sun is a high-speed (16 Mbytes/s transfer rate) platform interface board with Sun adaptor board and interface cables.

7D Supernode:
the Parsys SN1000

David M. Watson
Parsys Ltd
London
UK

The Supernode system, which utilises transputers as its computing elements, was originally developed at Southampton University, UK. The commercial systems can claim to be flexibly reconfigurable because of the crossbar switch interconnection. System characteristics are:

Basic idea	FPC
Paradigm	MIMD
Languages	C, Fortran, Pascal
Connectivity	Crossbar (reconfigurable)
Processors	Transputers (T800)
Parallelism	1024
Technology	VLSI

As far as the author has been able to discover, there are no other commercially available systems which offer an exactly similar configuration to this machine. The following system has some similarities, but lacks the crossbar connectivity:

Computing surface	Meiko
	Bristol
	UK

There are, of course, a very large number of suppliers who offer systems with a limited amount of parallelism based on single-card transputer implementations.

7D.1 Introduction

The Parsys SN1000 series architecture was generated under the European Community funded Esprit Programme's Project P1085, 'Supernode', whose objective was to provide cheap high-powered scientific computing, by the simultaneous use of large numbers (up to 1000) of moderately powerful microprocessors. The commercial marketplace, however, is becoming increasingly aware of the benefits of such powerful machines and their area of application is now much broader than was originally envisaged.

This contribution treats the Supernode architecture from the bottom up. It starts with some justification of parallel processing and then describes the system components and the way they are assembled to form complete systems.

All conventional digital computers are built from transistors connected together to form so-called gates which, in turn, are connected to form more complex building blocks. These are packaged as integrated circuits which are mounted on circuit cards and these are in turn plugged together to form a computer. The type of transistors used and the precise fashion in which they are connected together to form the gates define what is known as a logic family . The performance, power consumption, size and cost of a computer is very largely determined by the logic family used in its construction.

For many years the fastest logic family used in computers has been emitter coupled logic (ECL). This has the drawback, however, that it consumes comparatively large quantities of power per function, which limits the density of circuitry that can be achieved and thus drives up the cost and power consumption of the machine. The fastest and most powerful computers have thus been very expensive.

Recent advances in semiconductor processing have yielded a new logic family known as complementary metal-oxide silicon (CMOS) which has very low power consumption per function and can thus be packaged into very complex integrated circuits – so called very large scale integration (VLSI). It is this technology which has made the personal computer feasible due to the compactness and cheapness of the equipment which this high packing density makes possible. There has to be a drawback, of course, and this is that CMOS has a maximum speed somewhat lower than that of ECL, although even this may be overcome eventually. The loss in speed is much less than the reduction in expense, however, and so the CMOS computer is much more cost-effective. The aggregate power of a collection of many CMOS processors can thus be higher than that of an ECL processor of equivalent cost. The corollary is that a collection of CMOS processors of the same total performance as an ECL processor should cost significantly less.

Parallel processing is the art of making such a collection of processors perform the same job as a single expensive one. A number of techniques have been evolved for the interconnection and management of processors in this manner and they can be categorised in a number of ways. These include such headings as MIMD, SIMD, shared memory, message passing, pipelined, etc. The Supernode architecture is classified as an MIMD machine with separate memory and message passing by point-to-point serial links. The reasoning behind each of these choices is as follows.

MIMD: An MIMD machine consists of multiple independent computing units each of which operates simultaneously but independently on separate data. The other possibilities are SISD (a conventional computer), MISD (not a viable alternative) and SIMD (such as the AMT DAP). SIMD machines suffer drawbacks in terms of flexibility and the inability of the simple processors to perform complex arithmetic efficiently. The MIMD machine offers the best solution in terms of flexibility of operation to meet the requirements of a wide variety of algorithms.

An MIMD machine generally consists of a number of separate and independent complete processing units each with its own program, control unit and data. Some means must be provided to enable these units to communicate and cooperate. The different means of achieving these ends provide another level of classification of parallel architectures.

Separate memory: In order to simplify the cooperation and communication between programs on different processing units, many MIMD machines implement shared memory. This is an area of data storage accessible to more than one processing unit. It can be likened to a central filing area in an office, where each clerk can take away copies of the files and work upon them separately. Various techniques have been adopted for ensuring consistency of the data when more than one processor tries to change it at the same time and for avoiding the bottleneck such a shared resource causes when a large number of processors are employed. In general these techniques use large amounts of hardware and are not effective for numbers of processors above 10, although one manufacturer is designing a highly complex system which he claims will work with up to 100 processors.

Having separate memory overcomes these problems but places more of a burden upon the programmer, who has to ensure that the right data is properly distributed to the processors. It can also cause difficulties when a particular piece of information must be continuously updated and be available to all processors. Software techniques are evolving to solve even this problem.

Message passing: If separate autonomous programs are to cooperate then some protocol must be established to coordinate their operations. A system known as message passing has been developed which not only provides communication of data but also solves the problem of the management of the resources, since the messages act as tokens or permissions.

Point-to-point serial links: Some physical mechanism must exist for the passing of these messages. In a shared memory system this could be via the area of shared memory, but then some system must be established to alert the recipient of the message to its arrival and the sender to its collection. This is a further hardware overhead. A simpler mechanism is a communications channel, preferably with a minimum of circuitry, the simplest possible being a two-wire link down which data is serialised. If a processor has a fixed number of link connections associated with it then as the number of processors increases, so too does the number of channels and the communications bandwidth, thus avoiding saturation.

7D.2 The transputer

Conventional CMOS microprocessors are not readily connected together and programmed as parallel ensembles in the numbers necessary to achieve supercomputer performance, for the following reasons:

* By the time they have been surrounded by the other circuitry necessary to make them remember, communicate and synchronise they are bulky and power hungry
* The conventional languages in which they are programmed do not have the ability to describe operations in a parallel manner

Inmos wished to enter the microprocessor market with a unique product and designed one which was well adapted to the parallel mode of operation. It is known as the transputer and the Supernode is based upon it. A block diagram is given in Figure 7.14. The essence of this device is that it contains the majority of the components required to form the basic computational unit for an MIMD machine within one package.

It can be seen to contain two processor units – one for integer and memory address calculations and another for floating-point numbers. It contains a limited amount of memory which can be used for both programs and data and four serial links which can be connected to other transputers to form a communications network. It has an event controller which can be used to detect when external events, such as the depression of a keyboard key, have occurred and a peripheral and memory interface. This allows the connection of high-speed peripherals, such as disc or tape units, and further memory. The whole of the circuitry in the block diagram is contained in a single package about 3 cm square and, if no external memory is required, these can be connected into large working arrays with almost no other components.

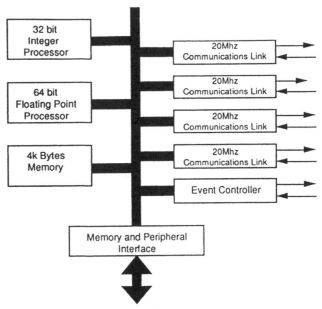

Figure 7.14   The Inmos T800 transputer architecture

The device shown, the T800, was developed within the same Supernode project as the architecture being described here. In terms of performance it is impressive, one transputer being able to achieve a computation rate of 2.25 MFLOPS. This is faster than the processor in any personal computer and is the equal of a small mainframe.

7D.3   Parsys architecture

If many processors are connected together by point-to-point links then, as the number of processors is increased, the ability to connect directly from one processor to another rapidly disappears if only a small number of links is available at each processor. For a large number of processors, therefore, it becomes necessary for messages to pass through intermediate processors if they are to travel from one side of the network to the other. If the amount of loading on intermediate processors in handling this traffic is to be minimised, then some optimal connection pattern must be found. The hypercube network has been proposed and used as such in, for instance, the CalTech Cosmic Cube and the Intel iPSC. As the number of processors grows, the maximum number of steps required to traverse the network grows slowly, but the number of links to each processor is also required to increase.

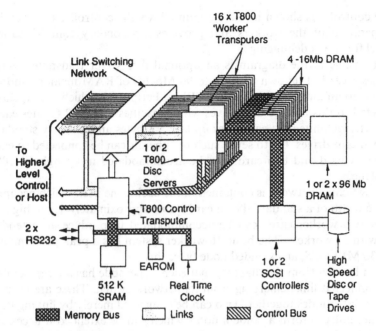

16 x T800
'Worker'
Transputers

4 -16Mb DRAM

Link Switching
Network

To
Higher
Level
Control
or Host

1 or 2
T800
Disc
Servers

1 or 2 x 96 Mb
DRAM

T800 Control
Transputer

2 x
RS232

EAROM

1 or 2
SCSI
Controllers

High
Speed
Disc or
Tape
Drives

512 K
SRAM

Real Time
Clock

▨ Memory Bus   ▭ Links   ▧ Control Bus

Figure 7.15 A single Supernode

The transputer has only four links, however, and if we are to build the
networks of hundreds of processors required to achieve supercomputer performance some other approach must be adopted. The original Supernode
concept was to build a compound processor from several transputers connected together such that there were enough spare links to form a hypercube of Supernodes. Within each node the connections were to be made
through a switching network which would be under software control and
allow an optimal network to be configured. The final architecture dispensed
with the fixed hypercube network between Supernodes and replaced it with
another switching network. The complete set of transputers can thus be
configured into any four-connected network in order to give the best routing of messages for the problem at hand. The Supernode grouping is still
retained, however, as a convenient module for construction, and is shown in
Figure 7.15.

In the diagram can be seen the 16 worker transputers with all their links
connected into a switching network, itself under the software control of a
further transputer. Experience has shown that the basic 4 kbytes of memory
within the transputer is not nearly enough for most applications and so a
further 4 to 16 Mbytes is added to each worker. Eight workers are accommodated on a single printed circuit card, whilst the control transputer and
its associated memory and interfaces occupy another card.

The control bus shown in the diagram allows the controller to supervise the operation of the workers and provides a secondary communication channel for use in debugging.

Also visible in the diagram is an optional disc server transputer which occupies a card of its own with up to 96 Mbytes of RAM memory and an interface to an industry standard SCSI bus. Peripherals which are typically connected to this bus are disc drives with capacities up to 1.2 Gbytes each, tape cartridge units with capacities up to 2.3 Gbytes and industry standard half inch tape drives. Up to seven such peripherals can be connected to each disc server card and two cards can be accommodated in a single SN1000 backplane.

The switching network is contained in the backplane itself which occupies half the width of a standard 48 cm card frame approximately 41 cm high. A further two worker cards can be accommodated to produce an extended node with 32 workers. The basic 16-worker system has a peak performance of 24-36 MFLOPS, an extended node twice this.

It can be seen from the diagram that each Supernode has a large number of unconnected links emerging from its network switch. These are used to connect Supernodes together. Two can be connected merely by linking their emerging links to form a tandem node, which can be extended if necessary to contain 64 workers and has a performance of 96-144 MFLOPS. A number of such machines have been manufactured.

Larger machines can be produced by the use of an outer level controller and outer level switch. These can be seen in Figure 7.16.

This has noticeable similarity to the previous diagram, complete Supernodes replacing the transputers of Figure 7.15, and demonstrates the hierarchical nature of the machine. In these larger systems the outer level controller supervises the node level controllers. Using this configuration machines can be built with more than 1024 workers and still have full reconfigurability. This ability to configure any network and change it under software control during the execution of a program is a unique feature of the machine.

Hosting: Initially, the machine was sold as an accelerator for conventional computers, the ones favoured being the IBM PC and Sun workstation series. In the case of the IBM PC an interface card plugs into the PC which carries a transputer and 2 Mbytes of memory. This connects to the Supernode via the transputer links. A similar card serves the same purpose in the Sun workstation or the MicroVAX. A recent introduction is a direct Ethernet connection which, with TCP/IP software support, allows direct access from networks. This removes the need for a host machine, although it is usually best to incorporate a cheap PC in the system as a console, particularly for diagnostic purposes.

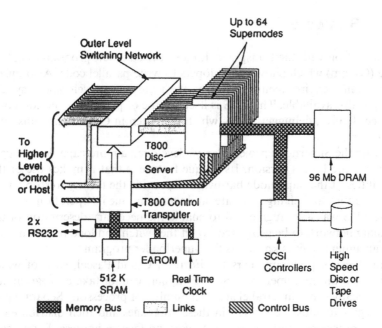

Figure 7.16   A complete Parsys supercomputer

Display: A display facility is provided as an option with a very high definition screen (1280 × 1024 pixels) with full colour. Four transputers are closely coupled to this screen and the remainder of the transputers to give very high performance graphics.

High-speed input/output: An interface has been built which can transfer data into and out of the system up to at least 60 Mbytes/s. This data is distributed automatically across the network of processors on input, or collected automatically on output. The device can transfer moving video data to and from the system and is of value anywhere that very large data rates are required. It is based on the standard Parsys printed circuit card and its mode of operation means that it can be used with any multi-transputer system.

TRAM mother card: A mother card is available which can be used to incorporate a number of the industry standard transputer modules known as TRAMs into a system. An increasing range of functions is available in this format and the first to be used are those providing Ethernet connectivity and low-end graphics.

7D.4   Software

In conjunction with the transputer, Inmos devised a new programming language (Occam) which allowed developers to write parallel code. A complete programming environment, known as the transputer development system (TDS) is also available. The TDS is itself a suite of programs – editor, compiler, configurer, debugger, etc. – which is written in Occam and runs on a transputer.

During the Supernode project Parsys developed a more capable debugger to replace the Inmos version. Its unique feature is that it makes use of the capabilities of the Supernode hardware to provide the facility to stop a program, examine and change its state, and then continue its operation.

The TDS was also augmented to enable the necessary description of the switching network to be generated, to set the switch and load programs into the transputers. This is known as the Superloader program.

Inmos also supply compilers for Fortran, C and Pascal, each of which can be used on the Supernode. Such compilers cannot take a program and automatically run it in parallel across a number of processors. Separate program segments must be written in these languages and then distributed to separate processors and be coordinated by an Occam harness. Parsys supplies a network communications package from Edinburgh University, known as TINY, which makes the use of these languages much easier.

Idris: Athough it provides a fully-tailored software development environment for transputer based systems, TDS does not provide very much support for running programs which need to control the hardware and perform I/O. It is also highly non-standard and cannot support more than one user. To deal with this problem, Parsys provide a UNIX-like operating system for the Supernode. The chosen system is Idris (Whitesmiths Inc., USA) which complies with the POSIX IEEE standard for UNIX systems, and proved easy to port to transputers. This operating system allows the transputers to be programmed in ANSI standard C, Fortran, Pascal or assembly-language. The compilers for these languages have no specific knowledge of parallelism. Separate programs written for each transputer are loaded and coordinated by the operating system.

Other software: Other environments are now becoming available which have similar facilities to those outlined above. One such is the Helios system currently available from Perihelion Ltd. A port of the Oracle database system will shortly be available on the machine, and will take advantage of the high bandwidth to parallel discs which can be available. Libraries of precompiled mathematical routines have been produced by Liverpool University. The availability of such modules makes the task of generating parallel programs much easier. In conjunction with FEGS Ltd, Parsys has produced a fully parallel solver toolkit for finite element equations. This has already been used to parallelise one commercial finite element package from PAFEC Ltd.

7E   GRIP:
   the GRIP multiprocessor

Chris Clack
University College London
London
UK

It is unfortunate that, in spite of considerable research interest in the technique, no commercial implementations of the graph reduction technique have yet reached the market. The program described here was carried out at University College London and at least resulted in a hardware implementation. GRIP (graph reduction in parallel) is a high-performance parallel computer designed to demonstrate the potential of functional programming as a technique for exploiting parallelism. The system characteristics are:

Basic idea	FPC
Paradigm	Graph reduction
Languages	Any functional
Connectivity	Bus
Processors	Motorola 68020
Parallelism	128
Technology	VLSI, PALs

A number of similar systems have been developed in university environments in both the UK and the USA. The majority of these are referred to in Multiprocessor Computer Architectures, *edited by Fountain and Shute.*

7E.1   Functional programming

Programming languages may be grouped into families with common characteristics. Two such families are the imperative languages and the functional languages. The former are the most well-known programming languages (such as Fortran and Pascal) and their common characteristic is that each gives a sequence of commands to the computer. By contrast, the characteristic of the functional languages (such as Miranda and MSL) is that a program consists of an expression to be evaluated in the context of a number of function definitions. Functional languages are often said to possess inherent parallelism because they do not insist on a predetermined ordering of instructions – it is left to the compiler (and, in a parallel machine, to the run-time system) to determine the most appropriate order of instructions for the underlying computer.

The functional programming research work at University College London is based on the thesis that functional languages provide a much easier route to the programming of parallel computers. The great expressive power of these languages enables functional programs to be shorter than their imperative counterparts; furthermore, the clean and simple semantics of functional languages means that the compiler is better able to automatically detect opportunities for parallelism.

At first sight, this type of programming might seem to provide a painless route to parallelism. It is certainly true that functional programming for parallel machines is possible without the need for any special parallel constructs in the language and without the need for detailed program tuning. However, it is important to realise that the compiler can only detect as much parallelism as the programmer has expressed in the program – many algorithms are inherently sequential and it is the job of the programmer to choose a parallel decomposition of the computation. For example, good performance on a parallel machine can be obtained by using a divide-and-conquer algorithm (which divides the task at hand into two or more independent sub-tasks, solves these separately, and then combines the results to solve the original task).

The advantages of parallel functional programming over parallel imperative programming are:

* The parallelism may be dynamically rather than statically defined, since it is detected automatically by the compiler and scheduled by the run-time system
* Communication and synchronisation between concurrent activities are handled transparently, rather than being coded explicitly by the programmer
* There are no extra language constructs and the same program will run without any changes on either a single-processor or a multi-processor computer. This has the added advantage that it is not necessary to change the program when the number of processors in an underlying parallel machine changes

7E.2 Parallel graph reduction

Figure 7.17 presents a simple model of a parallel graph reduction machine. In this model, the program is represented by its syntax graph, which is held in the shared graph memory. There are multiple processing elements which

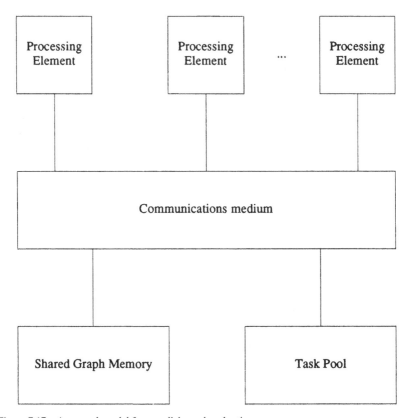

Figure 7.17   A general model for parallel graph reduction

concurrently execute *tasks* to transform sub-graphs of the program. Each task performs a sequence of transformations to evaluate (or reduce) a particular sub-graph to its final value. The final value physically overwrites the top node of the sub-graph, so that previous pointers to the sub-graph remain valid. Any task may initiate a concurrent sub-task to evaluate a subordinate sub-graph whose value it will subsequently require. A task may be *blocked* when it attempts to access a graph node which is currently being evaluated by another task; when evaluation of the node is complete, the blocked task can be resumed.

Task descriptors representing potentially executable tasks reside in the shared task pool and idle processing elements poll the task pool for work.

As long as the reduction process is indivisible, the graph can never be in an indeterminate state; the entire state of the computation is always defined by the current state of the graph and all communication is mediated by the graph. The overall view is that the graph serves as the communication and synchronisation mechanism between the concurrent activities [48,49].

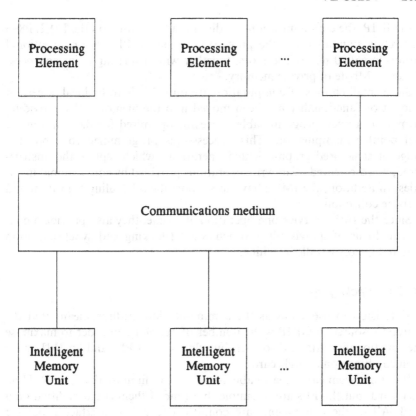

Figure 7.18   Physical structure of a parallel graph reduction machine

7E.3   GRIP system architecture and packaging

This section describes the GRIP machine, which has been designed to execute functional programs in parallel. Work on the GRIP project was carried out in partnership with International Computers Ltd and High Level Hardware Ltd. Whilst GRIP was designed for a specific purpose, its architecture has turned out to be quite general, and another group has already mounted a parallel dialect of Prolog on the same hardware [50].

Almost any parallel reduction machine can be thought of as a variation of the scheme shown in Figure 7.18. This is similar to Figure 7.17, except that the bottleneck on the shared graph memory has been ameliorated by physically distributing the memory (although it still represents a single address space) and the shared task pool has been distributed in a similar manner. Both the distributed shared graph and the distributed task pool are managed by intelligent memory units (IMUs).

In GRIP, the communications medium is a bus (based on the IEEE P896 Futurebus standard) and the processing elements (PEs) are conventional Motorola 68020 microprocessors, together with a floating-point coprocessor and 1 Mbyte of private memory.

Since small chunks of computation are quite likely to be local, a certain amount of functionality has been moved into the memories, by providing them with a microprogrammable processor optimised for data movement and pointer manipulation. This processor is programmed to support a range of structured graph-oriented operations, which replace the unstructured, word-oriented, read/write operations provided by conventional memories. In addition, the IMUs have to support the scheduling algorithm and garbage collection.

Since the IMUs service one operation at a time, they also provide a convenient locus of indivisibility to achieve the locking and synchronisation required by any parallel machine.

7E.3.1 Packaging

The decision to use a bus as the communication medium means that the scarcest resource in GRIP is the number of bus slots. In order to maximise the functionality attached to each bus slot, several PEs and an IMU have been combined on a single card.

It did not seem either reasonable or possible to fit more than one IMU on each card, but the PEs are so simple that four of them could be fitted on a card. All of the components are connected to a bus interface processor (BIP), which manages their communication with each other and with the bus. Figure 7.19 gives a block diagram of the GRIP card. This large single card can be replicated as often as is desired, up to a maximum of 21 on a half-metre Futurebus.

An added bonus of this architecture is that communication between a PE and its local on-board IMU is faster than communication with a remote IMU, and saves precious bus bandwidth.

7E.3.2 Host interfaces

Since GRIP is a research machine, its operation does not require very high bandwidth input/output. GRIP is attached to a UNIX host which provides all the file storage and I/O required. A 16-bit parallel DMA channel from the host is attached to an off-board extension of one of the PEs.

The host (an Orion) provides the development environment for all GRIP's firmware and software. In addition, each GRIP card is provided with a low-bandwidth 8-bit parallel diagnostics bus, which connects to a custom interface in the Orion. Through this bus, all the hardware compo-

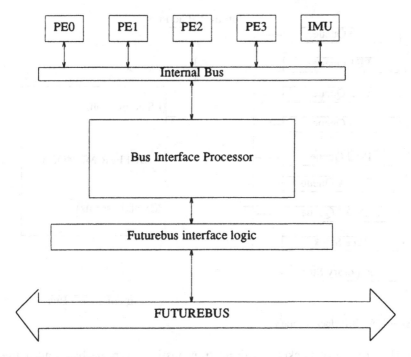

Figure 7.19 A GRIP card

nents on each card can be individually booted up and tested from diagnostic software running in the Orion.

7E.4 Bus architecture and protocols

In order to use the available bus bandwidth as efficiently as possible, the bus uses a packet-switched protocol (thus avoiding the latency of waiting for the IMU to effect a complex action and then send a reply). This led to the requirement for a packet-switching bus interface, the BIP, which is described below.

7E.4.1 The Bus interface processor

The BIP acts as a post office for the packet-switching system. It contains a fast buffer memory area which holds packets in transit, in which packets must be built before they are sent, and from which they may be read on receipt. The buffer memory is currently eight kwords of 34 bits, divided into a number of fixed-size packet frames.

The BIP also manages an input queue of packets for each PE and the

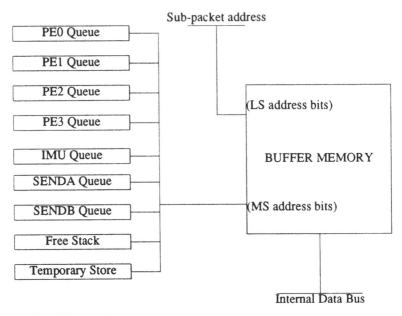

Figure 7.20   BIP block diagram

IMU, a queue of packets awaiting transmission over the bus, and a free stack containing empty packet frames. These queues contain packet addresses (not the packet data), which are used to address the packet data held in the buffer memory. Figure 7.20 gives a block diagram of the BIP organisation, and more details of the BIP design are given in [49].

7E.5   Intelligent memory architecture

The intelligent memory unit is a microprogrammable engine designed specifically for high-performance data manipulation operations on dynamic RAM. In this section the internal architecture of the IMU is outlined.

7E.5.1   Data path

The requirement for rapid data movement has led to the design of a rather unusual data path. The data path is based on a specially-programmed data multiplexor, built out of programmable array logic units (PALs), which provides two 40-bit registered outputs. Figure 7.21 gives the block diagram of the data path.

The M and G registers can be independently loaded from any of the five inputs, or from each other. In addition, a variety of masking operations are

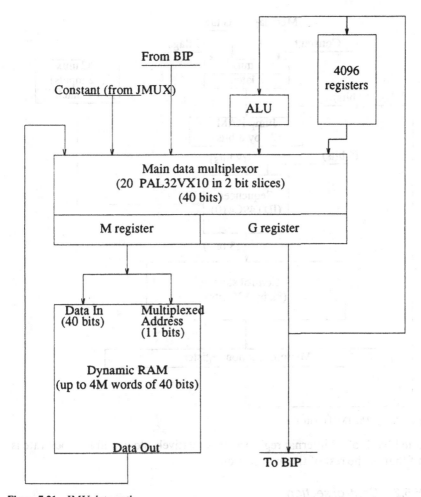

Figure 7.21 IMU data path

available, using a mask stored in the register bank to control the merge of M or G with one of the inputs.

The register bank consists of 4k 40-bit registers. A large number of registers are provided, because they are often used to hold long constants, thus allowing an 8-bit register address in the instruction to translate to a 40-bit constant.

The 'constant' input is actually driven by a 4-input 5-bit multiplexor (the J mux – see Figure 7.22), whose output is replicated eight times to cover 40 bits. Using a merge instruction under a mask from a register, a contiguous field of up to five bits can thus be inserted in any position in M or G.

The 32-bit ALU is built out of two quad-2901 parts, and contains a dual-

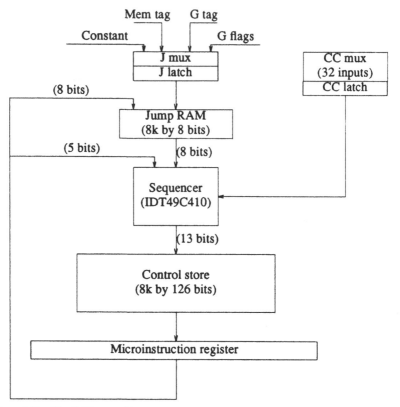

Figure 7.22   The IMU controller

ported bank of 64 internal registers. It is relatively slow, and its clock rate is half that of the rest of the data section.

7E.5.2   Control section

The IMU control section is conventional, except for the jump mechanism. Figure 7.22 shows its block diagram. There is one level of pipelining; the condition code (CC) and multi-way jump condition (J) are latched at the end of one cycle and used for conditional branching in the next. The sequencer is an extended 2910, with a 33-deep subroutine stack and a 16-bit address path.

The J latch output drives the least significant five bits of the Jump RAM, the other eight address bits being supplied by the microinstruction to select a page in the Jump RAM. The RAM translates this to an 8-bit address, which is fed to the sequencer together with five further bits from the microinstruction. This scheme allows 32-way jumps, provided they all land in the same 256-instruction page.

7E.6 Project status and future plans

GRIP is designed primarily to execute functional languages using parallel graph reduction, and all the software development effort has gone into supporting this aim. GRIP has been built and has shown promising early benchmark results. It now resides at the University of Glasgow, where it is the basis of further work on functional compilers, system software and industrial applications.

At University College London, work is currently under way to investigate a distributed memory architecture for parallel graph reduction. A prototype system has been designed which will run on networked UNIX workstations and it is intended that this should subsequently be ported to the nCUBE multiprocessor.

7F   AMT DAP:
*AMT DAP – a processor array in
a workstation environment*

David J. Hunt
AMT Ltd
Reading
UK

*This system is the latest of a very long line (in parallel computing terms). The
original work on the distributed array processor (DAP) systems was carried
out by a group at ICL in the 1970s. The basic AMT systems are very close to
the archetypal SIMD processor arrays, although the performance of current
devices is enhanced by 8-bit coprocessors.*

Basic idea	DPC
Paradigm	SIMD
Language	Fortran-Plus, C*
Connectivity	Mesh
Processors	1-bit & 8-bit
Parallelism	4096
Technology	VLSI

*Similar systems are those manufactured by MasPar (described in the next
contribution), and:*

Connection Machine 2	Thinking Machines Corp.
	Cambridge
	Massachusetts
	USA

7F.1   Introduction

A number of themes provide the basis for the DAP 500 and DAP 600 systems:

* Parallelism through the use of multiple function units is the key to ever
  increasing computational power

* For a very wide class of applications, an SIMD architecture is efficient in that only a single control unit is needed, and regular grid interconnect gives a match to many problem data structures
* Local memory associated with each processor gives high aggregate bandwidth thus avoiding the memory bottlenecks associated with scalar processors. In effect, the processing power is distributed throughout the memory
* VLSI technology is ideally suited to replication of functional units, thus giving a physically compact implementation
* There is an increasing emphasis on the use of workstations, either alone or as an adjunct to some central computer system. Hence, DAP is configured as an attached processor to a workstation or as a server on a network of workstations
* Data visualisation via a high-resolution colour display is important in monitoring the progress of a computation, and in interpreting its results. Hence, a small fraction of the high memory bandwidth of the DAP is made available for video output or other high-speed input/output operations

The DAP 500 [51] and DAP 600 are implementations, by AMT Ltd., of the DAP concept previously researched by ICL [52,53,54]. DAP installations include the University of Edinburgh and Queen Mary Westfield College, London. The latter operates a DAP service, bringing the total number of users to over 1000 worldwide, and representing a wide variety of applications.

7F.2 Architecture

In providing processing power through a set of individual processors, a fundamental design issue is the complexity of the individual processors: for a given quantity of hardware, should there be a few powerful processors or a large number of simple ones? DAP takes the extreme of the latter approach where the processors (PEs) are just one bit wide and there are very many of them: 1024 in DAP 500, or 4096 in DAP 600. Having very simple processors gives maximum flexibility in the higher-level functions that can be programmed.

The memory data path is also one bit wide for each PE, and at 10 MHz clock rate this gives an overall memory bandwidth of 1.3 Gbyte/s for DAP 500 or 5.1 Gbyte/s for DAP 600. The logic of 64 PEs fits in a 176-pin semi-custom chip, and the memory is provided using standard static memory components.

Figure 7.23 shows the basic principles of DAP operation. It shows a DAP 500, which has 1024 PEs arranged in a square array of 32 × 32, each with a

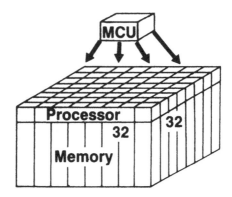

Figure 7.23   Principle of the DAP

one-bit wide memory below it, thus giving a cuboid of memory. The memory size is currently either 32 kbits or 64 kbits for each PE; a total of 4 or 8 Mbytes for the whole array. The DAP 600 has the same architecture, but has 4096 PEs arranged as a 64×64 array, and at least 16 Mbytes of memory.

Memory addresses are common to all PEs, so in a given instruction each PE accesses a bit of memory at the same memory address. Equivalently, a complete plane of memory is being accessed at the same time. Generally, each data item is held in the memory of a particular processor, with successive bits of each data item occupying successive locations. Thus a matrix of 16-bit values, for example, occupies 16 consecutive bit-planes of the memory. Some instructions provide access to one row of memory (corresponding to one row of PEs), or one word of memory (32 consecutive bits in a row), selected from a memory plane.

The instruction stream, common to all the PEs, is broadcast from a master control unit (MCU). To be more precise, the MCU performs address generation and decoding on behalf of all the processors, and a set of decoded control signals is broadcast. This means that little decoding is needed in individual processors.

7F.2.1   Processor element functions

Figure 7.24 shows the main components of one PE and its connection to memory, each of the data paths and registers shown being just one bit wide. The main components of the PE are three one-bit registers, named A, C and Q respectively, and an adder that performs arithmetic and logic functions. The detailed usage of the registers depends on how the DAP is programmed, but the Q register generally serves as an accumulator, and the C register holds a carry.

In a typical PE operation, the input multiplexor (at the left side of the fig-

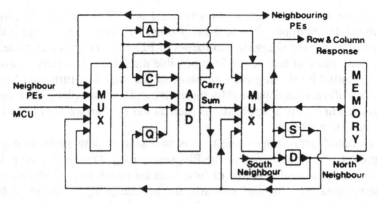

Figure 7.24 A processor element

ure) selects an operand bit from memory which is then input to the adder along with values from the C and Q registers. These three inputs are added, producing a sum which is optionally clocked into Q and a carry which is optionally clocked into C. An add operation on 16-bit integers, for example, is performed by 16 successive one-bit adds starting at the least significant bit, with the C register holding the carry between one bit position and the next.

The multiplexor near the right side of the figure selects data to be written back to the memory. In some cases the A register acts as a control input to this multiplexor. This means that for a given instruction, in those PEs where the A register is true the sum output of the adder is written to memory, but in those where A is false the old memory contents are selected and rewritten. This activity control is equivalent to switching off selected PEs in that the old memory contents are preserved, and is very important in implementing conditional operations both within functions and at the applications level.

An activity pattern may be loaded into the A register via the input multiplexor, and there are options to either write that value directly to A or to AND it with the existing A register contents. This latter option is very convenient for rapidly combining several conditions.

7F.2.2 Array interconnect

Although much processing is done with each PE working on data in its own local memory, it is important to be able to move data around the array in various ways, and two appropriate mechanisms are provided.

The first interconnection mechanism is that each PE can communicate with its four nearest neighbours in the array. Inputs from these North, East, South and West neighbours are shown at the left of Figure 7.24. Since the

PEs execute a common instruction stream, if one PE is accessing its North neighbour, for example, then so is every other PE. The overall effect is that a plane of bits in the Q registers in the set of PEs may, in one clock cycle, be shifted one place in any of the four possible directions. A matrix of words may be shifted by shifting each bit-plane of the matrix in turn, and longer distance shifts are implemented by successive shifts of one place. Such operations are important in applications such as the solution of field equations by relaxation methods.

The second array interconnection is two sets of data paths that pass along the rows and columns of the PEs respectively. One use of these data paths is in broadcasting a row of bits, such that each row of PEs receives the same data pattern, and similarly for broadcasting a column of bits. These broadcast operations each take just one basic clock cycle. Another use is in extracting data from the array, where the basic operations are to AND together all the rows or to AND together all the columns; variants of these operations permit data to be extracted from a single row or column.

Row and column data paths are important in areas such as matrix algebra. For example, in matrix inversion, they are used to extract the pivot column of a matrix and replicate it in every column. Another use is in a rapid global test implemented by ANDing all the rows in the array and then testing the result for all 1s.

7F.2.3   Master control unit

As already mentioned, the PE array is controlled by the master control unit (MCU). This is a 32-bit processor responsible for fetching and interpreting instructions, and its main components are shown in Figure 7.25. Instructions are held in a code store (separate from the array data store) which holds either 512 kbytes or 1 Mbyte, each instruction comprising four bytes.

7F.2.4   Fast input/output

In many applications, fast processing implies high data rates to or from external devices, and the DAP architecture provides this capability with only a small impact on processing performance. In the processor element diagram (Figure 7.24), the register shown as D may be loaded from the memory or written back to the memory, but does not otherwise take part in PE operations. Having loaded the plane of D registers from a plane of memory, the D plane may be shifted towards the North edge of the array, so that successive rows of the D plane are output at that edge. The D plane may similarly be used for input to the DAP by presenting successive data words as inputs at the South edge of the array.

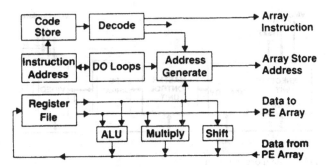

Figure 7.25   Functions of the master control unit

This shifting is done independently of the normal array instruction stream and is usually done at a higher clock rate. The D plane is controlled by one of a number of input/output couplers, rather than by the instruction stream, so this I/O facility may be thought of as a fast direct memory access (DMA) operation. For shifting the D plane, the coupler is independent of the array instruction stream and the operation is usually carried out at a higher clock rate. However, to load or store the D plane (which is necessary after each complete plane has been output or input), the coupler makes a request to the MCU along with the required memory address. This loading or storing suspends the instruction stream for one clock cycle.

When a DAP system has more than one coupler installed, the couplers arbitrate amongst themselves for use of the D plane, so the available bandwidth is shared between them. Couplers include buffering, which both matches the D plane clock speed to the external interface and avoids any crisis times associated with D plane arbitration.

For the DAP 500, the D plane connection at the edge of the array is 32-bits wide, and the overall bandwidth is 50 Mbyte/s, while only using 4% of the available memory bandwidth. For the DAP 600, the D plane connection is potentially 64 bits wide, but in practice most systems use only 32 bits, i.e. 1% of memory bandwidth.

An important coupler provides a video display facility. The patterns to be displayed are computed by the DAP in the array memory, then transferred to one of two frame buffers in the coupler for continuous refresh of a standard monitor via the usual colour lookup tables and A/D convertors. The screen resolution is 1024×1024 pixels, either 8-bit or 24-bit resolution.

Other couplers provide an external digital interface for input or output, either via a simple FIFO buffer, or via a more sophisticated double buffer arrangement with facilities for general purpose reordering of data as it passes through the coupler. External interfaces include a serial link.

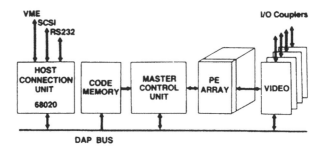

Figure 7.26   DAP system organisation

7F.2.5   System organisation

Figure 7.26 shows how the various DAP components connect together. With the DAP 600, an array support unit is added between the MCU and the array. During DAP processing there is a continuous flow of instructions from the code memory to the MCU and thence to the array. If I/O is in progress, then there is a concurrent flow of data between the D plane in the array and an I/O coupler.

The DAP bus along the bottom of the figure provides overall communication, including interfacing to a host computer system which provides program development facilities and access to conventional filestore and peripherals. A typical host is a Sun workstation running UNIX or a VAX system running VMS. The detail of the interfacing is managed by the host control unit (HCU).

The HCU performs a supervisory function including the allocation of DAP memory to user programs. In the event of a hardware failure it also provides diagnostic capability. The lowest level of control of DAP user programs resides in the MCU itself which runs a supervisor program in privileged mode to deal with scheduling of user programs and interrupt handling.

The I/O couplers are controlled by privileged MCU code in response to a supervisor entry from a user program, the necessary sequence of commands being sent to the coupler via the DAP bus. When a transfer is in progress, the coupler also uses the DAP bus to request the MCU to perform D plane loading or storing; this is carried out automatically by the MCU hardware.

The VMEbus may also be used to connect to medium-speed peripherals, taking advantage of the wide range of standard boards available in that format. A transfer on such a device is again initiated by a supervisor call from a user program, but the MCU passes on the request to the HCU for detailed management of the transfer.

7F.3 Software

7F.3.1 Fortran-Plus

The main programming language for DAP is Fortran-Plus [16] – an extended version of Fortran 77 having matrices and vectors as basic elements as well as scalars. This language has been the main influence on the parallel processing facilities in the proposed ISO/ANSI standard, currently referred to as Fortran 90.

A particular feature of the language is the facility for using masked assignments for local conditional operations, while IF statements are used for global transfer of control. The use and manipulation of Boolean matrices in masking, merging and selection are particularly useful in Fortran-Plus.

The language permits replication of vectors as well as scalars. This involves an explicit call to a function, to specify how the vector is broadcast; MATR gives a matrix of identical rows whereas MATC gives a matrix of identical columns. Various indexing constructs are also available: e.g. the extraction of a specified row or column of a matrix giving a vector result.

Fortran-Plus offers a range of precisions: integers from 8- to 64-bit length and reals from 24- to 64-bit length. There is a continuous tradeoff between word length and performance, and of course memory usage.

7F.3.2 Assembly language

Fortran-Plus provides a good match between the capabilities of the DAP hardware and the requirements of applications; the word length options and Boolean manipulation functions give great flexibility. However, in some applications special number representations may be required for optimum performance.

These can be programmed in the assembly language APAL. This necessarily involves bit-level operations and detailed coding but two aspects mitigate the amount of work involved: the ability to mix Fortran-Plus and APAL at the subroutine level, so it is often appropriate to have only a few critical routines in APAL; and the availability of powerful macro facilities in APAL, permitting in some cases an intermediate level language to be customised by the user.

7F.3.3 Run-time system

DAP programs are compiled on the host and downloaded into the DAP for execution. A standard host program controls the execution of the DAP program by calling routines that perform the following functions:

* Load a specified object program into the DAP
* Transfer a block of data between the host and the DAP in either direction
* Initiate processing at a named subroutine within the DAP program. The host program is suspended while the DAP is running
* Release the DAP resource; this also happens automatically when a host program terminates

A DAP simulation provides all the above facilities, but running entirely on a serial processor. Although the performance is much lower than that of a real DAP, this does provide a route for experimentation with short sections of DAP code. Interactive debugging facilities are available for both real and simulated DAP systems.

7F.3.4   Library routines

The Fortran-Plus compilation system incorporates extensive libraries of low-level routines that implement arithmetic and data manipulation operations as the appropriate sequences of bit-level operations. The presence of such routines is transparent to the user.

At a higher level, a wide variety of library routines is available to provide applications-related functions. These include:

* Matrix manipulation
* Signal processing
* Image processing
* Data reorganisation
* Complex mathematical functions
* Graphics

7F.3.5   Data mappings

In practice, many problems are larger than the PE array, and in this case the processing is carried out in sections that match the size of the array. The problem array is declared as a set of DAP-sized matrices, and the code works serially through the matrices of this set. Two possible data mappings for oversize problems are:

* Sheet mapping, in which each array sized section contains a neighbourhood of the problem array
* Crinkle mapping, in which each PE holds a neighbourhood of the problem array

Advanced users can employ more sophisticated mappings to suit their individual problems. To assist with this, a scheme known as parallel data transforms is available which includes a compact notation for describing regular data mappings, and a means for automatically generating code to perform the required transform.

7F.4   Application areas

DAP was created to tackle large computing problems such as the solution of field equations and matrix manipulation. It is very successful at such tasks, but has also proved suitable for other applications involving large structured data sets, including the following.

* Field equations
* Finite element analysis
* Linear algebra
* Quantum chromodynamic calculations
* Medical imaging
* Radar imaging
* Image processing
* Graphics
* Character handling
* Design automation

7F.5   Performance

Table 7.3 indicates the performance of the DAP 610 (running at 10 MHz) for processing matrix operands. The figures are given in MFLOPS or MOPS (millions of operations per second). The DAP 610 is an enhanced version of the DAP 600 which has an 8-bit coprocessor associated with each 1-bit processing element.

The DAP is generally much better able to achieve and sustain the quoted performance figures than a conventional processor, since operations such as address arithmetic and data movement usually take much less time than computing arithmetic results, whereas on a conventional processor these overheads are often greater than the arithmetic times.

Table 7.3 *Performance of the DAP 610*

Precision	Datatype	Function	Performance
1-bit	Logical		up to 40 000 MOPS
8-bit	Character		up to 4 000
8-bit	Integer		
		Add	1 600
		Multiply	250
		Multiply by scalar	up to 1 200
32-bit	Real		
		Add	48 MFLOPS
		Multiply	32
		Square	64
		Divide	24
		Square-root	44
		Maximum value	200

7F.6   Conclusions

The DAP has already shown its enormous potential, and its wide exposure to users has established a strong base of applications software and parallel algorithm techniques. The software is mature, permitting easy program development, and is ready to move forward with new advances in parallel programming languages. The emergence of DAP in a workstation environment makes it especially convenient to use, and the inbuilt display capability gives new insights into the nature of the computations as they are being performed.

7G   *MasPar MP-1:*
the design of the MasPar MP-1: a cost-effective massively parallel computer

John R. Nicholls
MasPar Computer Corporation
Sunnyvale, California
USA

The MasPar corporation was set up comparatively recently by ex-DEC personnel to exploit research which had been carried out in that company. The MP-1 systems are perhaps the first of the second-generation massively parallel designs to reach the market. This contribution concentrates on the hardware aspects of the system, whose characteristics are:

Basic idea	DPC
Paradigm	SIMD
Language	C
Connectivity	Mesh, crossbar
Processors	1-bit and 4-bit
Parallelism	16 384
Technology	VLSI

The system probably has most in common with:

Connection Machine 2	Thinking Machines Corp.
	Cambridge
	Massachusetts
	USA

7G.1   Introduction

By using CMOS VLSI and replication of components effectively, massively parallel computers can achieve extraordinary performance at low cost. Key issues are how the processor and memory are partitioned and replicated, and how inter-processor communication and I/O are accomplished. This contribution describes the design and implementation of the MasPar MP-1, a general-purpose massively parallel computer (MPC) system that achieves peak computation rates greater than 10^9 floating-point operations per second, yet is priced like a minicomputer.

MPCs use more than a thousand processors to obtain computational performance unachievable by conventional processors [55,56,7]. The MasPar MP-1 system is scalable from 1024 to 16 384 processors and its peak performance scales linearly with the number of processors. A 16k processor system delivers 30 000 MIPS peak performance where a representative instruction is a 32-bit integer add. In terms of peak floating-point performance, the 16k processor system delivers 1500 MFLOPS single-precision (32-bit) and 650 MFLOPS double-precision (64-bit), using the average of add and multiply times.

To effectively apply a high degree of parallelism to a single application, the problem data is spread across the processors. Each processor computes on behalf of one or a few data elements in the problem. This approach is called data-parallel [57] and is effective for a broad range of compute-intensive applications.

Partitioning the computational effort is the key to high performance, and the simplest and most scalable method is data parallelism. The architecture of the MP-1 [58] is scalable in a way that permits its computational power to be increased along two axes: the performance of each processor and the number of processors. This flexibility is well-matched to VLSI technology where circuit densities continue to increase at a rapid rate. The scalable nature of massively parallel systems protects the customers' software investment while providing a path to increasing performance in successive products [59].

Because its architecture provides tremendous leverage, the MP-1 implementation is conservative in terms of circuit complexity, design rules, integrated circuit geometry, clock rates, margins and power dissipation. A sufficiently high processor count reduces the need to have an overly aggressive (and thus expensive) implementation. Partitioning and replication make it possible to use low cost, low power workstation technology to build very high performance systems. Replication of key system elements happily enables both high performance and low cost.

7G.2 The array control unit

Because massively parallel systems focus on data parallelism, all the processors can execute the same instruction stream. The MP-1 has an SIMD architecture that simplifies the highly replicated processors by eliminating their instruction logic and instruction memory, and thus saves millions of gates and hundreds of megabytes of memory in the overall system. The

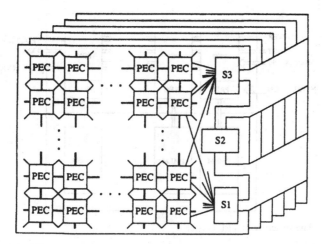

Figure 7.27   The MP-1 processor array

processors in an SIMD system are called processor elements (PEs) to indicate that they contain only the data path of the processor.

The MP-1 array control unit (ACU) is a 14 MIPS scalar processor with a RISC-style instruction set and a demand-paged instruction memory. The ACU fetches and decodes MP-1 instructions, computes addresses and scalar data values, issues control signals to the PE array and monitors the status of the PE array. The ACU is implemented with a microcoded engine to accommodate the needs of the PE array, but most of the scalar ACU instructions execute in one 70 ns clock period. The ACU occupies one printed circuit card.

7G.3   The processor array

The MP-1 processor array (Figure 7.27) is configurable from 1 to 16 identical processor cards. Each card has 1024 processor elements (PEs) and associated memory arranged as 64 processor clusters (PECs) of 16 PEs per cluster. The processors are interconnected via the X-Net neighbourhood mesh and the global multistage crossbar router network (discussed in Sections 7G.4 and 7G.5 respectively).

The processor cards are approximately 36 cm by 48 cm and use a high-density connector to mate with a common backplane. A processor card dissipates less than 50 watts; a full 16k PE array and ACU dissipate less than 1000 watts.

A PE cluster (Figure 7.28) is composed of 16 PEs and 16 processor memories (PMEMs). The PEs are logically arranged as a 4 × 4 array for the X-Net two-dimensional mesh interconnection. Each PE has a large internal register file, shown in the figure as PREG. Load and store instructions

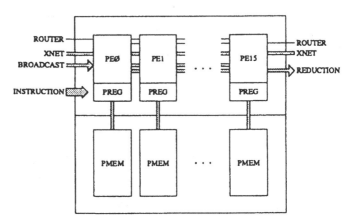

Figure 7.28   The structure of a PE cluster

move data between PREG and PMEM. The ACU broadcasts instructions and data to all PE clusters and the PEs all contribute to an inclusive-OR reduction tree received by the ACU. The 16 PEs in a cluster share an access port to the multistage crossbar router.

The MP-1 processor chip is a full-custom design that contains 32 identical PEs (two PE clusters) implemented in two-level metal, 1.6 μm CMOS and packaged in a cost-effective 164 pin plastic quad flat pack. The die is 11.6 mm by 9.5 mm, and has 450 000 transistors. A conservative 70 ns clock yields low power and robust timing margins.

Processor memory, PMEM, is implemented with 1Mbit DRAMs that are arranged in the cluster so that each PE has 16 kbytes of EEC-protected data memory. A processor card has 16 Mbytes of memory, and a 16 card system has 256 Mbytes of memory. The MP-1 instruction set supports 32 bits of PE number and 32 bits of memory addressing per PE, so the memory system size is limited only by cost and market considerations.

As an MP-1 system is expanded, each increment adds PEs, memory and communication resources, so the system always maintains a balance between processor performance, memory size and bandwidth, and communications and I/O bandwidth.

7G.3.1   Processor elements

The MP-1 processor element design is different from that of a conventional processor because a PE is mostly data path logic and has no instruction fetch or decode logic. SIMD system performance is the product of the number of PEs and the speed of each PE, so the performance of a single PE is not as important as it is in conventional processors. Present VLSI densities and the relative tradeoffs between the number of processors and processor

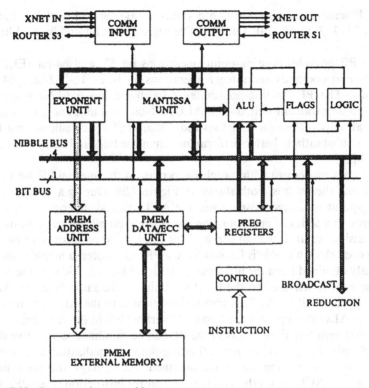

Figure 7.29 Processor element architecture

complexity encourage putting many PEs on one chip. The resulting design tradeoff between PE area and PE performance tends to reduce the PE architecture to the key essentials.

Each PE, shown in Figure 7.29, is designed to deliver high-performance floating-point and integer computation together with high memory bandwidth and communications bandwidth, yet have minimum complexity and silicon area to make it feasible to replicate many PEs on a single high-yield chip.

Like present RISC processors, each PE has a large on-chip register set (PREG) and all computations operate on the registers. Load and store instructions move data between the external memory (PMEM) and the register set. The register architecture substantially improves performance by reducing the need to reference external memory. The compilers optimise register usage to minimise load/store memory traffic.

Each PE has forty 32-bit registers available to the programmer and an additional eight 32-bit registers that are used internally to implement the MP-1 instruction set. With 32 PEs per die, the resulting 48 kbits of register occupy about 30% of the die area, but represent 75% of the transistor count. Placing the registers on chip yields an aggregate PE-PREG bandwidth of 117 Gbytes/s with 16k PEs. The registers are bit and byte addressable.

Each PE provides floating-point operations on 32- and 64-bit IEEE or VAX format operands and integer operations on 1-, 8-, 16-, 32- and 64-bit operands. The PE floating-point/integer hardware has a 64-bit mantissa unit, a 16-bit exponent unit, a 4-bit ALU, a 1-bit logic unit and a flags unit. The floating-point/integer unit uses more than half of the silicon area but provides substantially better performance than the bit-serial designs used in earlier MPCs.

Most data movement within each PE occurs on the internal PE 4-bit nibble bus and the bit bus, both shown in Figure 7.29. During a 32- or 64-bit floating-point or integer instruction, the ACU microcode engine steps the PEs through a series of operations on successive 4-bit nibbles to generate the full precision result. For example, a 32-bit integer add requires eight clocks; during each clock a nibble is fetched from a PREG register, a nibble is simultaneously obtained from the mantissa unit, the nibbles are added in the ALU and the sum is delivered to the mantissa unit. At the same time, the ALU delivers a carry bit to the flags unit to be returned to the ALU on the next step. The ALU also updates the zero and overflow bits in the flags unit.

The different functional units in the PE can be simultaneously active during each micro-step. For example, floating-point normalisation and denormalisation steps use the exponent, mantissa, ALU, flags and logic units together. The ACU issues the same micro-control instruction to all PEs, but the operation of each PE is locally enabled by the E-bit in its flags unit. During a floating-point operation, some micro-steps are data dependent, so the PEs locally disable themselves as needed by the exponent and mantissa units.

Because the MP-1 instruction set focusses on conventional operand sizes of 8-, 16-, 32-, and 64-bits, MasPar can implement subsequent PEs with smaller or larger ALU widths, without changing the programmer's instruction model. The internal 4-bit nature of the PE is not visible to the programmer, but does make the PE flexible enough to accommodate different front end workstation formats. The PE hardware supports both little-endian and big-endian format integers, VAX floating-point F, D and G format, and IEEE single and double precision floating-point formats.

Along with the PE controls, the ACU broadcasts four bits of data per clock onto every PE nibble bus to support MP-1 instructions with scalar source operands. The PE nibble and bit bus also drive a 4 bit wide inclusive OR reduction tree that returns to the ACU. Using this tree. the ACU can assemble a 32-bit scalar value from the OR of 16 384 32-bit PREG values in eight clocks plus a few clocks of pipeline overhead.

7G.3.2 Processor memory

Because only load and store instructions access PMEM processor memory, the MP-1 overlaps memory operations with PE computation. When a load or store instruction is fetched, the ACU queues the operation to a separate state machine that operates independently of the normal instruction stream. Up to 32 load/store instructions can be queued and executed while the PE computations proceed, as long as the PREG register being loaded or stored is not used by the PE in a conflicting way. A hardware interlock mechanism in the ACU prevents PE operations from using a PREG register before it is loaded and from changing a PREG register before it is stored. The optimising compilers move loads earlier in the instruction stream and delay using registers that are being stored. The 40 registers in each PE assist the compilers in obtaining substantial memory/execution overlap.

The PMEM processor memory can be directly or indirectly addressed. Direct addressing uses an address broadcast from the ACU, so the address is the same in each PE. Using fast page mode DRAMs, a 16k PE system delivers memory bandwidth of over 12 Gbytes/s. Indirect addressing uses an address computed locally in each PE's PMEM address unit and is a major improvement over earlier SIMD architectures [60] because it permits the use of pointers, linked lists and data structures in array memory. Indirect addressing is about one third as fast as direct addressing.

7G.4 X-Net mesh interconnect

The X-Net interconnect directly connects each PE with its eight nearest neighbours in a two-dimensional mesh. Each PE has four connections at its diagonal corners, forming an X-pattern similar to the Blitzen X grid network [61]. A tristate node at each X intersection permits communications with any of the eight neighbours using only four wires per PE.

Figure 7.27 shows the X-Net connections between PE clusters. The PE chip has two clusters of 4×4 PEs and uses 24 pins for X-Net connections. The cluster, chip, and card boundaries are not visible and the connections at the PE array edges are wrapped round to form a torus. The torus facilitates several important matrix algorithms and can emulate a one-dimensional ring with only two X-Net steps.

All the PEs have the same direction controls so that, for example, every PE sends an operand to the North and simultaneously receives an operand from the South. The X-Net uses a bit-serial implementation to minimise pin and wire costs and is clocked synchronously with the PEs; all transmissions are parity checked. The PEs use the shift capability of the mantissa unit to generate and accumulate bit-serial messages. Inactive PEs can serve as pipeline stages to expedite long-distance communication jumps through several PEs. The MP-1 instruction set [58] implements X-Net operations that move or distribute 1-, 8-, 16-, 32- and 64-bit operands with time proportional to either the product or the sum of the operand length and the distance. The aggregate X-Net communication rate in a 16k PE system exceeds 20 Gbytes/s.

7G.5   Multistage crossbar interconnect

The multistage crossbar interconnection network provides global communication between all the PEs and forms the basis for the MP-1 I/O system. The MP-1 network uses three router stages shown as S1, S2 and S3 in Figure 7.27 to implement the function of a 1024 × 1024 crossbar switch. Each cluster of 16 PEs shares an originating port connected to router stage S1 and a target port connected to stage S3. Connections are established from an originating PE through stages S1, S2 and S3 and then to the target PE. A 16k PE system has 1024 PE clusters, so each stage has 1024 router ports and the router supports up to 1024 simultaneous connections.

Originating PEs compute the number of a target PE and transmit it to the router S1 port. Each router stage selects a connection to the next stage based on the target PE number. Once established, the connection is bi-directional and can move data between the originating and target PEs. When the connection is closed, the target PE returns an acknowledgement. Because the router ports are multiplexed among 16 PEs, an arbitrary communication pattern takes 16 or more router cycles to complete.

The multistage crossbar is well-matched to the SIMD architecture because all communication paths are equal length, and therefore all communications arrive at their targets simultaneously. The router connections are bit-serial and are clocked synchronously with the PE clock; all transmissions are parity checked. The PEs use the mantissa unit to simultaneously generate outgoing router data and assemble incoming router data.

The MP-1 router chip implements part of one router stage. The router chip connects 64 input ports to 64 output ports by partially decoding the target PE addresses [62]. The full-custom design is implemented in two-level metal 1.6 μm CMOS and packaged in a 164-pin plastic quad flat pack. The die is 7.7 mm by 8.1 mm and incorporates 110 000 transistors. Three router chips are used on each processor card.

A 16k PE system has an aggregate router communication bandwidth in excess of 1.5 Gbytes/s. For random communication patterns the multistage router network is essentially equivalent to a 1024 × 1024 crossbar network with far fewer swiches and wires.

7G.6   Conclusion

Through a combination of massively parallel architecture, design simplicity, cell replication, CMOS VLSI, conservative clock rates, surface mount packaging and volume component replication, the MasPar MP-1 family delivers very high performance with low power and low cost. The massively parallel design provides cost-effective computing for today and a scalable growth path for tomorrow.

7H WASP:
the associative string processor

Ian Jaloweicki
Aspex Microsystems Ltd
Uxbridge, Middlesex
UK

The Aspex company was set up by staff from Brunel University, UK in order to exploit the ideas developed at the university. The system which they are marketing is noteworthy, both because it is a rare implementation of the associative paradigm, and because of the advanced technology being employed. The author of this contribution has chosen to concentrate on the latter aspect. The system characteristics are:

Basic idea	DPC
Paradigm	Association
Language	C, assembly
Connectivity	Linear near neighbour
Processors	1-bit
Parallelism	256k
Technology	VLSI, wafer scale integration (WSI)

As far as the author is aware, no similar systems are currently available, although one company offers a linear SIMD array of single-bit processors:

AIS 5000	AIS Inc
	Ann Arbor
	Michigan
	USA

7H.1   Introduction

An associative string processor (ASP) is a computer which processes data according to its contents. By its nature, it belongs to the class of data parallel machines, in that it is able to apply instructions to sets of data items. A key feature is content addressability, which enables items to be identified by their content, not their location in store.

The Brunel ASP is a massively parallel, fine-grain architecture, suitable for VLSI and WSI fabrication.

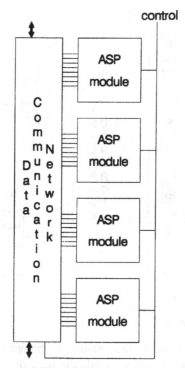

Figure 7.30   Connections between ASP modules

7H.2   ASP module architecture

Emerging from long-term research at Brunel University and being developed by Aspex Microsystems Ltd, UK, ASP modules and support software comprise highly versatile fault-tolerant building blocks for the simple construction of dynamically reconfigurable, low function parallel, high data parallel, second generation, massively parallel computer (MPC) systems.

7H.2.1   ASP modules

The potential offered by the ASP architecture stems from the realisation that heterogeneous architectures of this type could offer the most cost-effective solution for second generation MPCs. The fundamental building block of such systems will be the ASP module. According to application requirements, an appropriate combination of ASP modules is attached to the control bus and data communications network as indicated in Figure 7.30. The data communications network can be constructed so as to implement any general-purpose network topology (e.g. crossbar, mesh or binary n-cube) or

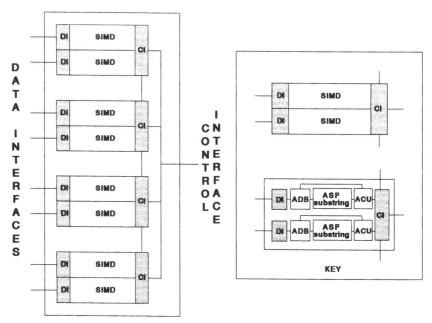

Figure 7.31   An ASP module

application-specific topology (e.g. shuffle-exchange or butterfly), to enable data transfer between pairs of selected ASP modules.

ASP modules comprise three different component types: the ASP substring, the ASP data interface (DI) and the ASP control interface (CI), as shown in Figure 7.31, which also indicates that the CI can support a local ASP data buffer (ADB) or an ASP control unit (ACU). System variants can be constructed whereby each ACU is an autonomous microcontroller, under the coordination of a single high-level control unit. Alternatively, the system may comprise no local controllers, where the CI is a port to a global controller which will provide all the system control.

7H.2.1.1 ASP substrings

An ASP substring is a programmable, homogeneous and fault-tolerant data parallel MPC incorporating a string of identical associative processing elements (APEs), a reconfigurable inter-processor communications network and a vector data buffer for overlapped data input/output, as illustrated in Figure 7.32.

As shown in Figure 7.33, each APE incorporates a 64-bit data register and a 6-bit activity register, a 70-bit parallel comparator, a single-bit full adder, four single-bit registers (representing carry (C), matching and destination (M and D) and active (A) bits) and control logic for local processing and communication with other APEs. In operation, data items are distrib-

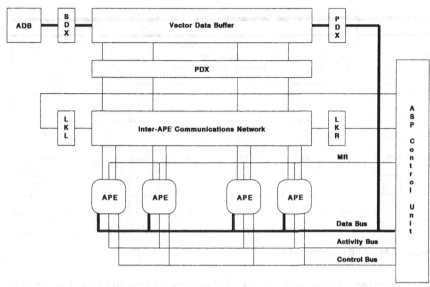

Figure 7.32 An ASP substring unit

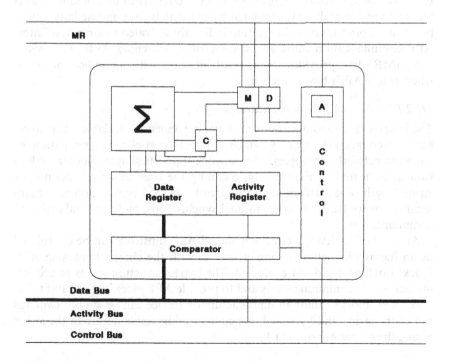

Figure 7.33 An associative processing element (APE)

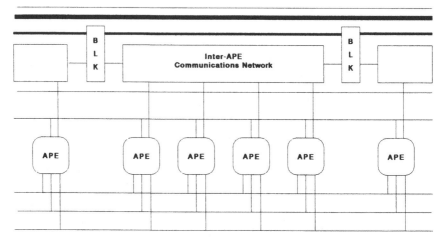

Figure 7.34   ASP block bypassing

uted over the data registers. Each ASP substring performs a kind of set processing, in which a subset of active APEs may be programmed to perform scalar-vector and vector-vector operations. Active APEs (denoted by the A-register) are either directly activated by the match data and activity values broadcast from the controller, or are indirectly activated as a result of inter-APE communication initiated by some other matching APE. The match reply (MR) line provides the control interface with an indication as to whether any APEs have matched.

7H.2.1.2   Inter-APE communications

The inter-APE communications network implements a scalable, fault-tolerant interconnection strategy which supports cost-effective emulation of common network topologies. The network supports simple, modular extension as indicated in Figure 7.34, enabling the user to simply extend the string length. The network supports circuit-switched asynchronous communication, as well as more conventional synchronous, bi-directional multi-bit communication.

At an abstract level, a circularly-linked ASP substring can be considered as an hierarchical chordal-ring structure, with the chords bypassing APE blocks (and groups of APE blocks). The bypass structure serves to accelerate inter-APE communications and to provide APE block-defect fault tolerance. APE blocks failing in manufacture or service can be simply switched out of the string and bypassed, the content-addressable nature of the string easing the reconfiguration task.

7H.2.1.3   Data input/output

The upper levels of the input/output hierarchy consist of paging information between an external global memory store and the ASP data buffers (if
present). At the lowest level of the buffering hierarchy, the vector data
buffer VDB (see Figure 7.32) supports a dual-port exchange of vector data
with the APE data registers and with the local memories. The first of these
is APE-parallel and therefore is a very high-bandwidth exchange. The second is APE-sequential and provides a slower exchange between the VDB
and the local memory, although this may be fully overlapped with parallel
processing and so does not necessarily present a sequential overhead.

7H.3   System development

System development of ASP modules is underway, employing a variety of
technologies intended to provide comparative data on implementation
issues. Initial system developments employ a custom VLSI ASP, and are
intended as a test bed for the development of the full scope of the system,
including system software, operating systems, languages, applications and
development tools. The current developments are the Trax and MPPC systems.

7H.3.1   The Trax machine

Trax-1 is a data-parallel machine designed for off-line analysis of very complex streamer chamber images. The machine is constructed in a VME crate
using triple-height Eurocards. Its architecture is shown in Figure 7.35.

The Trax ASP system is configured as a single string of 16k APEs, built
from an array of 64-APE VLSI chips (see Table 7.4) and one double-
buffered ADB of 16k 32-bit words.

Each VLSI chip has 64 APEs, each with a 64-bit data register and a 6-bit
activity register. The ADB will be connected to the APE array via eight primary data transfer channels. The ADB is also accessible to the intermediate-level ASP controller (IAC) via a single secondary data channel. Trax
I/O speed (ADB-ASP) is 320 Mbytes/s. The Trax system comprises the following major subsystems:

* A 16k APE array with dual 16k × 32-bit ADBs, configured as a single
  string and built from eight APE array cards. Each card contains 2k APEs
  and a 4 kword ADB array. All cards are connected to the host via a common SDT channel. Additional APE array cards may be added to upgrade
  the processor capacity.

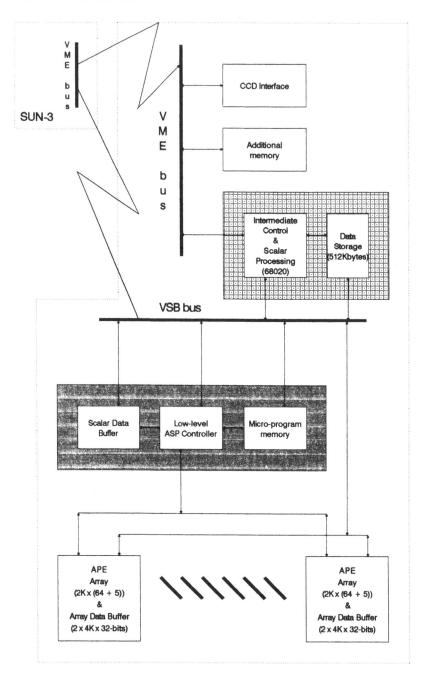

Figure 7.35   TRAX machine architecture

Table 7.4 *VLSI APE chip characteristics*

Chip area	7 mm × 8 mm
No. of pins	120
Clock rate	16 MHz
No. of APEs	64
No. of transistors	64k

* A low-level ASP controller (LAC) with 256 kbytes of writable micropro-gram store, 8 kbyte I/O scalar data FIFOs and a 16 kbyte scratchpad buffer.
* An intermediate-level ASP controller (IAC) containing a 16 MHz 68020 CPU, DMAC, 256 kbyte program store and 512 kbyte ASP data store.
* A high-level ASP controller (HAC), comprising the Sun host system, accessing the Trax hardware via standard VME and VSB backplane pro-tocols.

An ASP application program running on the Trax architecture can be divided into three distinct parts according to the level of the control hierar-chy. Procedures targeted at the HAC are grouped in high-level software ASP modules (HAMs), those targeted at the IAC are grouped into IAMs and those for the LAC are grouped into LAMs.

Trax systems provide all the necessary software support to develop, debug and run ASP applications, including programming tools, debugging tools, system software, run-time libraries and Unix device drivers. The Trax programming language is based on Modula-2, but interfaces to other pro-gramming languages at the high and intermediate expression levels are fea-sible.

7H.3.2 MPPC

A new ASP system currently under development is the massively parallel processing consortium (MPPC) computer. The purpose of the MPPC pro-ject is to build a real-time processor for on-line event detection in streamer chamber and other experiments. It is intended to implement a 64k APE machine in the same physical volume as the Trax system, using hybrid wafer-scale technology.

The architecture of the MPPC machine is essentially similar to that of the Trax system. All three levels of ASP controllers will be the same as those for the Trax. The ASP boards for this system will use hybrid modules known as HASP devices and pioneering high bandwidth direct interfaces to instru-mentation data sources as well as the more conventional buffered (ADB) interface. The HASP device currently under development will employ conventional ceramic thin-film hybrid technology, in which each 6 cm package will incorporate 1024 APEs by mounting 16 dies of the VASP64 circuit together with two 32-bit I/O channels. All necessary buffering will be integrated, as will the switching network for enhancing the inter-APE communications.

In the MPPC system, each module will have its own primary data channel and ADB to allow extremely high bandwidth direct data feed for real-time processing. The local ADB memories will be dual-ported and large enough to store more than one event, so that memory can be fed with the next event while the previous one is being processed.

The resulting processor board is designed to make maximum use of the components from the Trax-1 ASP boards. Each contains eight modules of 1024 APEs, which may be configured into a string of 8192 APEs. One memory buffer of 2 kwords is associated with each module to enhance data I/O.

7H.4   Wafer scale development

The architecture of the printed circuit cards and the hybrid modules is shared with the wafer scale integration ASP (WASP) being developed jointly by Brunel University and Aspex Microsystems. The ASP concept has been specifically developed to exploit the opportunities presented by the latest advances in the VLSI–ULSI–WSI technological trend, high-density system assembly techniques and state-of-the-art packaging technologies. Highly successful WASP1 and WASP2a (ULSI) and WASP2b (whole wafer) demonstrators have already been constructed. A next-generation device, WASP3, is primarily a test bed for the demonstration of a definitive highly fault/defect-tolerant ASP processor kernel with 256 APEs.

7H.4.1   Implementation

WASP represents a challenging and innovative method of implementing ASP modules on a single undiced quadrant of a silicon wafer. As indicated in Figure 7.36, a WASP device is composed from three different VLSI-sized blocks known as data routers (DRs), ASP substrings and control routers (CRs). The DR and CR blocks incorporate routing to connect ASP substring rows to a common data interface (DI) and a common control interface (CI) respectively. Moreover, both these blocks incorporate LKL and LKR ports to effect row-to-row extension of ASP substrings.

7H.4.2   Fault tolerance

Each of the DR, ASP and CR blocks has a defect/fault-tolerant design, so that APE blocks within the ASP substrings, individual ASP substring blocks and entire ASP substring rows (and hence entire WASP devices) can be bypassed.

Since APEs are identical and are content addressed, not only defects in manufacture, but also faults in service, can be accomodated by not including them in ASP substrings. Moreover, hierarchical bypassing allows both small and large clusters of faults to be similarly tolerated.

The WASP power distribution network is also defect/fault-tolerant. Each ASP substring row is independently powered; the power tracks run along the rows and are fed from external connections at both ends, within the DR and CR blocks. Each block contains a power isolator, so that bypassed blocks and rows can be isolated from the power network.

The creation of a working ASP substring starts with the simultaneous testing of all APE blocks, with those blocks failing to generate the correct test signature being bypassed. The testing strategy for subsequent ASP substring building depends on inter-APE communication timing constraints, since bypassing certain groups of adjacent blocks to achieve neighbour activation will require more than a single time slot. Therefore, in order to maintain the highest speed, ASP substring blocks which include such groups must themselves be bypassed, although they contain working APE blocks. Similarly, ASP substring rows including such groups of ASP substring blocks must also be bypassed, even though working substring blocks are thereby lost.

7H.4.3 Technological progress

WASP1 investigated the feasibility of the WASP concept with four 3.25 cm × 3.25 cm WSI devices on a 15 cm diameter CMOS wafer (1.5 μm, p-well, double-layer metal). Designed to 2 μm layout rules to improve yield, the highly-successful 720-APE WASP1 integrated five ASP substring rows, each comprising four ASP substring blocks and a simplified control router block.

WASP2 developed the concepts pioneered in WASP1 and has moved towards a processor with the generic characteristics of the device shown in Figure 7.36. Two variants have been assembled from the prototype ASP, DR and CR modules designed for the WASP2 demonstrator. The characteristics of these wafer scale processors are shown in Table 7.5.

These devices demonstrate the fundamental features of wafer interconnection structures, power distribution, signal distribution and wafer reconfiguration. Furthermore they are clear evidence that the manufacturing issues of monolithic wafer scale are within the scope of modern fabrication technology.

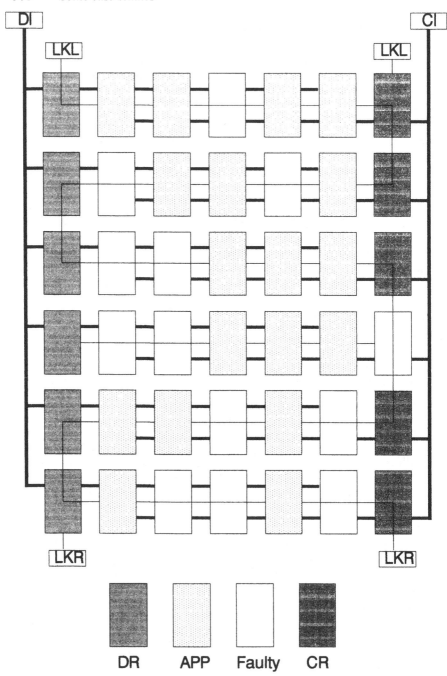

Figure 7.36   Generic WASP device floorplan

Table 7.5 *Characteristics of wafer scale devices*

	WASP2a	WASP2b
No. of APEs	864	6480
Area (sq. cm.)	15.2	89.2
No. of transistors	1.26M	8.43M
Power (W)	5.2 – 8.0	29.6 – 51.2
External clock (MHz)	6	6
Internal clock (MHz)	12	12

7H.5   Future Developments

Currently, a three-phase development of a 6cm × 6cm, 15 360-APE WASP device, for numeric-symbolic image processing, is scheduled. This project involves the design, fabrication and evaluation of three further phases of WASP devices.

In practice, WASP device configuration will depend on the packaging standards adopted (for particular application environments) for ASP module construction. Of the packaging standards being developed for aerospace applications in the 1990s, a lightweight SEM-E compatible module is assumed for the following projections.

SEM-E modules are based on a 16.25 cm × 15 cm thermal conduction plate with a substrate supporting microelectronic circuitry attached to each side. In service, the plate is clamped, along its top and bottom edges, to heat sinks. Currently, power dissipation is limited, by the thermal resistance of the clamps, to about 50 W, whereas the silicon wafers and the plate could support much higher thermal loads. Consequently, more efficient clamping methods are being researched. The mounting pitch for SEM-E modules is 15.25 mm.

Such assemblies could provide electrical and thermal support for the WASP wafers. In particular, a suitable mounting substrate could support four WASP devices and a local control unit comprising a simplified version of the LAC described above. The width of the SEM-E substrate and provision of decoupling capacitors in the central column limit the maximum WASP device width to about 6 cm.

Extrapolation from the results of WASP experimental development suggests that, with standard 1 μm CMOS fabrication technology, 10 ASP substring blocks could be accommodated within this width. With a die aspect ratio of 2:1, each block could accommodate 256 APEs. Thus, 15 360 APEs could be integrated in six ASP substring rows, within a 6 cm × 6 cm WASP device.

Since monolithic WASP devices must tolerate defects in manufacture, as

Table 7.6 *Performance forecasts for a two-substrate WASP device*

Configuration	1 or 2 MIMD processors
Performance	100 Giga-operations/s
I/O bandwidth	640 Mbytes/s
No. of processors	65 536 (fault-tolerant)
Package size	16.25 cm × 15 cm × 0.75 cm
Power dissipation	< 100 W

well as faults in service, not all of the implemented APEs will be harvested. Indeed, the harvest will vary from wafer to wafer. Moreover, it is unrealistic to expect all wafers to be usable. In practice, WASP defect/fault-tolerant circuitry targets harvests of at least 8192 APEs (a 53.3% harvest) on wafers passing standard parametric tests.

Consequently, assuming development of the WASP substrate and the SEM-E package described above, a 65 536 APE WASP module with eight 32-bit data channels can be conservatively forecast. Based on this extrapolation, Table 7.6 is deemed to be a set of realistic design targets. Such figures suggest that a performance of 1 TOPS (tera-operations per second) could be achieved with only ten modules.

71 WISARD:

Catherine Myers
Computer Recognition Systems Ltd
Wokingham, Berkshire
UK

There are very few companies indeed who manufacture cognitive systems based on dedicated hardware, rather than software simulations. Computer Recognition Systems Ltd took up the idea of Wisard, developed at the Imperial College of Science and Technology, London, in 1984. As the reader will discover in the following contribution, the actual implementation of the cognitive nodes is somewhat unusual, but extremely efficient. The system classification is as follows:

Basic idea	PC
Paradigm	Classification
Language	-
Connectivity	Random, reconfigurable
Processors	RAMs
Parallelism	2000
Technology	VLSI

As far as the author is aware, the only other cognitive systems which are approaching commercial development are those devised by Carver Meade at CalTech.

71.1 Introduction

One of the basic principles of a neural network is that its operation depends on the interaction of a large number of communicating, relatively simple, processing elements. Therefore neural nets lend themselves to implementation on highly parallel computers such as the Connection Machine.

There are, however, difficulties with this approach: as one example, a neural net may need much higher interconnectivity among its processing nodes than a general-purpose parallel machine is designed to provide. Conversely, processing elements in such machines are considerably more powerful than is required to implement nodes in most neural network models.

A different approach is to design a special-purpose machine to implement

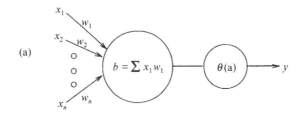

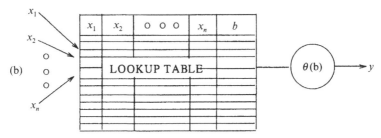

Figure 7.37   Neural network nodes (a) A standard design (b) A RAM-based design

the neural network (or one which may be configured appropriately for a class of neural networks). The WISARD (**WI**lkie, **S**tonham and **A**leksander's **R**ecognition **D**evice, named after its inventors) falls into this category [63]. It is designed to be a custom built machine, with the capability of massive parallelism amongst its nodes, which can perform classification of video images in real-time. If its output is used to drive, for example, a robot arm, the WISARD can be used to sort objects on a conveyor belt or to watch for and remove faulty objects from the belt. Because it is a neural network, the WISARD is trained to these tasks by being shown exemplars, rather than being programmed.

7I.2   RAM-based nodes

A standard node in a neural network might have the form shown in Figure 7.37(a), where θ is fixed and where the weights w_i are adjusted so that an appropriate output y is produced in response to each input $X = (x_1, x_2, x_3, \ldots, x_n)$. This type of node may be trained via error back-propagation or used in a Hopfield network.

However, there are several reasons why this sort of weight-adjusting node is difficult to implement in hardware. The adjustable weights themselves are not simple to devise electronically; the number of inputs to a node (n) is typically high – a node often receiving input from every node on the preceding layer – which leads to an alarming number of wires connecting processors; and the training rules often require complex computations such as the error differential or comparisons among all responses in the network. Worst of all, the training regimes are extremely slow. It is not uncommon for training of a moderately-sized network by error back-propagation to take several days on a Sun workstation.

RAM-based nodes do away with variable weights altogether, and so they circumvent most of these problems. Unfortunately, as shown in Figure 7.37(b), they don't look so much like a stylisation of a biological neuron; despite this, a network of RAM nodes has essentially the same capabilities as a network of more familiar weight-adjusting nodes.

The (n) binary inputs to a RAM-based node form an address in the range $0...2^n - 1$ into a 2^n-element lookup table, each location storing a value appropriate for the particular input pattern. This lookup table is easily implemented by a RAM, which gives these nodes their name. The value stored in the addressed table location is passed to an output function θ similar to that in a weight-adjusting node, which converts it into the final binary node output.

Such a node is trained by adjusting the stored values in the lookup table until every input X addresses a value such that the correct output y for that node is produced. In the case of the WISARD, the lookup table is initialised to contain 0s at every address; during training these are changed to 1s where necessary to obtain correct output. The WISARD's nodes use the output function $\theta(z) = z$.

WISARD nodes are almost trivial to implement, requiring only a small RAM, its address facilities and a read/write line which specifies whether the appropriate stored value should be read out of the RAM or a new value should be written in. No special hardware is needed to construct the node or use it (RAM-based nodes are discussed further in [64]).

7I.3   Structure of the WISARD

The memory of the WISARD consists of thousands of these nodes partitioned into groups, each group called a *discriminator*. Each discriminator is trained to recognise one class of object, and so the machine as a whole can discriminate between as many classes as there are discriminators. One such discriminator is shown in Figure 7.38.

Assume that the input to the WISARD is to consist of a 64×64 region of a thresholded TV image, and that it has been decided that each RAM-node will have $n = 8$ inputs (the basis of these decisions is discussed in a later sec-

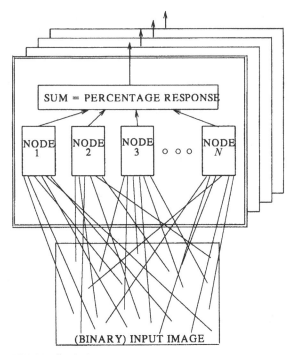

Figure 7.38   A WISARD discriminator

tion). Then if there are 512 nodes in a discriminator, the 4096 image bits can be mapped to the 4096 node input lines in a one-to-one mapping. The ordering is random, but is decided at initialisation and is fixed thereafter.

If this discriminator is to recognise pictures of the letter **A**, it is first shown one such training image. The bits of this image are mapped to the node inputs, forming one address into each node's lookup table. The value addressed in each node is set to 1, while all others in the table remain at 0. At this point, if the same image is shown again, it will address the same location in each node as previously, and therefore all 512 nodes will access 1s. If a new image is presented which addresses none of the same locations as the training pattern, all 512 nodes will access 0s. If an image is shown which partially overlaps the trained image, it will access some intermediate number of 1s.

The number of 1s accessed by a pattern can be summed, and the percentage of the total becomes the discriminator output or *response*: a measure of how similar the current image is to the class of images on which the discriminator was trained.

In the situation where the discriminator has been trained on just one pattern, P_1, the expected response to a new pattern Q is [65]:

$$ER_1 = N(O_{QP_1})^n$$

where O_{QP_1} is the fraction of bits in common between patterns Q and P_1, and where n is the number of inputs to a node and N is the total number of nodes.

Now, suppose a second image of an **A**, P_2, is also to be trained into the discriminator. Because P_1 and P_2 overlap, some values addressed by P_2 will already contain 1s. But as long as P_1 and P_2 are not identical, P_2 will also address different locations in some other nodes, and the 0s accessed there will now also be set to 1s.

If Q is now shown to the discriminator again, the expected response is:

$$ER_2 = N[(O_{QP_1})^n + (O_{QP_2}) + (O_{P_1P_2})^n]$$

Training continues for all of the training set – all examples of **A**s. After training on T patterns, the expected response to an untrained pattern Q is:

$$\sum_{i=1}^{T} P_i^n - \sum_{i=1}^{T-1}\sum_{j=2}^{T} O_{P_iP_j}^n + \sum_{i=1}^{T-2}\sum_{j=2}^{T-1}\sum_{k=3}^{T} O_{P_iP_jP_k}^n - \ldots (\pm) O_{P_iP_j\ldots P_T}^n$$

An important feature of discriminator training is that each training pattern need be shown only once. In contrast, in error back-propagation training, thousands of presentations of each training pattern may be required before the network learns. The problem with this faster training in WISARD is that it is one-sided. The discriminator learning to recognise **A**s cannot be taught anything about what is not an **A**. (This is a curious concept. Imagine what concepts a child would form about the class *dog* if he were shown a terrier, a Dalmation and a Pekinese and told all three were dogs, but never explicitly given examples of what was not a dog.) Further, one WISARD discriminator can only be taught to recognise instances of a single class – not to discriminate between multiple classes.

For this reason, the WISARD is provided with multiple discriminators – one for each class to be recognised. After the first discriminator has been trained to recognise **A**s, a second may be trained to recognise **B**s, a third **C**s and so on.

Then, when an unknown pattern Q is presented, each discriminator responds with a percentage indicating the similarity of Q to its own training images. The discriminator with the highest response wins and classifies Q. The confidence of this decision depends not only on the strength of the winning response but also on the weakness of the losing responses. This allows for some recovery from the absence of negative training which was mentioned above. Formally, confidence (C) is defined as:

$$C = \frac{(R_w - R_n)}{R_w}$$

where R_w is the winning response and R_n the next highest response.

If the WISARD is being used in an operation involving a conveyor belt where it is to sort alphabet blocks, it can order a robot arm to push **A** blocks into one pile when they are identified with high confidence, push **B** blocks into another pile when they are identified with high confidence, and push unrecognisable blocks into a separate pile.

7I.4   Configuring the WISARD

In the example above, several assumptions were made about the choice of number of nodes (N), the number of inputs to each node (n) and the like. For an understanding of the WISARD it is important to see what influence these parameters have on the operation of the system.

7I.4.1   Training set

When ER_1 is the expected response of a discriminator trained on one pattern to a novel pattern and ER_2 is the expected response after training on two patterns, the difference indicates the effects of training on a second pattern. The more similar the two patterns are, the larger the overlap will be until, when the two patterns are nearly identical, $ER_1 \approx ER_2$. Similarly, after training with T very similar patterns, $ER_T \approx ER_1$. In this case, the discriminator is said to have high specificity. An unknown pattern Q will be recognised by this discriminator only if it is very similar to all T patterns.

On the other hand, if the T patterns are very different, the overlaps between patterns will be low, and ER_T approaches 100% for every unknown pattern Q. In this case, the discriminator is said to perform with a high degree of generalisation – accepting a wide range of images as its trained class.

Choosing an appropriate training set therefore has a critical effect on the performance of the trained discriminator. If it is too specific, the WISARD reduces to a template matcher; only recognising images on which it was specifically trained. If it generalises too much, the WISARD discriminator will recognise any image and will therefore not be of much use as a classifier. Noise is of course equivalent to a degree of distortion in the image and therefore noisy images require a system trained with a high degree of generalisation.

7I.4.2   Node inputs

The equations defining discriminator response show that n, the number of inputs to each RAM-node in a discriminator, also has a strong influence on ER. The lowest reasonable value of n is 2. In this case, the lookup table in each node contains only 4 locations. Then, if the discriminator is trained on one pattern, the chance of an unknown pattern addressing the same location in a node as the first is 0.25. If $n = 8$, then the lookup table has 256 locations, and the chance that the new pattern addresses the same one as the first is 1 in 256.

So, high n increases specificity, low n increases generalisation. As a compromise, n is usually set in the range $4 - 8$, which allows some degree of tuning without allowing either effect to get out of hand.

7I.4.3 Coverage

Another parameter, the coverage, determines how many times each bit in the image is mapped to a node input. In the A-discriminator example above, coverage was 100% and each image bit was mapped only once. A discriminator with half the number of RAM-nodes could provide only 50% coverage, and each image bit would be connected to a node input with a probability of 0.5.

In practice, with large video images (e.g. 512 × 512 bits), coverage can often be as low as 50% without much loss of learning ability; while little is gained by increasing coverage above 100%. This is due to the large degree of redundancy in such a large input space.

7I.4.4 Limitations

Several limitations of the WISARD paradigm should be apparent at this point. First, and most important, the WISARD is inherently and simply a pattern recognition system. The discriminators have no semantic knowledge of their training sets. If the trainer (inadvertantly or mischieviously) included a disparate item in the training set, the discriminator would treat it as just as canonical as any other item. Likewise, the discriminator will not recognise a rotated, inverted or shifted version of a training image, a negative version of the image, or one with significantly different contrast – unless these cases are specifically provided for within the training set.

For these reasons, the WISARD is ideally suited for work in a controlled environment such as on a factory conveyor belt, where objects to be recognised appear in standard positions under constant lighting conditions.

7I.5 The CRS WISARD

Computer Recognition Systems Ltd (CRS) has been producing a commercial version of the WISARD machine since 1984. The machine itself occupies a cube about 50 cm on each side, with peripherals such as a video cam-

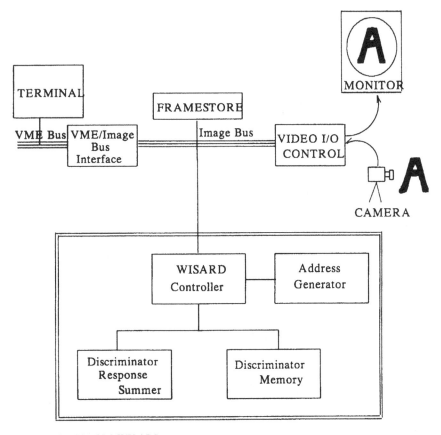

Figure 7.39 The CRS WISARD system

era, video display unit and terminal through which the user communicates with the operating system. It can also be provided with a disc to allow memory backup, a video recorder to allow off-site training or testing, and output units such as a robot arm. In Aleksander's research laboratory at Imperial College, London, a CRS machine outputs to a recording device which allows WISARD to name the class of the image being presented.

Schematically, the CRS WISARD is as shown in Figure 7.39. It consists of a controller which oversees access to discriminator memory and the discriminator response summer. An address generator can provide a random mapping of discriminator node inputs to input image bits; alternatively the mapping may follow some specified scheme. Addresses are generated during initialisation. The controller communicates with a framestore and a terminal; a video input/output controller captures camera images and also displays them on a monitor.

From the terminal, the user may first select the size and position of the

video image which is to be presented to the binary image input to WIS-
ARD. The user may also select the number of inputs to each RAM-node
and the coverage. Together the three parameters of input size S pixels, coverage V and number of inputs to each node n determine how many nodes N
are needed in each discriminator

$$N = \frac{VS}{n}$$

These choices are further bounded by memory requirements. Eight discriminators are provided in some 4 Mbytes of RAM. Accordingly, the
choice of S, V and n must satisfy:

$$500\,000 \geq N\, 2^n$$

The user may also set the confidence threshold in the range 0% to 100%.
When the confidence (C) exceeds this set threshold, a signal is sent out to
the output peripheral device.

There are three operational commands available, once all parameters
have been set. The user may clear all discriminators, train a discriminator or
classify incoming images.

During training, a 512×512 video input image from the camera is placed
into a frame store. A thresholded image of the correct size is constructed
and from this the WISARD controller fetches groups of bits (each group
forms the address for one node in the discriminator being trained). A 1 is
stored into the location addressed in each node.

During classification, the values addressed are not overwritten but are
retrieved and fed into the response summer. The tally for each discriminator
is output via the terminal, which lists each by number (and possibly by
assigned name) together with percentage response. Also shown are the discriminators with first and second strongest responses and the confidence
calculated from these two responses.

Rather than implementing discriminator memory as $N\, 2^n$-bit RAMs for
each discriminator, a single large memory is used with size $M = 8N\, 2^n$ bits
(see Figure 7.40).

This is partitioned into N virtual nodes, each containing 2^n locations.
Each location is eight bits wide – one bit to represent the value stored at
that node address in each of the eight discriminators. During training, only
one of the eight bit-planes is active, and that bit in each node is available to
be overwritten. During classification, nodes from all eight bit-planes are
active and respond with the value addressed.

In the CRS machine, operation within one discriminator is serial: each
node is accessed and operated on sequentially. (Classification can be 8-par-
allel if all discriminators perform their serial processing together.) However,
the machine is still fast enough that a full training or classification sequence

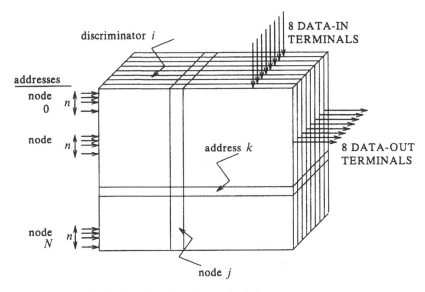

Figure 7.40   Use of a single RAM to implement discriminator memory

can be completed before the next input arives from the camera. The fetching of images into the framestore is independent of and parallel with reading and writing of discriminator memory.

7I.6   Conclusions

There are four major features of the CRS WISARD machine which have led to its successful use in several industrial applications:

Speed: Training and classification is possible at full video rate, and a discriminator can be trained to recognise a human face, for example, within about eight seconds of training.

Unskilled training: Obviously, use of the WISARD requires some understanding of how to set parameters and oversee training. However, it is not necessary for the user to know how to program or to understand which features of the input images are being used – only to provide a suitable training set.

Flexibility: The WISARD is a dedicated machine in the sense that all it is capable of doing is viewing examples of up to eight classes of video image, and classifying them via percentage discriminator response. Yet within this constraint, the WISARD can classify any sort of images: no reprogramming is required.

Robustness: Because the WISARD memory is distributed within each discriminator, memory representing a few nodes can fail without seriously degrading performance.

CRS WISARDs have been purchased by several firms which use the machines to watch items on a conveyor belt. The WISARDs variously check alignment of components on PCBs, check the accuracy of roller bearings, compare labels on phials of medicine with the contents, and check for rotten oranges by differences of skin texture. Banks in Ecuador and Scotland use WISARDs in counting and sorting banknotes with an error rate of one in a million. A food packing plant is using a WISARD to check that the cherries are aesthetically placed in the centre of cherry tarts.

8 Conclusions

The purpose of this book has been to introduce the reader to the subject of parallel computing. In attempting to make the subject digestible, it is inevitable that a great deal of advanced material has been omitted. The reader whose interest has been kindled is directed to the bibliography, which follows this chapter, as a starting point for continued studies. In particular, a more rigorous treatment of advanced computer architectures is available in *Advanced Computer Architectures* by Hwang.

It should also be noted that parallel computing is a field in which progress occurs at a prodigious rate. So much work is being done that some startling new insight or technique is sure to be announced just after this book goes to press. In what follows, the reader should bear in mind the developing nature of the field. Nevertheless, a great deal of material has been presented here, and it is worthwhile making some attempt to summarise it in a structured manner.

I have attempted to make clear in the preceding chapters that understanding parallel computing is an hierarchical process. A valuable degree of insight into the subject can be obtained even at the level considered in the first chapter, where three basic classes or types of approach were identified. Thereafter, each stage of the process should augment the understanding already achieved. It is up to each reader to decide on the level of detail required.

8.1   A taxonomy of systems

One straightforward way of presenting this type of material is in the form of a taxonomy. Some sciences, such as botany, use taxonomies as their very foundation. Here, they are simply useful tools for summarising a complex subject, providing at the same time an *aide memoire* and a convenient shorthand for use in discussion. This latter role is not without its perils, since reliance on such a shorthand can be a substitute for understanding, but on balance the technique is a useful one. An efficient taxonomy should have the following features:

(a) The overall structure should be hierarchical
(b) The highest level should be both the simplest and the mostsignificant, the lower levels more complex and less important
(c) There should be a minimum of redundancy

Naturally, the present author is not the first to attempt to derive an ideal taxonomy of parallel systems, nor will he be the last. For completeness, I note here some of the more significant previous attempts of which the reader should be aware.

Flynn: In his seminal paper on taxonomy of parallel computers [1], Flynn defined four categories of computer architecture based on the singularity or multiplicity of data streams. As we have already seen in Chapter 2, this concept proved so easy to grasp and to have such immediacy that his shorthand terms – SISD, MISD, SIMD and MIMD – are still in use (and useful) today. Unfortunately, the very simplicity of the approach has proved its undoing. The main drawback is not that the scheme cannot be stretched to cover most more recent ideas – it certainly can be – but that such stretching leads to the same shorthand symbol being used for quite different things. A second disadvantage is that, at the first level, the idea is not expandable – there are only four available categories, unless we follow Shute [66] and accept that the idea of zero instruction streams is a valid concept. Finally, the classification is really confined to hardware, which is rather limiting. The fact that Flynn's original ideas included two further levels of complexity is, unfortunately, never used and rarely even remembered.

Shore: In 1973, Shore developed an alternative taxonomy based on the organisation of a computer from its constituent parts [67]. His categories were: word-serial, bit-parallel; word-parallel, bit-serial; word-parallel, bit-parallel; orthogonal computer; unconnected array; connected array and logic-in-memory array. Aside from its shortcomings in failing to deal with such categories of system as the pipeline machines, this taxonomy suffered from the serious drawback of identifying its classes numerically, rather than by convenient acronyms or descriptive names. It is also apparent that the categories lack any ready connection with well-understood concepts – they say nothing about how various architectures are used, nor is it apparent whether the categories are exclusive or overlapping.

Hockney and Jesshope: In their book *Parallel Computers* [68], these authors spend more than twenty pages defining a structural notation as a basis for their taxonomy. Although this allows any system to be categorised with extreme precision in terms of the numbers and type of processors, connections, etc., it failed to gain general currency (in all but the most esoteric circles) because of its density and homogeneity. A machine such as the ICL DAP (a simple SIMD mesh) is described as:

$$C(64^2\,P)_l^{|-nn}; \quad P = B_p - M_{4K*1}$$

Whilst certain elements of this classification are immediately meaningful (implying 64×64 1-bit processors with four kbits of memory each), and the whole exhibits exemplary compactness in written form, the lack of a defined set of related categories makes any general discussion based on these ideas hard to achieve.

Shute: During the late 1980s, Shute developed a complex taxonomy (based on ideas put forward by Treleaven [69]) which attempted to include all parallel architectures of the calculator type [66]. Whilst he succeeded in including many of the more difficult categories, the basis of the taxonomy was of such complexity as to make it useful only for the more dedicated of taxo-maniacs.

Shute identifies three levels of classification – hard architecture, soft architecture and, for the sake of completeness, middle architecture. Within each level, classification proceeds in terms of parallelism, locality, granularity, regularity, generality and speed. Having examined each of these, Shute demonstrates a composite scheme, which he calls the Treleaven–Flynn classification, based on a four-dimensional grid having the axes: selection model; examination model; program storage mechanism and results storage mechanism. Because of its four-dimensional nature, the classification is difficult to reproduce graphically.

Although each of these systems has its own blend of advantages and disadvantages at the detailed level, they share one serious drawback – none takes into account the area of cognitive computation. It is quite reasonable to argue, as the authors of these systems undoubtedly would, that the areas of calculation and cognition are sufficiently different that they should be treated independently. Unfortunately, it is difficult for the intending user of parallel systems to decide on a choice of approach without some idea of how the two aspects of computation relate to one another. Further, a student of the subject cannot obtain a proper understanding by adopting too narrow an approach. It is mainly for these reasons that I chose to include both calculation and cognition in this book.

One further matter needs to be taken into account. The great advantage of Flynn's taxonomy was that its categories meant something in terms of how the various systems were likely to be used. Most more complex analyses have either lost, or never attempted to retain, this intuitive link with reality. It is for this reason that I deem yet another attempt to be worth-

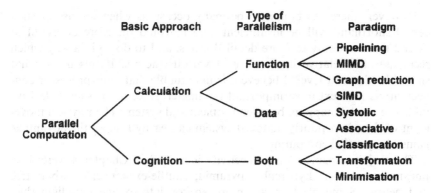

Figure 8.1 The first levels of a taxonomy

while. We will begin the process of building this new taxonomy by re-examining the first figure from Chapter 2 (reproduced here as Figure 8.1).

In this diagram I define the field of computation as being split into two categories – calculation and cognition. Systems based on the idea of calculation must be programmed, those utilising cognition are trained. Calculators are liable to produce results in numerical form (or some derivative of it), cognisers will usually produce decisions based on the category of the input data.

At the next level, the type of parallelism involved is defined. Calculators may embody either data or functional parallelism, cognisers combine both in a way which is not easy to disentangle.

In the third column, each of the three categories (data parallel calculation, function parallel calculation and parallel cognition) is further differentiated according to the paradigms which are employed by various implementations. In the author's opinion, this is the level of the taxonomy which should permit a discourse or discussion about parallel computing to be carried on without becoming submerged in unnecessary detail. It is fortunate (if not totally fortuitous) that we can, to some extent, subsume within this level the question of programming language or training technique since, as we saw in Chapter 3, particular categories of these apply to each specific paradigm. Indeed, some of the paradigms are, principally, programming techniques. It is perhaps at this point that the value of a classification based on paradigms becomes apparent – it is irrelevant that the important feature of a systolic system is the hardware arrangement, whereas that of a graph reduction system is the programming method. In each case the shorthand captures the essence of the paradigm. A final point here is that the classification is still sufficiently compact to permit modest expansion – either if some current idea (such as dataflow) is deemed worthy of inclusion, or if novel paradigms are discovered.

However, there are bound to be many occasions when the use of such verbal shorthand will be insufficient, and it would therefore be useful to extend the taxonomy to more detailed levels, and to do so in a way which recognises the relative importance of various factors. If this is so, what should be the next level? I believe it is unarguable that inter-processor connectivity is the next most important parameter, since it has such a decisive influence on the mapping between problem and system. The physical movement of data in a poorly matched system can easily lose all the advantage gained by parallel computing.

The major categories of connectivity identified in Chapter 4 were: bus; linear; mesh; cube; hypercube; pyramid; shuffle-exchange; crossbar; tree and neural. Some of these are more appropriate to one paradigm than another, but the number of likely alternatives is still great, so that presentation of the expanded taxonomy in the form of a tree becomes cumbersome, and the form used in Table 8.1 is more appropriate.

The reader should note two important points in relation to this table. First, I have suggested that any connectivity might be associated with the MIMD paradigm. This is because of the generality of application of the paradigm itself, and we see that the possibility is borne out in implemented systems. Second, there are good reasons why some paradigms are limited to one connectivity. A pipeline, for example, is inherently a linearly connected system. However, there are other cases where I have listed only the more likely arrangements – it is probably true to say that any paradigm could be implemented on any network, it is just that some combinations would be spectacularly inefficient!

It will come as no surprise to the reader that the next level of this taxonomy concerns the type of processing elements to be found in each system. Again, it would be possible to advance an argument which suggested that this aspect of a system is of no significance to a user, on the grounds that any function can be implemented on any processor, but I believe that this would represent an over-simplification. Leaving aside the question of processor autonomy, which tends to be linked closely with the computing paradigm, the processor complexity gives significant hints as to the categories of function which can be most efficiently implemented. Thus, binary image processing operations are unlikely to execute efficiently on a system constructed from floating-point processors, whilst an expert system might be difficult to implement on single-bit processors.

By this stage, of course, the utility of presenting the taxonomy as a full table is becoming moot. Such a table is certainly no longer understandable at a glance, as the earlier stages perhaps were. Nevertheless, that very complexity is a valuable reflection of the complexity of its subject matter – namely the huge variety of viable parallel systems which could be (and have been) configured.

Table 8.1 *A taxonomy including connectivity*

Basic Approach	Type of Parallelism	Paradigm	Connectivity
Calculation	Function	Pipelining	Linear
		MIMD	any
		Graph reduction	Tree
	Data	SIMD	Linear
			Mesh
			Cube
			Pyramid
		Systolic	Linear
			Mesh
		Association	Linear
			Tree
			Neural
Cognition	Both	Classification	Mesh
			Cube
			Tree
			Neural
		Transformation	Neural
		Minimisation	Neural

It is at this stage that we need to consider a parameter which I have barely touched upon in the preceding chapters – the number of many parallel elements present in any given system. This factor, in conjunction with the complexity of each processor, is an important determinant of the power of the system, although the reader should always bear in mind the difficulty of estimating the computing power of parallel systems (discussed in Chapter 6).

It ought to be apparent to the reader by now that we are at the limits of (some would say beyond!) what can usefully be incorporated in a taxonomy, and approaching the realms of what should be included in system data sheets. We will therefore complete this section by summarising those aspects of a parallel system which ought to be included for a reasonably full definition (see Table 8.2). Remember that it will not be necessary to consider every aspect of this complexity all the time – usually the first two lines will be sufficient.

The perceptive reader will note that there is no mention of performance in this short specification. This is not because the parameter is unimportant – on the contrary, it is because of its extreme importance that it cannot be compressed into a short form. The complexity of this problem was explored in Chapter 6 – intending users simply must spend the necessary time to understand the performance of a system in relation to their own problems.

Table 8.2 *A short definition of parallel systems*

	Meiko	AMT DAP
Basic idea	FPC	DPC
Paradigm	MIMD	SIMD
Language	Extended C	Fortran-Plus
Connectivity	Mesh	Mesh
Processors	32-bit integer	1-bit and 8-bit
Parallelism	128	4096
Technology	VLSI	VLSI

So far, then, we are equipped with a list of paradigms which give an insight into what is happening, and a set of headings under which to classify how individual systems work. What next?

8.2   An analysis of alternatives

The principal purpose of this book has been to introduce the reader to the various alternative approaches to the field of parallel computing. Although, at each stage, an attempt has been made to point out the advantages and disadvantages of various aspects, comparisons between alternatives have been confined to factual material such as the number of processors. The next stage, then, is to attempt a critical assessment of the ideas put forward. Bear in mind, however, that any such analysis must be, to some extent, subjective, and that one of the purposes of this book has been to put the readers in the position of being able to make their own judgements.

The key point to remember in what follows is the one which I have continually reiterated throughout the book: an appropriate mapping between problem and solution is vital to the successful application of parallel computing. If we take this principle as our unspoken foundation, then several other points seem to me significant, and I will consider them in the following sections.

8.2.1   The user interface

There are two quite different ways in which parallel computers may be used. The first is in the form of a black box, which performs some specified function (and none other), in a situation where the user interface consists of, typically, a switch. This kind of use need not concern us, since the contents of such a box are irrelevant to the user. The second mode of use is the same as that of a typical desktop PC – sometimes we use pre-written packages, sometimes we write programs, sometimes the computer is used as a process controller, etc. It is here that the user interface of a parallel computer is of vital importance, since a system that is hard to use rapidly becomes one which is not used at all.

Data parallel calculation systems present the most familiar immediate face to a user. Their standard languages are extensions of well-known favourites like Fortran and C, and, given the appropriate conceptual leap to thinking about parallel data structures as single entities, the high-level user is perfectly at home. At a lower level, however, where the design of new algorithms which map directly to the parallel structure is required, difficulties proliferate. One of the major problems concerns the bit-serial nature of the processors in many such systems. Such a processor configuration almost invariably means that the detailed structure of data must be taken into account – it becomes important, from the point of view of efficiency, that 10-bit numbers should be handled as such, and not as though they were 16-bit numbers.

A second problem to be overcome concerns the nature of the operations which are being performed. The three data-parallel paradigms – systolic, SIMD and association – all involve approaches which appear, to a conventional programmer, unusual. Systolic systems implement quite novel approaches to ordinary operations such as matrix multiplication. SIMD arrays are frequently programmed to execute functions on local neighbourhoods of spatially organised data sets. Associative processors usually seek to discover relationships rather than the results of straightforward computations. That all these oddities are inherent in the fields of application rather than the parallel computers themselves does not reduce the users' difficulties in coming to terms with them. There is, however, one mitigating factor. If there is a natural match between problem and computer (as there should be), this commonality of structure can reinforce any learning process which may be necessary.

With the exception of this slender ray of hope, however, it has to be recognised that, in the case of data parallel systems, there is very little that can be done to ease the transition between the high level, where programming problems are minimal, and the low level, where they are manifold.

Function parallel calculators probably demand more of a user at any level. This is mainly because the mapping of problem to structure can change significantly from one problem to the next, requiring constant vigilance to ensure efficiency. The typical programming level is therefore somewhat akin to that of algorithm design on a data parallel system, and is consequently more difficult than high-level programming on such systems.

On the other hand, because machines which embody functional parallelism are normally constructed from processing elements with more conventional instruction sets, the operations which are being performed will likewise be more familiar to a conventional programmer. Furthermore, although the optimum mapping of any problem onto a distributed system seems to require operator intervention, reasonably efficient mappings can be achieved by such tools as parallelising compilers. It is also likely that the quality of such tools will improve significantly as time passes, so the users' most difficult task will disappear, and function parallel systems will become no more difficult to use than conventional computers.

Using cognitive computers requires the greatest change of viewpoint of all. The calculator's programming is replaced by a training phase, during which two problems are likely to arise. First, the user must be sure that the choice of training material is appropriate for the purpose. Second, that the training is sufficiently complete to cover all conceivable eventualities. It is much more difficult to ensure both of these than, for example, to determine the validity of a conventional program (itself not always easy). Once this change of viewpoint has been accomplished, however, the concepts involved are markedly simple, even if the execution is not. The training phase is likely to be tedious in a way quite different from that of the familiar tedium of programming. Additional training is likely to be required for quite minor changes in circumstances, which a calculator program would take in its stride. Finally, a user must always bear in mind the probabilistic nature of the cogniser, and take this into account when considering any results.

Overall, then, we might say that cognisers require a significant conceptual leap, are inherently uncertain in a number of ways, and impose tedium; data parallel calculators are easy to use at a high level but become significantly more difficult to program for maximum efficiency; function parallel calculators require regular intellectual effort in their current state of development, but are more likely to eventually be supplied with tools which will make them indistinguishable from conventional computers.

8.2.2   *Generality of application*

One of the most frequent accusations levelled against parallel computers is their lack of generality of application. Since I have continually stressed the point that parallel computers should be deliberately matched to their applications, it would be inconsistent not to concede this point. Two things are worth bearing in mind, however. First, the criticism embodies the implicit assumption that ordinary serial computers are general in application. Whilst it is probably true that a typical serial computer is more versatile than a typical parallel one, no specific serial computer is completely general-purpose. No-one would trouble to use a scientific mainframe as a word processor, nor would any reasonable person attempt to undertake quantum chromodynamic calculations on an Apple Macintosh. Second, there are bound to be differences of degree within the generality of particular parallel systems. This is the issue on which I shall concentrate here.

At the first level, it should be apparent that data parallel calculators are likely to be more specific in application than function parallel systems. As I indicated in a previous chapter, this is partly because DPCs are often developed with a specific application in mind, whereas FPCs stem from particular computing approaches whose generality of application is unconstrained. At the present time, it would appear that cognisers are the most specialised of all, but this may merely reflect the rather limited amount of study given, so far, to the applications of these unusual systems. Within this overall view, however, there are some important differences to be considered between the various basic paradigms. It must, of course, be remembered that almost any problem can be forced into a shape in which it can be solved on any particular system – I am considering here more naturally mapped applications.

Pipelining is obviously universally applicable at the micro level but, equally, is extremely specific in its macro implementations. In the most extreme cases, both the individual functions of units and their detailed sequence are fixed. At the other end of the scale, programmable units and reconfigurable interconnections would permit substantially more generality, but only within the general class of problems where repeated, similar, operations are expected. Such applications are somewhat rare.

MIMD systems, on the other hand, are perhaps the most generally applicable of those discussed in this book. This is obviously a result of their considerable flexibility – the MIMD paradigm does, in one sense, include SIMD and several others as subsets of itself. Further, many MIMD systems implement rather limited parallelism, reflecting the equally limited parallelism to be found in many classes of problem.

Graph reduction systems form an interesting class. The mathematical foundation of the paradigm might lead one to suppose that such systems were very general in application indeed but, in fact, this turns out not to be so, perhaps because ordinary, single-processor computers are quite adequate for dealing with many problems that might otherwise map onto graph reduction systems.

The SIMD paradigm is indeed specialised to those applications where the data sets are both large and, usually, spatially structured. However, it should be borne in mind that, because we live in just such a spatially structured world, data sets of this sort occur more frequently than might be supposed. Images; solids, fluids and gases; engineering structures and fundamental forces can all be envisaged in such terms. This means that systems based on the SIMD paradigm are widely applicable within the areas of scientific computing and machine vision, and hardly applicable at all outside those areas.

Systolic systems, unless they are of the type which are really pipelines, are of very specialised application. Each such device has one dedicated function – the most generally applicable of these is probably matrix multiplication.

Similarly, associative processors are completely general in application within their own fields, and not at all so outside that area.

It is somewhat more difficult to make generalisations about cognitive systems. Many applications can be posed in terms of either classification or minimisation, but the paucity of available systems (other than in simulation), renders the validity of the exercise unproven.

8.2.3 Technical issues

The technical issues relevant to parallel computing are easily stated – they are those of scale, complexity and economy. By their very nature, the scale of parallel systems will always be a problem – if it is not, then the concept is probably being insufficiently exploited. For a parallel implementation to be worthwhile, it should offer improvements in performance (over conventional systems) which are measured in orders of magnitude. This means that a typical parallel computer (if one existed) is liable to be 10 or 100 times larger than a typical serial system – all other factors being equal. This consideration, in itself, can seriously limit the possible applicability of parallel systems.

The second factor – complexity – is mostly concerned with the interconnection of parallel systems. Again, it is inevitable that parallel systems will be more complex in this area than their conventional counterparts, although the complexity may be hidden at a technical level as in wafer scale integration.

As far as economy is concerned, I include it here as a technical issue because it is very heavily dependent on the two factors of scale and complexity just mentioned. Because parallel systems (with the possible exception of certain dedicated systolic devices) are both large and complex, they are inevitably costly. Of course, this does not define their cost-effectiveness, which is a separate issue.

In this analysis, we should ask if there are significant differences between the various types of parallel systems in terms of these factors. Unfortunately, the answers to this question are not quite straightforward. There is probably a natural limitation on the worthwhile size and complexity of pipelines, graph reduction systems and systolic arrays. Beyond a certain limit, the paradigm in each case tends to become inappropriate. However, the parameters associated with each of the other paradigms depend entirely on the scale of system which is chosen. MIMD computers are available having between four and 8192 processors; SIMD systems are made with between 64 and 65536 elements; cognisers ranging in size between a few neurons and several thousand have been constructed. Systems at the low end of each of these ranges are likely to be of quite moderate technical complexity, those at the upper end are at the very frontiers of what is feasible, and their associated costs are therefore very high.

One technical factor which is almost certain to differentiate between MIMD systems and all of the other paradigms covered in this text is the following. The technology which underpins MIMD systems is, for the most part, the same technology which is used in mainstream computing – at the very least the same processors, coprocessors and memory devices can be pressed into service for either. This is emphatically not so (except in the case of memory devices) for any of the other types of systems described in this book. The inevitable result of this is that the technology which these systems can use will be significantly poorer than that available to MIMD systems – perhaps by as much as an order of magnitude in such factors as packing density and clock rate. This will certainly act as a significant disadvantage for these systems.

8.2.4 Efficiency

As should have become apparent from reading Chapter 6, summarising the question of efficiency (or cost-effectiveness) is both difficult and of doubtful value. Nevertheless, a few very general remarks can be made, as long as the reader does not seek to extrapolate their validity too far.

Within the area of calculators, it is apparent that an inverse relationship exists between generality and efficiency. Thus, the more generally applicable a system is, the less efficiently it is likely to perform any specific task. In terms of our paradigms, this means that MIMD systems are likely to be the least efficient, graph reduction devices rather less inefficient, and the other, more specialised paradigms, most efficient of all. Of course, this does depend on utilising to the full, in each case, the potential for close mapping between problem and solution.

Cognisers present an even more difficult problem. One confusion lies in the fact that we only have one measure of efficiency available, namely task completion time. Thus, unless the same task has been attempted in a number of cases, we have no basis for comparison at all. A second difficulty is the immature nature of the whole field – so few neural systems have actually been implemented and applied to problems that we have no basis for judging the relationship between promised and achieved performance. Thus, at the time of writing, no supportable general judgement can be made about the efficiency of cognitive devices, other than drawing some rather tenuous connections between their performance and that of the human neural system, which is known to be superb for some problems and ineffective in other areas.

Table 8.3 *Parameters of alternative parallel systems*

System	Concept	Interface	Generality	Complexity	Efficiency
Pipeline	Easy	Easy	Poor	Low	High
MIMD	Hard	Hard	Good	High	Moderate
Reduction	Moderate	Moderate	Poor	Moderate	Moderate
SIMD	Easy	Easy	Moderate	High	High
Systolic	Hard	Easy	Poor	Moderate	High
Associative	Moderate	Moderate	Poor	Moderate	High
Cognitive	Hard	Easy	Unknown	High	Unknown

8.2.5 Summary

We can see from the above that parallel computing systems can be judged and compared on the basis of a number of factors including ease of understanding, ease of use, generality of application, technical complexity, efficiency and performance. Unfortunately, many of these factors are subject only to qualitative judgement, whilst others, which ought to be quantifiable, are extraordinarily complex. Consider Table 8.3. It should be apparent from this that there is no substitute for some understanding of the issues involved – perusal of the table is insufficient to obtain a complete analysis. Further, there is certainly no single measure which can be used in every case to select one system or the other. In some cases generality will be overwhelmingly important, in others efficiency will be paramount, etc. Any attempt to assign a numerical score for each factor and then sum the components for individual paradigms is certain to be misleading.

8.3   The future

Any book which concerns itself with a subject at or near the frontiers of development of any field should end with a consideration of future trends. It is, however, important to bear in mind two points. First, the speculation should be based, as far as possible, on an extrapolation of available data, rather than pious hopes for startling breakthroughs. It is apparent from Figure 8.2 that the power of computers (though it be measured in a far from perfect way) has been growing at a constant rate for more than five decades – in spite of the invention of such items as the transistor, microprocessors and parallel computing itself. There is therefore little reason to suppose that inventions such as neural or optical computers will have significant effects on this trend – although they may allow it to continue for longer than would otherwise be possible. Second, the process of extrapolation is always somewhat doubtful. In this spirit, therefore, I offer the following suggestions of future trends in a number of areas.

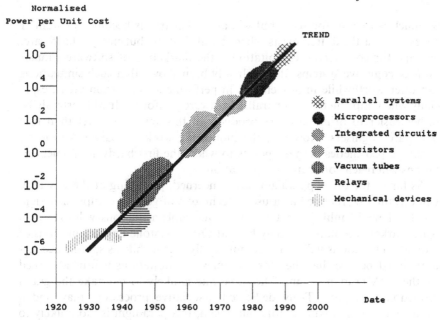

Figure 8.2   The upward trend of computing power

8.3.1   Commercial

As a rough guide, it seems to take about ten years to transfer new develop-ments in computing from their first useful manifestation in the laboratory to properly supported products in the marketplace. Thus, worthwhile labo-ratory implementations of SIMD arrays were available in the late 1970s and early 1980s – a decade later they were becoming available as commercial devices from AMT, AIS, MasPar, etc. Based on this notion, what can we expect in the next ten years? Clearly, we can expect increasing numbers of suppliers in the following areas:

SIMD arrays: As the levels of integration improve, such systems will become increasingly cost-effective and appropriate for, in particular, vision applications.

MIMD systems: There are two areas where these will increase their mar-ket penetration – the most powerful supercomputers for scientific comput-ing, and plug-in accelerator cards to improve the performance of worksta-tions. In the former case the parallelism will be apparent to the users and will be exploited to the full, in the latter case it will be completely hidden.

So much is easy to foresee – but will any other trends become apparent? I believe that a third area exists where parallel ideas, but not yet hardware, are ripe for commercial exploitation – the marketing of software simulations of cognitive systems. It has already been shown that such simulations can offer worthwhile improvements in performance in certain areas, especially when implemented on parallel hardware platforms. It will certainly be rather easier to bring software products of this sort to market than true hardware cognisers. However, the pioneering work of Carver Meade on cognitive prosthetics perhaps points to where the first hardware implementations will reach commercial exploitation.

As far as the other paradigms are concerned, pipelining at the low level will certainly be retained as a useful technique of general computer design, but I believe it unlikely that its high-level implementations will ever gain wide market acceptance. It may be that certain systolic implementations of individual functions will prove commercially worthwhile as specific accelerators but I believe that the more complex manifestations will be absorbed by the MIMD mainstream. The same fate is likely to overtake the graph reduction technique. Truly dedicated associative processors may find a place as database manipulators but, again, this paradigm is more likely to be absorbed as a component of more general systems.

8.3.2 Architectures

It is worth asking whether any particular architectural concepts are liable to come to the fore during the next decade. At the moment, two-dimensional near-neighbour meshes and hypercubes dominate the field. I think there are good reasons to suppose that the linearly connected system of processors will prove to be more popular in the near future. This architecture seems to have advantages in the areas of ease of construction, the ability to map to a wide range of data types, fault-tolerance and expandability that at least two manufacturers (AIS and Aspex) have already perceived and which may commend themselves to increasing numbers of producers and users.

In the longer term, if the area of cognisers is to thrive, new techniques for implementing highly-connected, three-dimensional architectures will be needed. It is perhaps here that optical methods may find one of their most important applications.

8.3.3 Technology

There are a number of developments in technology – principally, but not solely, semiconductor technology – which are bound to affect the design of parallel computers in the future. This is mainly because parallel computing depends for much of its validity on large scale and high connectivity. The developments which are likely to prove of most importance include:

Wafer scale integration: As I indicated in an earlier chapter, WSI will free parallel system designers from many of the problems which they now experience – once all the computing power can be constructed in one unit by means of a single, coherent, process, many of the special costs associated with parallel systems will begin to be reduced. We have already seen (Chapter 7H) that one manufacturer is implementing systems of hundreds of thousands of processors on single 25 cm diameter slices of silicon. This technique should certainly become more widespread.

Gallium arsenide: Circuits made from this material, which can operate at frequencies of hundreds of megahertz, are particularly apposite for parallel computers, because the requirement for compactness which such circuits impose is easily realisable for parallel architectures. There appears to be a natural match here which is certain to be exploited sooner or later. The ability to integrate optical devices on the same substrate will be a further encouragement to use this material.

Optical computing: At the start of this book I explained why I would not attempt to cover this topic. However, I would be remiss if I did not note, as a likely future trend, the extended use of optical computing techniques. I will leave it to others to expand on this theme, with the exception of two cautionary remarks. First, the timescale before any such implementations become available outside the laboratory is likely to be rather longer than a decade. Second, just as with most other advances in technique, optical computing is unlikely to be the universal panacea which some of its advocates claim.

3-D semiconductors: The implementation of semiconductor devices is substantially, at present, a planar process offering, in particular, two-dimensional connectivity. The implementation of, particularly but not exclusively, cognisers would be greatly facilitated if connectivity could be extended into three dimensions. Some work has already been done in this area.

Nanotechnology: Perhaps one of the most exciting developments for the potential of efficient parallel computers lies in the recent development of nanotechnology. These procedures, at present in their infancy, result in transistor equivalents which consist of only a few atoms or molecules. The major drawback of such devices – their inability to interface directly with more traditional circuitry – is mitigated in highly parallel computer structures where most devices need only be connected to each other. As in the case of optical computing, it will almost certainly be longer than a decade before such devices appear outside the laboratory.

8.3.4   User interfaces

It is already becoming apparent that, if the use of parallel computers is to become widespread, its existence will have to be increasingly hidden from all but the most dedicated users. I believe this will come about (as in other branches of computing) by the use of graphical and perhaps, eventually, vocal, interfaces. Work in these areas is already widespread, and is certain to expand further.

In the shorter term, I believe it unlikely that the concept of the compiler target language will become a central theme of software in this area, although the DARPA funding agency in the USA is looking further at such developments. More likely is that the C language (or its derivatives) will become a *de facto* standard software platform, principally because of commercial, rather than scientific, pressures.

8.4   Concluding remarks

Parallel computing, in all its various manifestations, is a fascinating and expanding subject. Its intensive study will always be the preserve of a limited number of experts, and the more technical sections of this book have been aimed at those who are starting down this path. However, I believe that its study, at a certain level, is of interest to a wider audience – in particular to those who may use such systems. I hope that in this book I have demonstrated that an understanding of some of the underlying issues of parallel computing need not be limited to a few experts, but is open to many.

Bibliography

Cognisers – Neural Networks and Machines that Think, R. C. Johnson & C. Brown, J. Wiley & Sons, 1988.

Artificial Intelligence – A Personal, Commonsense Journey, W. R. Arnold & J. S. Bowie, Prentice-Hall Inc., 1986.

Optical Computing: A Survey for Computer Scientists, G. D. Feitelson, MIT Press, 1988.

Digital Image Processing, R. C. Gonzalez & P. Wintz, Addison Wesley Publishers Ltd, 1987.

Multiprocessor Computer Architectures, Eds. T. J. Fountain & M. J. Shute, North Holland Press, 1990.

Programming Models for Parallel Systems, S. A. Williams, J. Wiley & Sons, 1990.

Programming in PARLOG, T. Conlon, Addison Wesley Publishers Ltd., 1989.

Cellular Logic Image Processing, Eds. M. J. B. Duff & T. J. Fountain, Academic Press, 1986.

An Introduction to Neural Computing, I. Aleksander & H. Morton, Chapman & Hall, 1990.

Multi-Computer Architectures for Artificial Intelligence, L. Uhr, J. Wiley & Sons, 1987.

Interconnection Networks for Large-Scale Parallel Processing, H. J. Siegel, Lexington Books, 1985.

Reconfigurable Massively Parallel Computers, Ed. H-W. Li, Prentice-Hall Inc., 1991.

Semiconductor Devices – Physics and Technology, S. M. Sze, J. Wiley & Sons, 1985.

The Science of Fractal Images, Eds. H-O. Pietgen & D. Saupe, Springer-Verlag, 1988.

Advanced Computer Architecture, K. Hwang, McGraw-Hill, 1993.

References

[1] M. J. Flynn, Very high speed computing systems, *Proc. IEEE* **54**, pp. 1901–9 (1966).

[2] R. M. Lougheed, D. L. McCubbrey & S. R. Sternberg, Cytocomputers: architectures for parallel image processing, *Proc. Workshop on Picture Data Description and Management*, pp. 281–6 (1980).

[3] C. Rubat de Merac, P. Jutier, J. Laurent & B. Courtois, A new domain for image analysis: VLSI circuit testing with ROMUALD, *Pattern Recognition Letters*, pp. 347–57 (1983).

[4] Meiko Ltd. commercial literature, (1966).

[5] M. J. Reeve & S. Wright, The experimental ALICE machine, in *Multiprocessor Computer Architectures*, eds. T. J. Fountain & M. J. Shute, North Holland Press, pp. 39–56 (1990).

[6] C. Kirkham, The MANCHESTER DATAFLOW project, in *Multiprocessor Computer Architectures*, eds. T. J. Fountain & M. J. Shute, North Holland Press, pp. 141–54 (1990).

[7] W. D. Hillis, *The Connection Machine*, MIT Press (1985).

[8] K. Bromley, S-Y. Kung & E. Swartzlander (eds.), *Proc. Int. Conf. on Systolic Arrays*, Computer Society Press (1988).

[9] F. Rosenblatt, The Perceptron: a probabilistic model for information storage and retrieval in the brain, *Psych. Rev.*, **65**, pp. 386–408 (1958).

[10] J. J. Hopfield, Neural networks and physical systems with emergent collective computational properties, *Proc. Nat. Acad. Sci. USA* **79**, pp. 2554–8 (1982).

[11] D. O. Hebb, *The Organisation of Behaviour,* Wiley, New York (1949).

[12] J. J. Hopfield & D. W. Tank, Neural computation of decisions in optimisation problems, *Biol. Cybern.* **52**, pp. 141–52 (1985).

[13] E. W. Dijkstra, Co-operating sequential processes in *Programming Languages*, ed. F. Genuys, Academic Press (1968).

[14] T. J. Fountain, M. J. B. Duff & K. Matthews, The CLIP7A image processor, *IEEE Trans. on PAMI*, **10**, (3), pp. 310–18 (1988).

[15] J. Reid, Fortran 90, the new Fortran standard, *.EXE Magazine*, **6**, (3), pp. 14–18 (1991).

[16] R. W. Gostick, Software and algorithms for the distributed array processors, *ICL Tech. J.* May, pp. 116–35 (1979).

[17] INMOS, *The Occam 2 Reference Manual*, Prentice Hall (1988).

[18] J. R. Glauert, Specification of Core DACTL1, (Internal Report No. SYS-C87-09, University of East Anglia, UK, 1987).

[19] S. Kirkpatrick, C. D. Gellat & M. D. Vecchi, Optimisation by simulated annealing, *Science*, **220**, pp. 671–80 (1983).

[20] G. E. Hinton & T. J. Sejnowski, Learning and relearning in Boltzmann machines, in *Parallel Distributed Processing*, **1 and 2**, MIT Press (1986).

[21] D. E. Rumelhart, E. David, G. E. Hinton & R. J. Williams, Learning internal representations by error propagation, in *Parallel Distributed Processing*, **1 and 2**, MIT Press (1986).

[22] P. H. Bartels, R. Manner, R. L. Shoemaker, S. Paplanus & A. Graham, Computer configurations for the processing of diagnostic imagery in histopathology, in *Evaluation of Multicomputers for Image Processing*, eds. L. Uhr, K. Preston, S. Levialdi & M. J. B. Duff, Academic Press, pp. 239–78 (1986).

[23] T. J. Fountain, An analysis of methods for improving long-range connectivity in meshes, in *Pattern Recognition - 4th Int. Conf.*, ed. J. Kittler, Springer-Verlag, pp. 259–68 (1988).

[24] P-E. Danielsson & T. Ericsson, Suggestions for an image processor array, (Internal Report LITH-ISY-I-0507, Linkoping University, Sweden, 1982).

[25] T. J. Fountain, *Processor arrays - Architecture and Applications*, Academic Press (1987).

[26] M. J. B. Duff, Pyramids - expected performance, in *Pyramidal systems for computer vision*, eds. V. Cantoni & S. Levialdi, Springer-Verlag, pp. 59–73 (1986).

[27] G. R. Nudd, T. J. Atherton, N. D. Francis, R. M. Howarth, D. J. Kerbyson, R. A. Packwood & G. J. Vaudin, A hierarchical MSIMD architecture for image analysis, *Proc. 10th ICPR*, Atlantic City, USA, pp. 642–7 (1990).

[28] M. R. B. Forshaw, Array architectures for image processing 1 - connection matrices, (Internal Report No. 87/3, Image Processing Group, University College London, 1987).

[29] F. A. Briggs, K. Hwang, K-S. Fu & B. W. Wah, PUMPS architecture for pattern analysis and database management, *Proc. IEEE Wkshp. on CAPAIDM*, Hot Springs, USA, pp. 178–87 (1981).

[30] C. C. Weems & D. T. Lawton, The image understanding architecture, *Int. J. of Computer Vision*, **2**, pp. 251–82 (1989).

[31] T. J. Fountain, The use of linear arrays for image processing, in *Proc. Int. Conf. on Systolic Arrays*, San Diego, USA, pp. 183–92 (1988).

[32] A. Turing, On Computable Numbers with an Application to the Entscheidungsproblem (1937).

[33] T. J. Fountain, A survey of bit-serial array processor circuits, in *Computing Structures for Image Processing*, ed. M. J. B. Duff, Academic Press, pp. 1–14 (1983).

[34] J. Beetem, M. Denneau & D. H. Weingarten, The GF11 supercomputer, *Proc. 12th Ann. Int. Symp. on Computer Architectures*, Boston, USA, pp. 108–18 (1985).

[35] T. J. Fountain, Introducing local autonomy to processor arrays, in *Machine Vision*, Ed. H. Freeman, Academic Press, pp. 31–56 (1988).

[36] J. V. McCanny & J. G. McWhirter, On the implementation of signal processing functions using one-bit systolic arrays, *Electron. Lett.* **18**, pp. 241–3 (1982).

[37] C. G. Langton (ed.), *Artificial Life*, Addison-Wesley (1989).

[38] R. Philhower & J. F. McDonald, Interconnection complexity study for a piggyback WSHP GaAs systolic processor, in *Proc. Int. Conf. on Systolic Arrays*, San Diego, USA, eds. K. Bromley, S-Y. Kung & E. Swartzlander, pp. 555–64 (1988).

[39] *The Transputer Databook*, Inmos technical publication (1988).

[40] W. Purvis, Programming the Intel i860, *Parallelogram* **31**, pp. 6–9 (1990).

[41] *Massively parallel computers*, eds. M. Maresca & T. J. Fountain, Special issue Proc. IEEE, (April 1991).

[42] E. R. Brocklehurst, (NPL Report DITC 192/91, 1991).

[43] K. Preston Jr., The Abingdon cross benchmark survey, *Computer*, July, pp. 9–18 (1989).

[44] A. R. Rosenfeld, A report on the DARPA image understanding workshop, *Proc. 1987 DARPA Image Understanding Workshop*, Los Angeles, USA, pp. 298–302 (1987).

[45] C. C. Weems, E. Riseman & A. Hanson, An integrated image understanding benchmark: recognition of a 2 1/2 D 'mobile', (Internal Report No. COINS TR88-34, University of Massachusetts, USA, 1988).

[46] Thinking Machines Inc. commercial literature, (1993).

[47] H. T. Kung, Systolic Algorithms for the CMU WARP Processor, in *Systolic Signal Processing Systems*, ed. E.E.Swartzlander, Marcel Dekker, pp. 73–95 (1987).

[48] C. Clack & S. L. Peyton-Jones, The four-stroke reduction engine, in *Dataflow and Reduction Architectures*, IEEE Comp. Soc. Press (1987).

[49] S. L. Peyton-Jones, C. Clack, J. Salkild & M. Hardie, GRIP - a high-performance architecture for parallel graph reduction, *Proc. IFIP Conf. Functional Programming Languages and Computer Architecture*, Springer-Verlag, pp. 98–112 (September, 1987).

[50] T. J. Reynolds, L. A. Spacek & A. J. Beaumont, BRAVE - a parallel Prolog, (Internal Report No. CSM–91, Computer Science Dept. University of Essex, October, 1986).

[51] D. Parkinson, D. J. Hunt & K. S. MacQueen, The AMT DAP 500, *Proc. 33rd. IEEE Comp. Soc. Int. Conf.* (February, 1988).

[52] P. M. Flanders, D. J. Hunt, S. F. Reddaway & D. Parkinson, Efficient high speed computing with the distributed array processor, in *High speed computer and algorithm organisation*, Academic Press, USA (1977).

[53] D. J. Hunt & S. F. Reddaway, Distributed processing power in memory, in *The fifth generation*, Pergamon-Infotech, UK (1983).

[54] S.F. Reddaway, J. B. G. Roberts, P. Simpson & B. C. Merrifield, Distributed array processors for military applications, *MILCOMP85. Military computers, graphics and hardware*, Microwave Exhibitions & Publishers Ltd., UK (1985).

[55] S. F. Reddaway, DAP, A Distributed Array Processor, *First Annual Symposium on Computer Architecture*, IEEE/ACM, Florida (1973).

[56] K. E. Batcher, Design of a Massively Parallel Processor, *IEEE Transactions on Computers*, **C-29**, pp. 836–40 (September 1980).

[57] D. L. Waltz, Applications of the Connection Machine, *Computer*, pp. 85–97 (January 1987).

[58] T. Blank, The MasPar MP-1 Architecture, *Proc. IEEE Compcon Spring 1990*, IEEE (February 1990).

[59] P. Christy, Software to Support Massively Parallel Computing on the MasPar MP-1, *Proc. IEEE Compcon Spring 1990*, IEEE (February 1990).

[60] K. E. Batcher, The Architecture of Tomorrow's Massively Parallel Computer, *Frontiers of Massively Parallel Scientific Computing*, NASA CP 2478 (September 1986).

[61] E. W. Davis & J. H. Reif, Architecture and Operation of the Blitzen Processing Element, *3rd. Int. Conf. on Supercomputing*, **iii**, pp. 128–37 (May 1988).

[62] R. Grondalski, A VLSI Chip Set for a Massively Parallel Architecture, *International Solid State Circuits Conference* (February 1987).

[63] I. Aleksander, W. V. Thomas & P. A. Bowden, WISARD - A radical step forward in image recognition, *Sensor Review*, **4**, (3), pp. 120–4 (1984).

[64] I. Aleksander & M. J. Dobree-Wilson, Adaptive windows for image processing, *IEE Proceedings*, **132E**, (5), pp. 233–45 (1985).

[65] I. Aleksender & H. B. Morton, *An introduction to Neural Computing*, MIT Press, Boston (1989).

[66] M. J. Shute, Categorising parallel computer architectures, in *Multiprocessor Computer Architectures*, eds. T. J. Fountain & M. J. Shute, North Holland, pp. 1–38 (1990).

[67] J. E. Shore, Second thoughts on parallel processing, *Comput. Elec. Eng.* **1**, pp. 95–109 (1973).

[68] R. W. Hockney & C. R. Jesshope, *Parallel Computers*, Adam Hilger (1981).

[69] P. C. Treleaven, D. R. Brownbridge & R. P. Hopkins, Data-driven and demand-driven computer architectures, *Computer Surveys*, **14**, (1), pp. 93–143 (1982).

Index